Ashok K. Banker's best-selling books have been published in sixteen languages in fifty-eight countries. Apart from his immensely popular retellings of ancient Indian epics including the *Ramayana* and the *Mahabharata*, he is also known for his Kali Rising crime fiction series, the acclaimed literary novels *Vertigo* and *Byculla Boy*, and the non-fiction book *The Valmiki Syndrome*.

AF215168

EPIC
Loves

Stories from the Adi Parva
of the **MAHABHARATA**

Ashok K. Banker

SPEAKING
TIGER

SPEAKING TIGER BOOKS LLP
125A, Ground Floor, Shahpur Jat, near Asiad Village,
New Delhi 110049

This edition first published by Speaking Tiger Books 2022

Copyright © Ashok K. Banker

ISBN: 978-93-5447-326-5
eISBN: 978-93-5447-331-9

10 9 8 7 6 5 4 3 2 1

Typeset in Minion Pro by SŪRYA, New Delhi
Printed at Shree Maitrey Printech Pvt. Ltd., Noida

Contents

SHAKUNTALA AND DUSHYANTA

1

A great king entered a vast jungle. He was accompanied by his army, hundreds of horses, elephants, warriors armed with swords, spears, maces, javelins and other weapons. They roared and cheered to show their might as they rode through the forest. Conch blowers sounded their shell trumpets, dhol drummers pounded their kettle drums. The chariot wheels rumbled, the elephants trumpeted, the horses neighed. All the denizens of the forest, animal, insect and human, wondered at this great noise and stopped still in fear.

The king was exceedingly handsome and well loved. The women of his kingdom showered flowers and praises—and coy invitations—upon him when he rode through the streets. Wealthy and powerful, he wanted for nothing. His enemies feared him enough to show great respect and avoid confrontation—those that were foolish enough to oppose him in battle met with devastation and ruin, and were massacred or enslaved. Brahmins paid homage to his greatness, kusalavya bards sang his praises. But after the king had conquered all the realms he desired to possess, and had partaken of all the fruits of pleasure, he grew restless of kingship and sought new thrills and pursuits.

His favourite pastime was the hunt. Unlike earlier kings of his line who preferred to ride out alone or in small packs, hunting stealthily, he rode out with small armies, making a great show of it so that everyone knew that the king's hunt was passing by. All heads turned to watch the glamour of his entourage. Many of his citizens even ran behind his train or followed on horse or by wagon. But each time he went farther and farther into the deep jungle, and eventually, all fell back and turned homewards. Finally, only he and his retinue continued, making their way noisily forward, with great merriment and clash of music and voices. Even his chariot was designed to produce the loudest sound, its heavy iron-clad wheels rumbling ominously, the effect intended to strike fear into the hearts of his enemies; it had become his trademark as a king at arms. Despite its ponderous rumbling, the chariot was drawn by powerful bhoja stallions and capable of achieving great speeds, often compared to the swiftness of Garuda by those who observed it from afar.

That day, the king came to a new place, a forest within the great aranya, the unexplored wilderness that still covered much of the earth. It was a beautiful grove comparable to Nandana itself, the fabled garden of the king of the gods in his heavenly realm, Indraloka. Magnificent bilva, arka, khadira, kapitha and dhava trees grew in great profusion. Its landscape was varied, and ranged from mountains and valleys to great plains spotted with great boulders. There was no sign of water or human habitation. The king and his retinue rode on for several yojanas, marvelling at this new place they had discovered, so far removed from civilization. In the forested parts of this country, they were amazed at the profusion of game. The greatest herds of deer they had ever seen abounded here, as did every other manner of forest creature. So unaccustomed were these beasts to the sight or scent of humans that they stood still at first and stared in puzzlement at the new arrivals, unafraid and unshy. With great enthusiasm, the king and his best men embarked on their hunt. They slaughtered deer by the score. Entire families of tigers were massacred by arrowshot alone. Those that were only wounded he dismounted from his chariot and slew with his sword. The hunt continued for days and he had recourse to every manner of weapon which he employed in the killing of all manner of beasts. He brought down lions with spears, smashed the skulls of wild boars with maces, flung javelins into the thick hide of elephants. Roaring with exultation like the very predators he killed, he took pleasure and pride in his kills, massacring the animals of that unspoiled forest. At last, in alarm and panic, the creatures of the region began to flee before the thundering advance of this manic herd of two-legged killers, entire herds dispersing and stampeding, deer crying out and leaping in all directions to flee their tormentors, even the long-fanged cats slinking away silently to hide in the deep shadows and glare balefully at their new rivals.

In the nights, while the king and his jubilant band of followers feasted on the choicest portions of the meat they had hunted, some predators worked their vengeance. Men were dragged off screaming into the darkness, heads chomped to pulp and limbs crushed between iron jaws, bones smashed by rampaging elephants or bellies ripped open by razor-sharp boar tusks. But these losses were minor compared to the slaughter of the animals. As always, man was the cruellest predator of all, hunting for pleasure rather than need. The carcasses they piled up could have fed a force a hundred times their size for weeks. Most would rot uneaten, beautiful beasts slain for man's cruel pleasure.

The forest had its revenge on the invading force. The riverbeds were parched, the ponds dry. Not a drop of water was to be found for miles and miles. Search as they may, they could find no trace of water, running or still. Surely the animals must slake their thirst somehow. But the animals could not speak, nor did the forest yield its secret. And so the king and his entourage thirsted mightily even as they tired of the salty meat of their kills and craved other foods. Yet these deprivations only infuriated the king further and rather than withdraw his men, he drove them further into the new country each day, slaying more and more creatures in prodigious numbers. The sheer scale of the massacre grew to epic proportions. Some say at the very least he slew several hundreds, but most insist the number of slaughtered beasts ran into the several thousands. Enraged by extreme thirst and blood-rage, the king was like a conqueror possessed, waging war against the animals of that region like a mad buffalo run amok.

2

Ravaged by thirst and exhaustion, their numbers already depleted by the attacks of vengeful animals, the king's retinue dwindled further as men began to drop for want of the most simple succour: water. By degrees, their blood lust diminished, as the king's anger waned. His own head pounding with lack of water, body parched and blood heated, he ceased his killing spree. Onward they rode, further into unknown territory. Across plains, over mountains, through valleys, they had no choice but to push on—already they had come too far from the last source of water. Turning back was no longer an option. Men fell like the beasts they had slain, dropped by the invisible arrow of thirst, to lie dying or dead in strange lands. The predators that followed the human force crept up under cover of night and consumed these fallen, often tearing them to shreds while still alive. The angry forest wreaked its own revenge on its ravagers.

Finally, when his force had been reduced to a fraction of its original size, even their horses and elephants half-dead from lack of water, and it seemed as if every last one of them would die there in that unknown country, and his own strength halved, the king came to a rise.

Goading their mounts, he and his men rode up to a ridge overlooking a vast valley. Reining in their exhausted mounts, they gazed upon an extraordinary sight. Below lay a great forest, lush and beautiful like nothing they had seen before. There was water there in plenty—they could see a great river snaking its way through the valley, waterfalls plunging from the surrounding cliffs, ponds and pools visible through gaps in the trees. The trees were emerald green, filled with a profusion of colourful birds of every description. The air was filled with their cries. There were animals in the woods below as well, roaming freely, even more unspoiled and innocent than the ones they had seen earlier. The sounds of lions roaring could be heard, yet a herd of deer continued to graze unafraid. The sight of ripe fruits hanging from the trees made their parched mouths water, and the pristine unblemished beauty of that arboreal vision brought tears to the eyes of these battle-hardened men.

Riding along a sloping pathway that led down, they entered the valley and cried with relief at the sight of water and nourishment. Slaking their thirst and eating their fill of luscious ripe fruits, they lay on the soft cool grassy mounds, beneath the gentle shade of great trees, and recovered their strength. Their urge to hunt was satiated and all they desired was to regain their energy that they might return home. But the king grew eager to explore further. Wishing to continue alone, he bade all his men except two—a priest and an advisor—to remain and indulge their fill of nourishment and rest until he returned. Then, accompanied only by the brahmin and the minister, he proceeded upon his chariot.

So lush was the grassy undergrowth that it all but muffled the rumbling thunder of the king's war chariot. The sun was warm and energizing, yet never harsh, even as the day wore on from morning to afternoon. Cool scented breezes blew and all the animals they saw were innocent and unafraid. They saw lions resting beside grazing deer, and everywhere the trees were dark with swarms of shatapadas, buzzing and busily making their sweet treacly honey. The king knew then that this was the innermost heart of the strange realm they had discovered, and that the first forest they had entered had been as the gateway to this heavenly country.

At length, they came to a grove at the delta of the river they had glimpsed from the ridge above. The trees here were as smooth and slender as flagpoles, and nestled within the perfect spot was a vast ashram. From the sight of the numerous yagna chaukats they saw everywhere, and the sheer number of thatched huts of all sizes, it was evident that a great number of rishis resided here. It was an idyllic place fit for the most austere yatis and valakhilyas.

'What place is this?' asked the king of the brahmin.

The brahmin stared in wonderment, enraptured by the beauty and calm of the place. 'It can be none other than the fabled ashram on the banks of the sacred river Malini. I have heard tales of it from sutas but never thought I would live to see it with my own eyes. It is the domicile of Rishi Kanva, descendent of Kashyapa.'

The king gazed out across the hermitage for a while, but neither he nor his companions saw any living soul in sight.

The king handed the reins of the chariot to his advisor. 'Stay here until I return,' he commanded, then disembarked from the chariot.

Continuing alone on foot, he entered the grove, passing through it to the ashram beyond. The ashram overlooked the river and his attention was diverted by the cries and sight of chakravaka birds frolicking in the water noisily. The ruddy geese sent up loud cries, unafraid of any predators as they thrashed and splashed water with their wings. The king smiled at the sight, wishing now that he had carried his bow and quiver, then continued through the ashram. He found every hut empty, every yagna chaukat cold and unlit, and not a single person in sight. Yet there was no doubt that many lived here, for he found garments and belongings, sacrificial oblations and items for the living, as well as signs from ritual sacrifices performed by brahmins everywhere. Where were the denizens of the ashram? He saw various items and arrangements that he recognized from his own studies of the Vedas—some he knew to be preparations for rituals spelled out in the Rig Vedic chapters of the great Books of Knowledge, others related to the Sama Veda, Yajur Veda or Atharva Veda.

Clearly, many great rishis resided here and pursued their Vedic studies and rituals with complete dedication. 'This must be what Brahmaloka looks like,' he thought, awed.

Not finding anyone through the entire length and breadth of the ashram, yet certain that many must reside here currently, the king began to call out as he went. His voice echoed in the woods. Finally, just when he was about to give up and retrace his steps, a voice answered. He was surprised to hear a woman's soft tones respond, coming from the direction of the river.

A vision came into sight, freshly bathed, her long black hair still wet from the river. Clad in the humble attire of an ascetic, she was dark of hair and eye, dusky of skin and beautiful beyond description. Though surprised to see him, she was nonetheless the epitome of charm and grace and received him with great honour and respect. Offering him a seat, she gave him water for the arghya, and he washed his feet, hands and face and accepted her offer of refreshment. After observing all formalities, she then enquired who he might be and what he desired. Even though it was evident that she was bursting with curiosity, her questions were brief and polite, which impressed him further.

'I am Raja Dushyanta and I am told this is the ashram of the fabled Rishi Kanva. Is it so?'

'It is, sire,' replied the woman. 'But my father is not presently here.'

'Where has he gone?' asked Dushyanta, doing his best not to stare. Her beauty captivated him and he could feel his heart quicken, his blood race.

'He has gone on an errand,' she replied. 'He may be a while returning but please do us the honour of waiting until he returns.'

'And where are the other rishis who reside here? For I see that there must be many, surely?'

'Aye, sire, indeed. The rishis of this ashram are

extremely austere in their vows and dedication. There are yatis, valakhilyas and other devout sages. Presently they are all on pilgrimage and my father and I are here alone.'

Unable to contain his eagerness to know the maiden better, Dushyanta began to ask her questions, always polite and courteous, but also enquiring more than any casual visitor might. He learned that her name was Shakuntala, and that she lived here in service to her father Rishi Kanva and the other rishis of the ashram. While she spoke, Dushyanta kept stealing glances at her, admiring her beauty, her youth, her perfection. For her part, she seemed unaware of her own beauty and wore it casually, unselfconsciously, unlike the apsaras of his court who preened and primped themselves all day. Her damp hair hung by her side, waist-long, and it drew his attention time and again to her voluptuously undulating body and shapely hips. He listened as she praised her father and described his qualities and reputation as a man of great self-sacrifice and dedication to the brahman.

Dushyanta could not help ask. 'Yet how is it that a rishi of such severe vows happened to father a daughter, especially one as beautiful as yourself? And how is it that you live here with him in this remote wilderness far from civilization? After all,' he added teasingly, 'a flower so radiant in beauty should not conceal its lustre in the deep forest!'

She blushed shyly at these comments but replied sincerely, 'My Lord...'

'Dushyanta,' he said quickly. 'I am lord only to those who serve me. You are by no means my servant nor could you ever be. Pray, address me simply as Dushyanta.'

She seemed to contemplate this for a moment. 'I have been raised always to address people correctly, my lord. I cannot disobey my father's orders and simply address a king by his name. It would not be right.'

He smiled. So innocent and pure of heart, yet so radiantly beautiful too. He had never known such a woman before. 'Then I shall have to call you Rani.'

Her doe eyes flashed up, staring at him. 'My Lord? I do not comprehend your meaning.'

'If you call me Lord or King, I shall call you Lady or Queen. It is only right.'

She covered her mouth with her hand. 'But that cannot be. I am but a rishi's humble daughter, with no possessions or property to my name. I am no lady, far from a queen!'

'You are possessed of regal bearing, rich in intelligence and wit, with a jewelled smile, precious voice, an aspect fitting for the goddess of wealth herself, almighty Lakshmi...' he let his words trail off, enjoying her startled expression. 'Queen is barely sufficient. Perhaps I should call you Devi. For you are no less than a goddess in body and mind!'

Her hand shot out as if to cover his lips before he could say more, the innocent instinctive reaction of a child, but she stopped herself before her hand could touch his mouth, withdrew it, and lowered her eyes to the ground shyly. 'Nay, my good Lord Dushyanta. You cannot call me, a simple brahmacharini, a goddess! You might anger Sri herself!'

He laughed. 'Then resolve this at once. Agree to call me Dushyanta and I shall call you Shakuntala.'

She glanced up at him, and he saw the fire of energy spark in her eyes. Not quite mischief, but it showed that she had great force of will.

He smiled winningly. 'It is the only way.' He added softly: 'Shakuntala.'

Swallowing nervously, she bobbed her head once, then said in barely a whisper, 'Aye, Dushyanta…sire.'

He wagged a finger in warning. 'Just Dushyanta, nothing more. Or I crown you Sri on earth incarnate!'

'No!' she cried, genuinely distressed. 'Dushyanta. Please do not.'

At the sound of his name spoken by that nightingale voice, in that passionate tone, his heart stirred powerfully. It was all he could do to keep himself from taking her in his embrace and demonstrating his passion for her right there and then. But Dushyanta knew that this was no palace chattel or serving maid. This was indeed a lady, even if she did not know it. He would treat her as such. 'Thank you, Shakuntala.' He resumed his seat calmly, with an effort. 'Pray, continue. You were about to explain to me how your illustrious father Rishi Kanva came to sire a daughter and why you continue to live in this remote if beautiful forest with him like any shaven-head brahmachari—though you are clearly not one.'

She nodded, taking his words at face value and seeming not to hear the irony in his phrasing—or the subtle innuendo. 'I shall tell you, for it is no secret.'

3

'In times of yore, the great brahmarishi Vishwamitra began to practise great austerities. The tapas power he accumulated grew to a great store, enough to dislodge even mighty Lord Indra from his seat if he chose to rise up against the devas. Indra summoned the apsara Menaka, fabled for her beauty, and requested her to seduce Vishwamitra that he might cease his powerful penance.

'Menaka was afraid of Vishwamitra's legendary temper. "Great Shakra, you know that when provoked he is capable of unleashing destruction even against one as powerful as thee. I dare not disturb during his meditation. He once caused the death of the great Vasishtha. On another occasion, he created the river Kaushiki from the force produced by his penance, and to this day, it rages so wilfully that few can cross its tempestuous waters. Later he renamed it Para. Do you recall that sacred river? On its banks lived Vishwamitra's own wife, cared for by the righteous rajarshi Matanga, who became a hunter to survive the great famine. After the famine ended and Vishwamitra returned home, he thanked Matanga for maintaining his wife by officiating at his ceremony, an event which you yourself attended, Lord Indra, and I saw you drinking soma there in Vishwamitra's presence. Vishwamitra is a nakshatra, and he is possessed with the energy of an entire constellation of stars. He created the constellation Shravana through his own energy. If he kicks the earth hard, earthquakes ripple throughout the world. If he wishes, he can uproot the great Mount Meru and whirl it around like a mace. Every aspect of his features is as radiant as the sun, and as deadly as Yama. How can a mere apsara such as myself dare to interrupt his great tapasya? Speaking of Yama, the lord of death and dharma himself fears Vishwamitra. As do Soma, the maharishis, saddhyas, vishwadevas and valakhilyas."

'When Shakra pressed Menaka, entreating her to undertake this chore, she continued to argue thus. Finally, she agreed reluctantly on certain conditions. "If you would have me do this, then you must guarantee me your protection and use your own powers to make me seem innocent. I shall go before Vishwamitra. Let Marut the wind god strip me of my garments. Let Manmatha, lord of love, use his power to entice the brahmarishi. Create an environment that seduces him and makes him conducive to my charms. I shall act innocent. Let him be seduced by me rather than me seducing him wilfully."

'Indra saw the sense in Menaka's suggestion. He enlisted the aid of Vayu and Kama, the lords of Wind and Love. Menaka entered Vishwamitra's ashram where the great sage sat absorbed in his meditative trance. Pretending to be innocent of his presence, she moved coquettishly around him, dancing and cavorting playfully. From the fruits and trees around, Kama drew fragrances and scents that evoked passion while Vayu swirled them into Vishwamitra's senses, stroking the sage's body with arousing caresses. His senses provoked, the brahmarishi opened his eyes for an instant, and his gaze alighted on Menaka. At exactly that instant, Marut sent a sudden gust of wind to snatch the filmy garment from the apsara's body, leaving her unclothed and exposed in all her radiant beauty. Menaka gasped, then reached for her stolen garment, but even as she stretched out her body, it was whipped further away from her by another puff from the same wind. She had to bend low and reach far to pick it up and as she did so she struck a pose that no man could look upon without feeling a great surge of passion. Given a perfect view of the naked apsara, perfect in body and grace, masterful in movements, filled with the strength and glow of youth, Vishwamitra was overcome with desire for her. Unable to stop himself, he proposed to her that they cohabit. Genuinely awed by the power and reputation of the great brahmarishi, Menaka agreed coyly. Without reclaiming her stolen garment, she came into his arms and he clasped her to himself as a starved man clasps food.

'For an untold length of time the apsara and the brahmarishi indulged themselves in that solitary place, losing their wits completely to the act of procreation, until the days and weeks and months melded into each other and seemed to form but a single endless day. All the great tapas energy accumulated by the brahmarishi, which could have given him power enough to dislodge the king of gods had he so desired, was emitted in the act of coition and absorbed in the form of seed by Menaka. Of that act and energy was conceived a female child. When her womb grew heavy, Menaka went to the banks of the river Malini, in the Himalayas. There she stayed until her time came to give birth. Leaving the child on the banks of the Malini, Menaka returned to Indra's assembly, her task accomplished.

'Left alone on that desolate Himalayan plain by the river, the baby's presence attracted numerous predators. Growing bolder by the passing hour, they crept closer to the child, and would have surely consumed her in moments. But the shakuna, the birds who view all from their vantage point high in the sky, floating like kites suspended on invisible strings, saw her plight and descended to protect her. They took it upon themselves to keep the predators at bay. Soon after, Rishi Kanva, who had gone up to the Himalayas to meditate, chanced upon her when he went down to the river for his ablutions. Seeing her alone there in that desolate place, he knew that she would not survive long if left unattended. He brought her home, and raised her as his own daughter. The shastras say there are three kinds of parents. One gives a body. The second protects. The third kind provides food. Therefore Kanva adopted the child he sought to protect and nourish as his own daughter. Because he found her surrounded by shakuna birds, he named her Shakuntala.'

4

Dushyanta was simultaneously thrilled and inspired by Shakuntala's narration of the circumstances leading to her own birth. More than a little aroused by her frank account of the seduction of her biological forebear by the alluring nymph, he saw that she exhibited no coyness or mischief. To her, it was merely a factual account which she had narrated as best as she knew. There was no attempt on her part to arouse or titillate. He could hardly blame her if the facts of the account themselves were provocative. Now he was even more enamoured of her. For it was clear to him that her beauty was matched by intelligence, wit and a noble spirit. Unable to stop himself, just as Vishwamitra was possessed of desire for her mother Menaka, Dushyanta clasped Shakuntala's hands in his own. She reacted naturally, trying to pry herself free, but he held on. Looking into his eyes, she saw his passion and the force of his desire and was overwhelmed.

'Shakuntala, I was right at first. You are no less than a princess or noble woman in your own right. The story of your birth confirms it. Your very aspect speaks of your high origins and breeding. I am overcome with longing for you. From the instant I first laid eyes on you, your hair wet from the river, your hips sinuous in your simple hermetic garment, your eyes doelike and bright in the shade of the jambu tree, your innocence, your sincerity, your intelligence, your beauty, all have charmed and overcome me. I cannot resist my senses a moment longer. Consent to marry me. I will shower you with gold necklaces and garments, ornaments and gems, treasure from a dozen faraway nations, wealth and furs, whatever your heart desires you shall possess. My entire kingdom shall be at your disposal, and I myself your servant. Marry me this instant.'

Shakuntala took a moment to recover from the shock and surprise of this passionate outburst. Trembling a little, she finally managed to say, 'Raje, great king that you are, I cannot answer you myself. I beg of you. Wait until my father returns and ask him for my hand in marriage if you desire me.'

Dushyanta's heart was filled with joy for her answer meant that she herself was not averse to the union. It was all he needed to know. 'I cannot wait a moment longer, my love. Let me take you in the gandharva rite of marriage. It is one of the eight accepted forms of marriage and recognized by all civilized people. In this rite, you only need to consent and we can join together willingly as man and wife. It is a marriage of love.'

Shakuntala shook her head. 'I do not know of this gandharva marriage. I am unaware of such matters. How can I agree independently? I ask you again, wait until my father returns. Ask him for my hand in marriage. If he consents, I shall not refuse you.'

But Dushyanta's passion overflowed and he could not bear to wait. 'Shakuntala, I would not mislead you. Let me explain to you the eight kinds of marriage that have the sanction of dharma. They are brahma, deva, arsha, prajapatya, asura, gandharva, rakshasa and paishacha. Manu, the first mortal created and formulator of the natural laws by which all mortals abide peaceably, has set out in no unclear terms what each of these forms entail. The first four are sanctioned for brahmins, the first six for kshatriyas. Kings may resort to all eight forms freely. The asura form is only sanctioned for vaisyas and sudras. The form of marriage I propose, the gandharva vivah, is eminently acceptable provided both participants are willing and feel genuine passion for one another. Tell me that you do not feel passion for me and I will stop persisting. But I know that the emotion I see in your eloquent eyes mirrors my own desire. I feel the pulse of your blood in the vein of your wrist. I feel your warm breath on my cool palm now. I see all the signs of passion and desire awakened in you, just as they are in me. Therefore, the gandharva form of marriage is most appropriate for us and in keeping with dharma. Tell me if I am wrong in any respect.'

Shakuntala regained control of her breathing and admitted: 'Great king of the Kurus, I do not deny the truth in what you say. I am satisfied also by your explanation of the forms of marriage and the righteousness of this form. It is true that I am willing and therefore nothing else prevents us from joining together in this mutual union.'

Dushyanta moved to take her in his arms, his face

revealing his delight. 'Then speak no more, my love. Let us be man and wife this instant.'

'Wait,' she pleaded firmly. 'I shall agree to be your wife, Dushyanta, on certain terms and conditions. Only if you agree to them will this union occur. Are you willing?'

'Of course. Did I not say that you may demand anything of me that you desire? Even without naming your conditions, I am agreed to them!'

'Then, give me your word that even though there is no one else to witness our covenant, you will still honour it as a sacred and secret pact. Promise me only this one thing, Dushyanta. If I bear a child by you, and if it is a son, then give me your guarantee that our son will succeed you as king.'

Dushyanta stared at her, unable to believe his ears. 'Is that all? My beloved, it would be the greatest joy of my life to make our son the heir to the Kuru throne! What more could I desire? You shall be cared for as a queen deserves, surrounded by all the wealth and comfort of the world. Our child, when he or she is born, shall want for nothing. All this is my dharma as a husband, it is your right to demand as the wife of a king!'

With those words, Dushyanta dispelled any shred of doubt that might have remained in Shakuntala's mind. Unable to resist him any longer, overcome by her own emotions and her joy at such a fine mate, she succumbed to his embraces and returned his passion tenfold.

After they had dallied awhile together in mutual passion, Dushyanta lay with Shakuntala. Had the choice been left to him, he might never have left her presence or that idyllic grove.

But in his absence, his men had received word from the capital that a political rebellion was brewing. It had taken a great deal of time and effort to seek him out, but finally the message reached his advisor and priest who were waiting at the outskirts of the grove and they entered that sanctum to bring him the urgent missive. Dushyanta knew that he must return at once or risk endangering his entire kingdom and throne. He told Shakuntala to come with him at once but she could not leave without meeting her father and telling him all that had transpired. Unsure when Rishi Kanva would return, Dushyanta felt he had no choice but to leave alone for the present time. But he promised that he would send fresh forces to bring her to the capital at once.

'My love, I shall dispatch a four-fold army, with infantry, cavalry, elephants and chariots, to fetch you in royal style. You shall enter the city of the Kurus like a queen. Then we shall live together the rest of our lives in perfect love.'

So saying, he climbed aboard his chariot and rode away. Shakuntala's heart ached to see him leave and she felt bereft. The same heated passion that had brought her such joy and fervour only hours earlier now left her feeling cold and lonely. Before Dushyanta came, she had stayed alone here in this desolate grove in perfect happiness, never feeling the lack of anything or any person. But now that she had known the joy of union and the love of a man, the same grove, the same solitary existence, all seemed empty and sad.

Somehow, she passed the time until her father returned. By the time he was back, she had begun to think of the many ways he might react to the news of her unexpected marriage and dalliance. Embarrassed, she would not come before him and hid in the shadows of her hut. But not for nothing was Rishi Kanva a great sage. Through the power of his divine sight, he saw all that had occurred and understood everything. Then he sought out his daughter and said to her gently, 'Bhagyavaan, what you have done today is nothing to be ashamed of. What the Kuru king said to you was indeed true. All was in accordance with dharma. Even without mantras recited, a gandharva marriage is acceptable between two willing persons. Indeed, among kshatriyas it is the preferred way! Your choice of husband is distinctive: Dushyanta is a good king and a good man, and does his best to live according to dharma. The son of this union will be an even greater king than his father, mighty in power and wealth and influence, and his sway will extend to the far corners of this earth.'

Shakuntala was overjoyed and overwhelmed with relief. As she washed her father's feet with the arghya water and prepared his repast for him, she asked timidly, 'Does that mean you will grant me your blessings, father?'

He smiled and put a hand on her head, blessing her. 'Always, my fortunate one! Not only that, ask me for any boon you desire. Consider it my wedding gift to you both!'

Shakuntala's mind had been filled with anxiety over the rebellion that Dushyanta's men had spoken of when they came to fetch him. To her innocent mind, it had seemed like the end of his kingdom and the world itself. Her sleep had been filled with nightmares that her newly betrothed husband and mate might be slain in battle even before he could send for her and her entire future would be crushed before it even began. With these fears in her mind, she asked her father, 'Grant that the kings of the Kuru race should always be true to their word and never be dislodged from their thrones, no matter how great the challenge.'

Rishi Kanva saw her concern for her husband and applauded it silently. 'So be it,' he proclaimed. And in his mind, he thought, 'This is truly my daughter. Even at such a moment, she did not ask for anything for herself. Only for her husband. Dushyanta is a lucky man to have her as his wife.'

5

Dushyanta returned home to his capital city and was instantly plunged into a nest of political intrigue and power play. Taking advantage of his long absence, his rivals had begun a deadly conspiracy against him and all those he relied on. He found he could trust no one completely and that even the most reliable advisors and ministers had formed alliances designed to protect their own interests. The web of political deal-making stretched wide and deep and it was not possible for any king to completely uproot it. Wisdom lay in compromise, acceptance and in making one's own deals to ensure stability for the present. Over time, when the opportunity presented itself, he could eliminate the worst of his rivals and enemies in carefully orchestrated ways, without upsetting the entire apple cart of politics. Not for nothing was Hastinapura also called Gajashraya, the City of Elephants. Her politics were as ponderous as a ton-heavy gajagamini.

The battle for political survival and stability demanded all his energy and time as well as the forming of alliances. Forced to use whatever means he possessed, he married into various powerful dynasties of neighbouring kingdoms, ensuring their cooperation and thus eliminating potential rivals. In time, he was sucked into the vortex that is the game of kings and forgot all about his dalliance with Shakuntala. The entire time spent on that trip seemed like a fever dream. The hunt, the terrible slaughter of countless beasts, the blood lust that had overcome himself and his men, the deadly thirst that had almost killed them, the beautiful hidden forests within forests, the idyllic valley, the heavenly grove, the unspeakably beautiful maiden all alone in the empty hermitage, her extraordinary tale of her birth, the powerful lust that had overcome him—all seemed like fragments from a half-remembered dream in the light of awakening. His memory began to deceive him. He began to think that perhaps it had been Shakuntala herself who had seduced him, just as her mother Menaka had seduced the brahmarishi. She had done it subtly, no doubt, with carefully orchestrated details. Perhaps it had all been planned by some rivals of his throne—misdirecting them into that remote aranya, leading them farther and farther inland into a place where they almost died of thirst, and then finally, when they were almost dead from lack of water, letting them find that grove. Naturally, it had seemed idyllic and perfect. Shakuntala must have been posed that way, freshly bathed, hair loose and wet, emphasizing her figure and beauty, body clad in only that simple transparent garment. The more he thought about it, the more he became convinced that he had been seduced and deceived, that it had been the intention of his rivals and the woman to lure him there and trick him into begetting a child upon her, so that they might claim his throne. Even her condition of marriage: that her son would be heir to the Kuru empire. Why would an innocent unworldly rishi's daughter demand such a condition? Why would she even think of it? No, surely there was mischief at work there. She had been too perfect to be true. He must have been half-deluded by thirst and the strangeness of the forest, and she must have drugged or influenced him somehow, either through the water she gave him to drink or the fruits she offered him to eat. Yes, he had been tricked and she had been the instrument of his enemies to unseat him when all other means failed.

Convinced of this, Dushyanta deliberately ignored his promise to Shakuntala and continued living as before. He grew harder and harsher in his kingship, forced to make hard choices and take difficult decisions in order to retain his power and authority. As time passed, the incredible hours he spent in Shakuntala's arms began to seem more and more dreamlike, less real. Until finally, a day came when he felt he must rid himself of the memory itself, and act as if it had never happened. He sought the advice of his ministers and of advisors well versed in law and dharma and they too advised the same course of action. Since only Shakuntala and he had been present when that pact was made, all he had to do was deny any such pact existed. She had no other means of proving her claim. Who would believe the word of some wanton woman from the wilderness against the word of a Kuru emperor?

And so, Dushyanta forgot Shakuntala.

Meanwhile, back in the ashram of Rishi Kanva, Shakuntala did indeed conceive from the union. Her gestation was a long one, for she was determined that she would deliver her child on royal silks in the palatial settings he deserved. A prince, a future king, a Kuru emperor, he could not be born here in the wilderness. She extended her gestation through the power of her will, certain that Dushyanta would live up to his promise and send for her. But the months passed, and then a whole year went by with no sign of her husband or his representatives. Still she held the baby in her womb, nursing it within, refusing to birth it anywhere except where she felt it was intended to be born. But still no army came, no escort, not even a messenger from her beloved. She waited and waited, and as the first year became a second, and then the third year loomed, she knew at last that something must have befallen him. Some complex weaving of political forces had prevented him from sending for her. Perhaps he feared that his representatives would lead his enemies to her, that she and the child might be in danger? Perhaps there were other issues at stake that she did not know of, that she could not possibly understand out here in the forest, and he did not wish to send her a message for fear it might be intercepted and used against him? Her mind always found some way to rationalize and justify the delay, never once blaming him for the lapse. It was never Dushyanta who was at fault, merely circumstances, or the weight of kingship, or some unknown cause.

When three years had passed, she permitted her son to be born.

Contained within her womb for such a long time, he had grown strong and powerful. The moment he was born, he began to grow at a prodigious rate. In no time at all, he was the equivalent of any other three-year-old boy. At an age when other children could barely walk, he could run and jump and his bones were strongly knitted and body much larger than a one-year-old's. His progress continued at the same rapid rate. His teeth and nails and bones were particularly strong. Even falls from heights did not break his bones. His bite could rival that of a lion. Living in a jungle, he was fond of wandering off into the deep woods on his own, at an age when most children could barely walk a few steps from their mother before falling down. He ran for miles, watching the animals of the forest and growing fascinated with them. He played with lion cubs in the presence of the mother lion, who looked on and yawned indulgently. He climbed on baby elephants and rode foals. In time, his play turned rougher as he grew bolder and more mischievous. He would wrestle with lions, tie up elephants to trees, ride wild buffalo, grapple with large tusked boars and force them to the ground, sit upon the backs of tigers and compel them to take him where he pleased. He feared no beast and because of this, the animals came to respect him and let him do as he pleased. They became his companions and friends.

By the time he was six years old he was as strong and well built as any young man. Even if one added the three years he had spent in the womb, he still looked nearly twice his age. Awed by his growth, valour and rapid progress, the rishis of Kanva's ashram called him Sarvadamana, He Who Subjugates Everything. In addition, he had a birthmark on his palm, roughly shaped like a chakra. It was the symbol of a king and every rishi who saw him agreed that he could become nothing less than a samrat, a king of kings.

Finally, the day came when all the rishis and sadasyas of the ashram came to Rishi Kanva and told him that the time had come for young Sarvadamana to be installed as yuvaraja. Rishi Kanva agreed. 'A married woman cannot stay forever in her parents' home. Sooner or later she must go to her husband's house, otherwise people will speak ill of her and her marriage.'

Shakuntala had long since realized that her husband would not send for her. But she had not wished to dishonour her father by saying so and had held her tongue. Now, when he urged her to go to Dushyanta, she made only a feeble protest. 'He said he would send for me.' Her father sighed, 'Nine years is long enough to wait. Now it is time to go to him and confront him with his son.' Shakuntala did not protest further. The very next day, Sarvadamana and she left for Gajashraya, the City of Elephants, accompanied by a contingent of her father's most trusted disciples.

On arrival, she went straight to the palace and sought an audience with her husband. Dushyanta was holding court with the full sabha in attendance. Kings, queens, princes, princesses, nobles of every major house, ministers and advisors, priests and diplomats, emissaries and visiting dignitaries, the cream of Arya royalty was present. When the roughly-clad woman came forward with her son dressed in a fur cloth, he failed to even recognize her.

'Dushyanta,' she said, and at the sound of her voice and at the sight of her appearance, the court's hustle and bustle died down instantly. Who was this woman, dressed in rags, calling the king by his first name? What gumption! What arrogance! What ignorance. Tch tch. 'It is I, Shakuntala, whom you took as your wife in the ashram of my father Rishi Kanva. I have brought before you the fruit of our union, your son. Remember our pact and take him into your house. Crown him your yuvaraja as promised and make him heir apparent to the Kuru crown.'

In the great commotion that followed, Raja Dushyanta was rendered speechless. Of course he remembered Shakuntala now. His eyes, accustomed to seeing women with painted faces and bejewelled ornaments and silks, had barely given her a second glance. Yet once she had presented herself, there was no mistaking her. At once, the memory of that passionate encounter, so long buried and forgotten, came to the fore of his mind—and his heart. He was filled with a surge of overwhelming love and joy. My son? Our son? He almost ran down the steps to embrace Shakuntala and the handsome young boy who stood beside her, looking unmistakably like a young Dushyanta. Forgotten were the ravings of his besieged mind about her being part of a conspiracy against him. Forgotten were all his suspicions and doubts. Forgotten were the years he had spent making backroom deals and doing whatever had to be done to hold the Kuru empire together and stabilize his throne. Shakuntala was here! His love, his only true love. And he had a son by her.

Together they would live now, as king and queen, with a young, strong prince to succeed him. He was weary of the coquettish princesses and spoilt concubines that had paraded through his bedroom over the years. None had meant a fraction of what Shakuntala meant to him. Even after years married to so many women, that single day he had spent with her in the forest outweighed them all. He had regained his true love, his only love. Everything would be different now. He could be happy once again.

But then he came to his senses and heard the murmurs of the court. All eyes were on him, awaiting his response. He realized he had begun to stand, his hands still on the armrests of the throne. Hearing the curious whispers of his closest advisors and catching the mood of the comments flying around the hall, he resumed his seat. This could not be. He could not accept Shakuntala or her son. It would undo everything he had worked for, over these past nine years. The struggles of a decade would be ruined. Rebellions would break out once more, fomented by rumours of the king losing his head and handing over his kingdom to an unknown brahmacharini's bastard child. His alliances would be worthless, his marriages and backdoor deals rendered impotent. His allies would turn against him, even the people might revolt, unwilling to accept this unknown heir apparent whom they had never heard of before. People would ask if a king's every get from the wrong side of town was to be granted a crown and a throne, or if this was an exception. He would be the butt of jokes and vile rumours. The very authority of Hastinapura would be undermined.

His grip tightened on the lion's heads that adorned the ends of the armrests, pressing hard on the delicately inlaid silver.

'Sadhini,' he said coldly, speaking loudly and harshly that all might hear him. 'What nonsense do you spout? I have never seen you before in my life. How dare you come before the throne of Hastinapura and make these wild accusations? Neither by dharma, kama or artha did I ever make any pact with you, marital or otherwise. Now go from here before I have you removed by force!'

At these words, the mood of the court changed at once. He felt the surge of relief and regret that swept across the sabha hall. His rivals and enemies were regretful that he had not committed an error of judgement, giving them cause to vent more complaints against him, while his friends and well-wishers were relieved that he had responded so strongly and clearly.

But on no one else in that court did Dushyanta's response have a greater impact than on Shakuntala. At once her face altered, her beauty shrinking. Her eyes turned as red as copper as tears welled up uncontrollably. Her lips trembled. And though she remained decorous and made no aggressive movements towards the king—the armed soldiers around her made such a move ill-advised— yet through her eyes she communicated more anger than men might do by brandishing swords. Silent for a long tortuous moment, when she spoke again it was with the accumulated pain and sorrow of a decade of patient waiting and unshakable faith. In a single moment with a few words, Dushyanta had shattered her expectations and faith, humiliated her and reduced her life to ashes and shame. 'Raje,' she said, addressing him by his proper title, 'Great Samrat of the Kuru empire. Consider your words again. You know that what I say is truth and nothing but truth. You yourself were witness to our pact. I urge you: Do what is righteous under dharma. Do the right thing. By lying to me you lie to your own self. By doing so you steal truth from yourself. You do not sin against me, you sin against yourself! And he who can commit such a transgression against himself, what might he not do to others? Listen to your heart and your conscience. There is a being that dwells within each man, and he dwells within you as well. He knows everything you do, good or bad. He is that which is a part of god within us and which makes us godlike. Not for nothing is Yama lord of dharma as well as death. Those who follow dharma may be excused an error of judgement. But the one who denies his errors cannot be forgiven. Yama will hunt him down and punish him. I have been faithful to you in every respect. Patiently and silently I waited nine long years, though you said it would be no more than nine days till you sent for me. You said you would send a four-fold army to bring me with all due pomp and ceremony to this very palace. As befitted a queen, you said! And yet, after keeping me waiting in the forest for nine years, when I come to you without complaint or accusation, you treat me this way? Why do you turn this cruel face to me, Dushyanta? This is your dharma. You have no choice but to obey! If not, may your head be splintered into a thousand pieces! The ancients teach us that a son is a part of the husband's body that is rejuvenated and brought back into this world by the wife. That is why the other word for wife is jaya, for with her by his side a man is ever victorious! Because bearing a son saves one's soul from the realm of hell known as put, therefore a son is known as putra.'

Shakuntala looked around at the court filled with richly clad and bejewelled spectators. She had no friends or well-wishers there. She was an island of dharma in an ocean of injustice. She wept and wrung her hands in misery and appealed to the stranger who sat upon the throne, his cold, hard face turned away from her, contemplating some distant pillar or detail of the fine architecture of his hall.

'What shall I say to convince you further?' She went on. 'I am a true wife who follows every word of the shastras. I keep house diligently. I bore you a son. I am devoted to you, even when you were absent for nine years I never once thought ill of you. I am a part of you now, and together we have made a better part of ourselves in this, our son. I am the means by which you can achieve dharma, artha and kama. I am the only friend who will be with you to the very end of your life.'

But still Dushyanta was as unyielding as a stone statue and as unrelenting as iron. Weeping copiously, Shakuntala broke down, retreating into the familiar territory of the shastras and Vedic knowledge and lore with which she had grown up, as the daughter of a maharishi, and keeper of an ashram full of learned brahmins.

'A man who has a wife can pursue grihastha-ashrama.

A man who has a wife can find happiness. A man who has a wife has a friend in solitude, an associate in ceremonies, and a caretaker in times of suffering. Even in exile, a wife refreshes her husband when all else is lost.

'A man with a wife can be trusted. A wife is a man's best means of salvation. When a man dies, the wife will even accompany him to the afterworld, for even after death the marital bond does not end unless you wish it to end. A wife who dies before her husband will not continue on her way but will wait for him to arrive that they might proceed together.'

She continued in this vein for an unknown length of time, her voice growing shriller, her words a litany, her message reduced to a plaintive drone.

Finally, at a gesture from the advisors, the soldiers came forward, intending to escort her out of the palace.

At this, she came to her senses and pushed them away, warning them not to come closer. They stepped back warily but remained close at hand, in case she attempted something more desperate.

Instead, she changed her mode of appeal. She held out her hands, palms joined together, in an appeal to Dushyanta.

'If you will not accept me as a wife, whatever your reasons, then at least accept this, your own son. The Vedas tell us we should utter these words when a son is born: "Born of my body, born of my heart, you are I myself returned to life again. May you live a thousand autumns. You extend my life and lineage infinitely. Therefore live well, live happy forever." Look at him, Dushyanta, this is

your son, you can see it on his face, his body, his smile.
Just as the ahavaniya fire is kindled from the garhapatya
fire, so has his body been kindled from your own. It is as
if you divided yourself into two and this is the younger
half. Remember how we conceived him? You were on
a hunting expedition and lost your way. To my father's
ashram you came and begged me to marry you in the
gandharva style. I was reluctant but you convinced me
it was righteous under dharma and I agreed and we
indulged in wedlock.'

Dushyanta's voice was quiet in the silent hall. 'Woman,
I do not even know you. We have never met before. I do
not even know your name.' 'Do not say that!' she cried.
'I am Shakuntala! I told you the story of my birth. My
mother was Menaka, the foremost of apsaras. Of all the
six supreme apsaras—Urvashi, Purvachitti, Sahajanya,
Menaka, Vishwachi and Ghritachi, she was the one born
from Brahma and the best of them all. Urged by Indra,
aided by Vayu and Kama, she descended from Indraloka
to earth and seduced Brahmarishi Vishwamitra. The fruit
of their union was I, so named because after birth I was
protected by shakuna birds. The sage Kanva adopted me
and raised me as his own daughter. It was to his ashram
that you came that day nine years ago and we met. What
sins did I commit in what past life that you deny me now,
I do not know. If you choose to forsake me, then so be
it, I shall return meekly to my father's ashram and live
out the rest of my life in solitude. But do not deny this
boy his legacy. He is your own son!'

Dushyanta's face was never crueller than in that

moment. 'Shakuntala, if that is your name... Even if a trace of what you say were true, even if that were so, yet tell me this. How do I know this son is mine? Should I simply take your word for it? Why should I believe you? Your father was a kshatriya who turned brahmin to achieve his own ends, not because he had some higher goal. Even as a brahmin, he succumbed to lust. You claim he sired you upon Menaka, the celestial courtesan? Look at your state! How can you compare yourself to that legendary epitome of womanhood? And this boy you claim is my son, conceived nine years ago? Look at him. Everyone, look at him. He is not nine years old! He is huge. He is perhaps twice that age. His body is like the trunk of the shala tree, his arms are like a wrestler's arms. What nine-year-old boy could have such a physique? Everything you say is nothing but lies. I do not know you or acknowledge him. Go away from here at once and do as you wish. You are nobody to me.'

6

At this terrible pronouncement, even the collective emotions of the sabha hall seemed to turn towards sympathy for the ascetic woman with the young boy. Even Dushyanta's fiercest political opponents within the court smiled thinly, inwardly cursing the king's clarity of purpose. They had been hoping beyond hope that he would have relented and acknowledged the woman, for it was clear that there had been some relationship between them at some time. Ascetics as high-minded as she did not make such claims lightly. Rishi Kanva was a legendary if obscure brahmin. Nobody from his ashram would lie outright, that too on such a royal scale. Probably the king had indeed encountered the woman during one of his many hunting expeditions. There had even been one famous such expedition nine years ago, where he had gone missing for several fortnights. Everyone recalled it well because it was that absence that had fuelled the crisis in the administrative scene, and changed the landscape of Hastinapura's politics. It was also notable because ever since that day, the king had never once ventured away from the capital for more than a few days, no more than a fortnight, and only in the rarest of emergencies. His iron hand and constant presence here had been the very reason why they were unable to work their machinations and pursue their own agenda as forcefully as before. So the more the woman had argued, her passion and intensity—and her painful sincerity, above all—had won their minds over, making everyone believe that there was some truth to what she claimed, if it wasn't the whole truth. The setting was ripe for a controversy. But by denying her so brusquely and cruelly, the king had eliminated any accusations they might have levelled against him. By himself refusing to acknowledge her or the boy, he had left no room for controversy. By law, the court then had to abide by his decision and ignore the woman and her son. It was an unfortunate missed opportunity.

Now, the soldiers moved forward again, this time authorized to haul the woman and boy out of court and out of the city, never to be seen again. Even they moved slowly, faces revealing mixed emotions. This was not some hardened criminal threatening the king. A brahmin woman of such high birth, with such obviously austere upbringing, she was a person to be respected, admired, not apprehended and exiled. But they had their dharma to fulfil. And so they moved closer, blocking her way to the king in case she should attempt something untoward.

'Is this your dharma?' she asked. Her voice was clearly audible in the hushed hall. Everyone was listening with rapt attention, aware that the unexpected drama was almost at an end. Many were openly shocked at Raja Dushyanta's final words and the uncompromising harshness he had displayed. It was evidence of how much he had changed in these past nine years. No more the playful king who cavorted with concubines and indulged in every fleshly pleasure, leaving the administration of the kingdom to his advisors and allies. This was an emperor in every sense of the word, ruling the empire he had himself consolidated and strengthened in the past decade, with a firm rein and unshakable resoluteness. Imperial. That was the one word that described his response. The words of an emperor, who had once been a king, who had once been a man. Thus did kingship change men from flesh and blood to iron and gold with hearts of steel.

'Is this the way you treat your own wife and son?' she asked. The soldiers, only yards from her, looked at one another, unsure what to do. Their leader gestured and they retreated to their earlier positions, remaining close enough to apprehend her instantly should she make any foolish move, yet far away to allow her a few more moments to speak her mind—and heart. What could be the harm? From the way they looked down at the polished floor of the hall, even they felt sympathy for her, especially after the king's cruel denials.

'You accuse me... Me! ...of such things, yet what of yourself? Is your moral vision so obscured? You see the faults of others even if they are as tiny as mustard seeds but your own, though they are as fat as bilva fruit, you ignore! You dare denigrate me and deny me the truth of my own birth? Who are you to deny me? My mother was indeed Menaka. It is true that as one of the greatest apsaras to the gods, she was able to keep herself well bathed and cared for, clad in the finest garments and most precious ornaments. I have lived the life of a sadhini, in a humble forest ashram, working with my bare hands, with no comforts or luxuries. I have no fine clothes, no jewellery, and I am covered with the dust and grime of a long foot journey. But nine years ago, when you saw me for the first time, freshly bathed from the river, my hair loosed by my waist, you claimed that I was no less than an apsara to your eyes! You showered compliments upon my beauty like leaves in autumn. Perhaps much of my beauty has waned with time, for these past nine years have been very hard on me. Perhaps I was never beautiful and you lied to me that day. But it is not my opinion or claim we are debating, it is your own! By your own admission, you are either a liar or a man without dharma! While I have spoken only the truth, in every single word and detail. The difference between you and me, great Dushyanta, is like the difference between a mustard seed and Mount Meru! For I have abided by dharma in every single respect, but you ignore even common decency.'

Now she took a single step forward, raising her hand accusingly to point at the throne upon the dais. The advisors and ministers nearest to the king cringed, for all knew the wrath of a brahmin could be terrible and feared a brahmanic curse. Even the servants fanning the king and standing by with wine and fruit blanched visibly and stepped aside, seeking to distance themselves from their liege in the event that the sadhini issued some terrible pronouncement. The sabha hall's silence deepened to a deathly absence of sound. Not one person coughed or shifted in their seats or moved so much as a tinkling

in puerile arguments. It is a fact of life that the truly evil person always insists that he is truly good and that those who are genuinely good are truly evil! Thus do the fools of the world try to separate morality into black and white and shades of grey, insisting always that they themselves are pure white, or at worst, a subtle shade of grey. In fact, grey itself is a shade of black. The truly wise do not grade people at all, they accept all humans as equal and only behaviour as good or evil.'

Shakuntala took another step forward, her eyes blazing like rubies in her ebony face. A rumbling sound began to grow as she spoke. The congregation looked around, at each other, then at the walls and pillars and ceiling, wondering at the sound, yet too awed by the sadhini's passion and the power of her eloquence to make any move. Each one feared that by moving he or she would attract the wrath of the brahmin onto himself or herself, and that fear kept them rock still, even as the rumbling built and grew into something ominous, as if a thundercloud had formed upon the ceiling of the hall itself and threatened to unleash a vajra at any instant.

'Your denial of my words hurts me deeply, I do not deny it. But I do not address that. It is your denial of your own flesh and blood that I cannot tolerate. It has been said in our shastras that a man who denies his own son can never ascend to higher worlds. The gods themselves destroy his prosperity! So by denying the son of your own body you are invoking the wrath of the gods themselves and leading your entire kingdom and dynasty into ruin!'

With a crash, the rumbling broke into a boom. A

blinding miasma forced everyone to shut their eyes momentarily. When they opened their eyes again almost at once, nothing had changed, yet clearly some supernatural force had spoken in that sound, expressing its wrath.

Shakuntala continued. 'The pitris, our ancestors, have said that the son establishes the family and continues the lineage, and thus, a son can never be abandoned. Pitr Manu even said that a man need not beget a son through biological conception alone. That is one way, to beget a son upon one's wife. But he also spelled out five other ways in which sons can be had—they can be obtained, bought, reared, adopted, or begotten on women other than one's wife. All these qualify as sons. Yet you who have begotten your own son upon your own lawfully wedded wife, deny him!' The rumbling grew again, this time increasing in intensity and depth, like some great invisible giant gnashing his teeth and growling in anticipation of a death blow. 'Sons support the dharma of men, enhance their father's fame, and bring happiness to their father's hearts. Sons are the rafts of dharma upon which ancestors are transported to the heavenly realms and steered away from the hellish worlds! The shastras also tell us that one natural pond is better than a hundred dug wells. In turn, a sacrifice is better than a hundred natural ponds. But a son is better than a hundred sacrifices. And truth is better than a hundred sons! Can you estimate then, the extent of your falsehood in denying the truth of your own son's existence?'

Now the mood in the sabha hall began to turn to one of near-panic. For everyone feared that the power of the sadhini's anger would scorch all present. She would at any time unleash the full potency of her tapas energy and all would be turned to ashes. But still none dared move.

Only Dushyanta sat silent and still, staring down from his throne without expression. Neither anger nor sorrow nor fear passed across his face. Only the steadfast expression of a monarch who had seen entire armies ground to dust and empires crumble and fall, the face of a man who looks upon his own certain death and does not fear or thwart it, merely watches it approach.

'Your transgression is not against me, or even your own son,' Shakuntala said in a voice that seemed made of the thunder itself, her eyes flashing with a ruby fire that resembled lightning in the belly of a cloud. 'It is against truth itself! For I can accept your denial, your turning me away, your lack of love for me, everything. What I cannot and will not accept is your lies! You deny the truth of my identity. The truth of our marriage. The truth of our union. The truth of our son's birth and existence. This is unacceptable to me. Truth is greater than all the Vedas, greater than dharma, it is the supreme brahman itself, it is the ultimate godhead. Therefore I pronounce this judgement upon you, king of the Kurus. Once you are dead, my son will rule over your kingdom, sit upon your throne, wear your robes and your crown, eat from the same golden plate and drink from the same silver chalice, and he shall reign undisputed and unrivalled. None will dare challenge his supremacy, none will win in battle against him, none will triumph against him in statecraft. He shall be emperor not just in name but in truth! This, I declare to be true and so shall it come to pass!'

And with a great thundering boom, forcing all present to shut their eyes and cry out in terror, the entire world turned to blinding white. Every mind went blank for an instant, every mouth opened to release an involuntary scream, and it was as if the entire congregation were merged with some celestial congregation, as if the court of the gods themselves was superimposed upon this court of Dushyanta; and those celestial courtiers, the devas themselves, spoke in their rumbling booming voices with one single tone, and all they said was, 'It shall be so.'

Then a single great voice, like a gruff grandfather of all creation, spoke: 'Shakuntala speaks truth. This son is the son of Dushyanta. He must be maintained by Dushyanta, and because of this, he shall be known as He Who Is Maintained, Bharata.' The final word boomed forth like a blast of thunder from a thousand thunderclouds, etching the word into the memories of all present.

And then the world flashed again to black and when the blindness passed, all was as it had been before.

7

Dushyanta descended from the throne dais. All eyes were upon him, all throats silent.

He reached the floor of the sabha hall, the same polished level on which Shakuntala and her son—Bharata, he would henceforth always be known by the name Bharata—stood. He smiled and held out his arms.

'My love,' he said. 'My wife! My son.'

A great gasp of excitement rippled through the congregation.

Dushyanta gestured at the royalty, nobility and aristocracy seated around on gilded thrones of their own, the pride and majesty of the empire gathered together. 'Had I accepted you at your first word, as I dearly desired to do, these same people would have renounced me. Had I embraced you and acknowledged you as my wife and Bharata as our son, they would have turned against me. Sedition, conspiracy, assassination, rebellion, secession, these would all have been the order of the day. For only through a show of cruel strength can an emperor hold an empire together. Such is the way it has always been and so shall it always be. There was no place for you or our son in the life of the emperor of Hastinapura. And

Dushyanta the king who loved you at first sight and married you...why, he would have been assassinated within days, if not moments, of accepting a simple rishi's daughter as his wife and a boy of such obvious dharmic power as his son and heir. Alliances would have toppled, coalitions collapsed, and war would have broken out over the issue of succession alone. Even the people would have been hard-pressed to accept you as their queen or Bharata as their yuvaraja. Therefore I was compelled to lie to you, and deny you. But now, now that all this great gathering has witnessed my denials, heard your responses and witnessed for itself the great voice of the gods that spoke thereafter, and heard what that voice had to say, nobody can dispute your righteousness, nor the veracity of your claims.'

Shakuntala had listened to all this with wide, staring eyes. No more tears fell from her face, but her anger and grief had begun to dissipate, unveiling the beauty that lay beneath. Now, she cocked her head in hesitation, asking doubtfully, 'You...you knew this would happen? You... deliberately compelled me to speak?'

Dushyanta approached her, bowing his head low, his face expressing regret and genuine pain. 'Never have I had to show such cruelty before, not even when I pronounced a sentence of death or slaughtered innocents in order to achieve a military goal. Yes, I admit it, my beloved wife. I provoked you into speaking out, knowing that as a brahmin's daughter and one brought up in the way of dharma, you would not tolerate lies. Therefore I did not simply deny you and turn you away. For nine years I lived in anguish and self-recrimination. I did not know how to send for you and make you my queen without causing the kingdom to revolt against me. It was a seditious time, a turbulent decade. What would have been the point of making you my queen for a night, only to see the kingdom burn and both of us assassinated and our son slain? My only recourse was through dharma. Therefore I waited for you to come to me. You took a long enough time! And when you came before me, I knew I must provoke you into speaking out, to saying exactly the kind of things you said. The honest person is always predictable for he or she will always do what is right! So did you. And your anger and your righteousness prompted the gods themselves to intervene, when the court of men had failed to speak for you,' he gestured at his own court, 'and to pronounce judgement on your behalf. For we still live in an age when dharma and fidelity are rewarded, not punished or ignored. And now, all the world knows that Shakuntala is my lawful wife and Bharata my lawful son and heir. None dare dispute it,' Dushyanta raised his voice to a menacing baritone, glancing around at his courtiers, 'or they risk incurring not just my wrath but the wrath of the gods themselves!' Not one person met his eyes with a challenge or denial. If anything, all bowed their heads in acquiescence.

Shakuntala smiled then, and in that smile her radiant beauty was visible for all to see, the beauty of a mortal woman born of the apsara Menaka, most beautiful of all female creations. Dushyanta came to her and embraced her, tentatively at first, then openly, and Bharata, laughing and happy at the reunion of his parents, joined in the embrace, and with one movement, the entire court rose to its feet, and began applauding and cheering. The hall filled with their deafening cries of joy and support, and not a single one dared offer any opposition.

'I love you,' Dushyanta said softly to his wife, clasping her and acknowledging her before the entire world. 'Rule with me and be my queen. It is time to fulfil all my promises to you and for us to resume the marriage we entered into so briefly that auspicious day.'

And Shakuntala was pacified and appeased and filled with love and joy.

Thus was Bharata, son of Dushyanta and Shakuntala, born and made heir to the throne of the Kuru nation. In time, he ascended to the throne, exactly as Shakuntala had predicted, and Dushyanta had desired, and in time he brought about the enduring peace that his father had struggled to maintain. Living up to his name, he maintained and was maintained. He came to be known as Chakravarti, monarch of all realms, and as Sarvabhauma, sovereign of the world. He performed many great yagnas, and his grandfather, Rishi Kanva was the officiating priest at all of them. And from his lineage was engendered the modern Indian state of Bharat, better known now as India. Thus did one of itihasa's greatest love stories engender a nation.

GANGA AND SHANTANU

1

Mahabhisha was a king of the Ikshvaku clan. Truthful and courageous, he was renowned for having performed one thousand Ashvamedha sacrifices and one hundred Vajapeya sacrifices. For his devotion and sacrifice, he attained entrance to the heavenly realms and was honoured by the devas.

One day the devas, accompanied by many rajarshis including King Mahabhisha, went to pay homage to Lord Brahma. Ganga, queen of all rivers on earth, also came to pay her respects. As always she was clad in a flimsy garment as white as moonlight. Just as she presented herself before Brahma, a wind blew away her insubstantial vastra and she was left completely exposed. Embarrassed, all present averted their faces, except for King Mahabhisha who found himself unable to avoid admiring Ganga's beauty. He was powerfully aroused by her womanly splendour. Aware of his unabashed gaze, Ganga too felt her emotions stir and was curious as to who this rajarshi might be who dared to look upon her undaunted when even the devas had lowered their eyes. As Mahabhisha continued to stare at her nakedness, completely lost in contemplation of her beauty, Lord Brahma took offence at his rudeness. 'Shameless one, for this you shall be reborn once again on the earthly realm.' But because his sin was only a minor one, the Creator also decreed that once his mortal life was ended, Mahabhisha would once again attain the heavenly realms. Mahabhisha did not protest or object to the punishment, which only increased Ganga's curiosity. He only asked Brahma-dev, humbly, if he could be born as the son of a great king in his own lineage. After considering who a suitable candidate might be, he proposed the name of Pratipa. His request was granted and he prepared to descend one last time to the mortal realm to accept his danda without complaint.

After a last glance at her admirer who had willingly accepted punishment for the simple act of gazing at her, Ganga departed the court of Brahma.

2

Now, around this time, a similar penalty had been imposed upon the eight Vasus. These divine dwellers in the heavenly realms had committed a grave error and as a result were also cursed to take rebirth in human form on earth for a single lifetime.

The great Brahmarishi Vasishtha, son of Varuna, lived upon Mount Meru, king of mountains. In that idyllic place, he performed his austerities and sacrifices. Requiring a plentiful supply of ghee to offer during his sacrifices, he had need of a cow. He appealed to Sage Kashyapa who fathered upon Surabhi, daughter of Daksha, a magical cow capable of fulfilling every desire. Despite her magical properties, Vasishtha only used the cow sparingly to obtain the milk product he required for his sacrificial offerings.

One day, the divine Vasus came to Mount Meru. It was common for devas, rajarshis and other divine personages to rove the idyllic forests of Mount Meru. The Vasus came with their wives and made love upon that scenic slope. Afterwards, wandering near the ashram of Vasishtha, the wife of Dyau chanced upon the magical cow. Realizing by the power of her own divinity as well as the cow's extraordinary qualities that it was no common animal, she tested its nature. She was astonished by its powers and rushed back to her husband. Vasishtha was away at this time. Urged by his wife, Dyau came to see the cow and was equally amazed by its celestial beauty and powers. He saw the ashram and immediately knew that it was Vasishtha's hermitage. He told his wife, 'I know of this divine cow. It belongs to Varuna's son, Vasishtha, who lives here. Apart from its ability to produce anything one desires, this creature's milk grants anyone who drinks it ten thousand years of undiminished youth!'

Hearing this, the wife of Dyau was struck by a thought. Her dearest friend Jinnavati, daughter of Rajarshi Ushinara, was the most beautiful young woman and dearly desired to retain her youth and beauty forever. 'How wonderful it would be if we could give this cow's milk to her to drink. She would be able to stay young and lovely always!' The only way to do so would be to take the cow as well as its calf to Jinnavati, in order to draw the milk fresh before drinking. Dyau was hesitant but his wife seduced him with amorous promises and he succumbed. With the help of the eldest Vasu, Prithu, and their other brothers, they stole the cow and her calf and took her to Jinnavati's domicile.

Vasishtha had left the ashram to collect fruits. When he returned and found the cow and calf missing, he grew concerned for their welfare. Worried they might have got loose from their tethers, he searched for them in the forest. But when he could not find them anywhere, he knew something was amiss. Resorting to his divine sight, he perceived that they had been stolen by the Vasus to please the wife of one of them. Enraged, he cursed the Vasus. As divine beings who had never set foot on earth, the worst punishment possible for them was to be sent down to the mortal realm where they could never enjoy the same powers and pleasures they enjoyed in heaven. Therefore he cursed them to be reborn in human form for a single lifetime.

Feeling the effect of the curse, the Vasus raced back to Mount Meru. They prostrated themselves before Vasishtha and pleaded for clemency. But for a very long time, he remained adamant. Finally, acknowledging that all of them were not equally responsible for the transgression, he modified his curse. 'As you only did your brother's bidding, you will be permitted to return to the heavenly realms after spending a year on earth. But Dyau, who was fully aware of his crime, shall remain in the world of men for the entire duration of his mortal lifetime. In addition, because he was seduced into committing this crime by promises of amorous pleasure, therefore he shall be denied the pleasure of cohabitation during his time on earth. He shall remain celibate and shall sire no offspring. He may devote himself to the pursuit of dharma in order to learn right from wrong, and attain skill in the use of weapons, remaining always among men and neither gaining pleasure from nor giving satisfaction to women.'

3

Remorseful and stricken, the Vasus left the heavenly realms and were making their way to the mortal world when they met Ganga, who had only just departed Brahma's court. She heard their voices and saw their agitated state and enquired what the matter was. They told her the story. She sympathized with their plight and told them of King Mahabhisha who had just been penalized with the same penalty, albeit for a different reason.

When the Vasus heard that Mahabhisha was to be reborn as Shantanu, the son of King Pratipa in the great line of Puru and Bharata, they saw an opportunity. 'Great goddess of the river, grant us your grace. We have never entered the womb of a mortal woman before. Our divinity shall be diminished if we do so now. You are the purest epitome of womanhood in all the worlds. Descend upon earth and allow us to be born as your children.'

Ganga had sympathy for the plight of the Vasus but she was hesitant for one reason. 'In order to do as you wish, I would have to cohabit with a mortal man. His semen would have to enter my womb.'

'Let the man be this same King Shantanu in whose mortal body Mahabhisha will take rebirth. Shantanu is destined to be a great king and Mahabhisha's illustriousness is already legendary. We would be honoured to have such a personage sire us in the mortal world.'

Ganga thought of the way Mahabhisha had stared openly and unashamedly at her nakedness in Brahma's court and also of the powerful emotions that had stirred within her when she returned his unabashed gaze. There had been a great sharing of erotic energy between them at the time, and she could still feel her loins stir with desire for him. If she consented to help the Vasus, she would have an opportunity to unite with Mahabhisha in his mortal form as Shantanu, and fulfil her suppressed desires. It would not be for selfish fulfilment but for a righteous cause.

She agreed to do as the Vasus requested. 'Very well. I will agree to cohabit with King Shantanu on earth and give birth to you. But once born, you will have to live out your lives as mortal men. Is that acceptable to you?'

The Vasus discussed the matter and said, 'Seven of us are permitted to return home after spending one year on earth. Therefore, all you need do is to hurl each of your newborn sons into your own waters after birth. Through your divine channel which connects all three worlds, we shall ascend back to heaven. Cruel as this may seem, it is in fact a blessed release, for to stay mortal is greater suffering for us than for the mortal children to be drowned at birth.' They added wistfully, 'Only our brother Dyau shall have to remain on earth for the entire span of his mortal life. That is part of the curse.'

'It is good,' Ganga said thoughtfully, thinking of

Shantanu. 'Slaying the seven of you may release your souls for ascension but it deprives Shantanu of his sons. This way, at least one will remain with him to be his heir.'

'It shall be so,' they agreed, 'but there are certain conditions. The eighth son cannot have children of his own or mate with any woman.'

Ganga nodded sadly. 'If that is what the curse demands, so be it.'

4

King Pratipa was a deeply devout man. He spent every moment he could spare in meditation. His favourite spot was a certain place on the banks of the Ganga. One day while he sat cross-legged, lost in silent contemplation, Ganga rose in human form. Emerging from the river in droplets and spray that coalesced to form the shape and solidity of a human woman, she stepped onto the bank and approached Pratipa. So absorbed was he in meditation, he did not notice her approach. So she sat on his right thigh.

Opening his eyes, Pratipa was unperturbed by this sudden appearance of a beautiful woman. As a king and a warrior he had seen and experienced all the ways of the world. He asked Ganga kindly, 'Bhagyavaan, what is your desire?'

Ganga replied coyly, 'I desire you, great king. Take me and love me. I offer myself freely of my own will. I am brimming with desire and cannot be spurned.'

Any other man might well have accepted her without question or further comment, but Pratipa was a spiritual man more concerned with seeking the delights of the soul than the pleasures of the flesh. 'Lady, you are beautiful and desirable. But I do not know you. I cannot cohabit with any woman without knowing her in some detail. It would be against my dharma.'

Ganga replied, 'Not with me. Making love to me can never be forbidden or against dharma. This much I assure you. I bear no ill will or malice towards you, and have no ulterior motives. I genuinely desire union with you. Love me as I wish to love you.'

But still Pratipa resisted temptation. 'In that case, you are greatly desirable, that I cannot deny. But alas, you have chosen to seat yourself on my right thigh. That is reserved for daughters, daughters-in-law and grand-daughters. If you desired to have pleasure with me, you should have seated yourself on my left thigh as that is the proper place for a lover to seat herself. This choice suggests that it is not appropriate for us to cohabit, no matter how great your desires. It would most certainly be against dharma and I cannot condone that.'

Ganga was not disappointed despite the rejection, for she had known all along what she was doing. 'O king, you say the right thigh is the proper seat for a daughter-in-law. Therefore make me your daughter-in-law. Unite me with your son. I am sure a king as magnificent as you are in appearance and wisdom will have an equally illustrious son. It would be my privilege to mate with him and add my contribution to the famous Bharata line.'

'So be it,' said Pratipa gladly. 'However, wise and insightful as you are, you must also know that I have no son and heir yet.'

'I do know this,' Ganga admitted. 'Yet I am of divine

nature and can wait as long as need be without aging or losing my beauty. Therefore I shall gladly wait until you sire a son, for I have decided that he alone shall satisfy my desires. Whenever you have a son and he becomes of marriageable age, bring him here to this very spot and I shall appear to offer myself as his mate. I shall bear him many sons and enhance the reputation and glory of your dynasty, of this you can be assured.'

'It shall be as you say, divine one,' Pratipa said, understanding that his lineage was being blessed by a being of great power.

Ganga rose to leave, then paused and turned briefly. 'King Pratipa, I ask only that you do not reveal my divine nature to your son. Do not tell him who I am, even if you suspect the truth yourself. Also tell him that if he wishes me to bless your bloodline then he must never question what I do, no matter what the circumstances. These are the only two conditions I lay upon you. If they are acceptable to you, then know that your descendants shall be blessed with divine power and fame as a result of this union.'

Pratipa accepted all her conditions and watched as she walked slowly from the bank onto the rushing waters of the river. She stepped across the raging surface of the Ganga as if she were stepping on kusa grass. Dolphins leaped and sang in greeting, turtles swam around her in homage and her power over the river was evident. When she was in mid-river, her body itself turned to water and fell back into the spate from whence it had come, leaving only her clear grey eyes lingering in mid-air for a moment. Then they too melted into spray and were absorbed by the river. The sound of the Ganga's roar filled Pratipa's ears once more and in its steady torrent, he recognized the voice of the beautiful stranger who had accosted him. But he kept this knowledge of her divinity and true identity a secret within his heart for all time and spoke of it to no one.

In time, Pratipa and his wife performed austerities to obtain the blessing of an heir. Despite their advanced age a son was born to them. This was in fact Mahabhisha reborn under the terms of his danda. Pratipa's son came to be known as Shantanu, because he was created after his father had achieved the state of quietude, Shanti, and gained control of his senses. Indeed, the moment he knew he had a son and heir, Pratipa began preparing him for kingship, and himself for retirement. Shantanu grew up to become a magnificent young prince, intelligent, well-versed in the Vedas and shastras, an expert archer. When he was of age, his father summoned him to the throne chamber and sent away everyone else.

When they were alone he confided in Shantanu. 'My son, your mate in life has been pre-ordained already.'

Shantanu was an obedient son who was willing to do whatever was asked of him. 'Father, if you have chosen a wife for me, I am sure she is no less than Sri herself descended on earth. Whomever you choose is acceptable to me.'

Pratipa was pleased by his son's response but this was no ordinary arranged match he was referring to.

He attempted to explain, choosing his words carefully in keeping with Ganga's wishes. 'The match is somewhat unorthodox,' he admitted to his son. 'For one thing, you cannot ask who she is, nor seek any knowledge of her family, lineage, background or any other details of her life.'

Shantanu was surprised but did his best to be supportive. 'Whatever you say is dharma for me, father,' he replied, though he did wonder at the strangeness of an arranged marriage wherein nothing was known about the bride or her family background!

Pratipa clapped a hand on his son's shoulder. Even at his young age, Shantanu had a neck that the court scribes described as being 'as thick as a conch shell' and shoulders and arms as strong 'as elephant tusks'. The exaggerations were not far off the mark; Shantanu took pride in building his own strength and his many activities kept his body fit and strong. Pratipa had no doubt the boy would grow up to be a great warrior and conqueror of his enemies. It was his judgement as a lover and husband that now concerned him.

'All you need know,' Pratipa said, 'is that she is no ordinary woman. Her beauty is extraordinary, and you will find great pleasure in her company. You shall enjoy great satisfaction in her charms.'

Shantanu was not sure how to react to his father's description of a woman as being sexually attractive, so chose to say nothing. But his father's next words genuinely shocked him.

'She first offered herself to me,' Pratipa confessed, 'a long time ago. I refused only because I did not deem it appropriate.'

Shantanu could not contain his curiosity. His princely upbringing and instruction urged him to remain silent but the boy in him got the better of his grooming. 'Why, father?' he asked. 'If she was so attractive, why did you refuse her?'

Pratipa smiled a wistful smile. 'I loved your mother well enough for one lifetime. Carnal pleasure was never a great attraction for me. It is the spiritual delights of the mind that attract me far more than those of the flesh. But also, the signs were not right.' He frowned, looking into the distance thoughtfully. 'Indeed, looking back on that day, I later thought...'

'What, father?'

'I thought perhaps she never intended to seduce me, she only pretended to do so. It was you she was after all along.'

'Me?' Shantanu was flabbergasted by the idea of a woman pretending to seduce his father in some past time in order to seduce him at some future date. 'But that makes no sense at all. You said this happened before I was even born!'

Pratipa nodded. 'That is why I know, and you know as well, that she could be no ordinary woman. No ordinary mortal woman. Do you follow my meaning?'

Shantanu did. His father was suggesting that the mystery woman was some kind of...goddess? Avatar of a goddess? An apsara or gandharva perhaps? They were considered supremely beautiful. 'Who do you think she—'

Pratipa raised a finger, his wrinkled face turning

severe. 'Enough. No more questions about her. That is a firm condition she laid down. This is why I had this talk with you, so that you would understand and accept these terms before you went to her.'

Shantanu glanced around, his emotions roused. 'Where is she then?'

'First promise that you are ready to accept her conditions.' Pratipa spelled them out clearly and carefully for his son.

Shantanu considered for a moment: mate with a woman who was clearly of divine or otherworldly origin, unspeakably beautiful—if she could have such an effect even on his ascetic father she must be unspeakably beautiful—and capable of giving a man immense carnal pleasure, who wished to confer herself on him, indeed, had desired him since even before he was born, and produce beautiful magnificent children with her, of whom one would rule his kingdom someday and be a legendary and historical king of the Purus? What was there to consider? Except…he desperately wished to know who she was and what her purpose was in seeking him, Shantanu, for so long. What part did he play in this divine erotic game? But that was the first and most important condition: he could never ask who she was or anything else about her.

He hesitated only briefly, but for a boy of his impetuous age and great appetites, even that hesitation was a foretelling of things to come. Perhaps I shall find a way to learn her secret without her knowing, he thought to himself; some way to know everything without breaking the promise. Yes, I am sure I shall be able to do so. For he was a prince of a great empire, inheritor of a great legacy, and of the age when anything seems doable, even the most extraordinary feat imaginable.

Aloud he said simply: 'I agree.'

5

Soon after this curious conversation, King Pratipa installed Shantanu upon the throne of Hastinapura and retired to the forest with his wife, where they spent the rest of their days in pursuit of spiritual ascension.

Shantanu went on to fulfil all the promise of his childhood and youth, becoming a powerful young king. Intelligent and gifted with many physical skills, he grew renowned for his archery. Like many kings of his line, he spent his spare time hunting in the forest. His favourite game animals were deer and buffalo. One day, while hunting alone on the banks of the Ganga, he encountered a vision. The most beautiful woman he had ever seen seemed to suddenly appear out of nowhere. He had been watching the bank carefully, tracking a deer, and she could not possibly have come from the treeline, which meant she must have come from the river, but there was no sign of a boat or raft. One look at her though, and it suddenly failed to matter where she had come from. She was the supreme epitome of womanhood, comparable to the great Lakshmi herself, as that great deity was described in puranas and tales of gods and demons. Her physical form was perfect in every respect, with not a single fault or blemish. When she smiled at him, her teeth flashed white, brilliant and perfect. Her face was so beautiful he could have gazed at her all day and never tired of looking at her. Enhancing her beauty further, she was dressed in golden bejewelled ornaments of a design he had never seen before, scintillating pieces of great workmanship and art. Her splendid body was barely concealed by flimsy translucent garments that swirled around her in the gentle lotus-fragrant wind from the river.

At the sight of her, Shantanu's every hair stood on end, and he dropped his bow as well as the arrow he had been holding. He was stunned by the sight of this extraordinary beauty. Even more astonishing than her beauty was the fact that she gazed at him with a look that bordered on pure adoration. She came closer, her filmy garments moving about her as her ripe, full body undulated with each step, and as she approached, he could see that the look in her eyes was pure, flaming desire. Her own gaze moved up and down his own body, admiring his masculine figure and assets. Never before had he been admired so boldly by a woman, never before had he looked so unabashedly upon a woman of such perfection.

'Who are you?' he asked in a voice hoarse with desire. 'Are you a god perhaps? An asura? Gandharva, apsara, yaksha, pannaga?' Belatedly it occurred to him to add, 'Are you human at all? You cannot be! Human, I mean. You are surely a goddess of some kind.'

Through all these questions, and the spaces between them, spaces in which he could hear nothing but the thundering of his own waves of lust washing upon the shore of his mind counterpointed by the roaring of the Ganga in spate, she remained silent. Only the wanton abandon in her eyes and the sultry movements of her body, clearly aimed at arousing him further, served as her replies.

Finally, he said, 'Goddess or otherwise, whoever you are, please be mine!'

He said these words gently, not in command. And as he said them, he moved slowly towards her, raising his hands in a gesture of wanting, of pleading.

She smiled slowly, and he could not help but smile back, and that simple act of exchanging smiles seemed as intense and satisfying as coupling with most other women. He realized then that he had never truly known love, desire or lust—not until now. What he felt now, this was true desire, real lust, and perhaps true love. He knew only that he wanted her and was willing to pay any price to have her in his bed, in his life. At that precise moment, consumed though he was by his desires, the words of the prophecy that Pratipa had made before leaving for the forest came to him: 'She will come to you one day, and change your life forever.' So this was she, and this the day of their union! His father had spoken wisely: even at first sight, he knew his life had been altered forever.

'I shall be yours only in marriage,' she replied softly, her voice as musical as the song of the river itself. 'And only on the conditions your father laid down. Do you recall those conditions? Can you promise them to me once more? If you can make those little promises and abide by them, we can be married this very day and spend this night itself together, as man and wife.'

He swallowed. Nervousness was never one of his traits. A strong, powerful man with great gifts of mind and body, he had been raised without reason to doubt himself or his abilities. Yet before this vision of a woman, he felt tongue-tied and as nervous as an errant disciple before a stern guru. 'Yes,' he said softly.

She smiled. And took a step closer. Now he could smell her fragrance, the soft musky perfume of womanhood mingled with something indefinable: it smelled like the river itself, lotus flowers and fresh glacial water and the Himalayan wind that travelled down with it. It was intoxicating as soma and almost drove him to his knees. It was all he could do not to crush her in his arms and have his way with her there and then. And from the look of mischievous teasing in her own eyes, he knew that she was well aware of the effect she had on him.

'Let me repeat it for our mutual benefit,' she said, stepping slowly around him, like a bride around the sacred yagna fire at the time of the nuptials. 'You shall never ask me who I am or whence I come. You shall never question anything I do or try to stop me. You shall never even speak harshly to me of those acts or attempt to dissuade me by word or tone of voice, gesture or expression. So long as you give me complete freedom to do as I please and go where I please to do it, I shall be your queen and obey your every command, make your every desire a reality. The instant you break these vows, I shall leave you at once and you shall never see me again in this form.'

He did not know if she had circumambulated him once, twice, thrice or more. All he knew was that she had stopped, and was before him once again, her body, her beauty, her face, her voice, all driving him to unbearable heights of lustful longing. 'Give me your answer now or go your own way,' she said. 'The choice is yours. I shall not repeat myself nor come before you again if you refuse.'

At this he paused. So he had a choice. That was good. Some part of him, the most kingly mature part, the part that had been schooled so thoroughly in the Vedas and shastras, the science of kingship and governance, the legal aspects of society, that still sane part whispered that it was a fair offer: he was free to reject it and go his own way. There was no coercion involved.

Of course, sometimes the most powerful form of coercion is the illusion of free will itself. Thus does destiny tempt and seduce us time and again. 'I chose', we say proudly. But what other choice did we truly have?

He could refuse her conditions. They were strange, unacceptable conditions. It did not matter whether they were being demanded by a woman or a man; what spouse could demand unconditional acceptance of any act of commission by their spouse? Without fear of censure, without even the power to dissuade or comment? That was not a marriage; it was an autocracy!

And yet.

And yet.

He desired her more than he had desired any woman before.

Or anything.

He wanted her.

He must have her.

And she wanted him just as badly. That was evident in her eyes, her body, her every movement, the gentle shudder she released when her hip had accidentally brushed against his rear as she circumambulated him. The quick intake of breath when she leaned closer to him and spoke her most recent words. The blazing flames of desire in her eyes. Those could not be feigned so well. She desired him and had carried the torch of desire aflame and alight for a great length of time. He was new to this party. She had been waiting here a long time and her passion burned brighter and sharper for that long wait.

And within himself, he felt a stirring of some ancient memory. As if he too had seen her once before, and desired her. A memory, half-formed, of her in the same flimsy garments, wind-blown, then laid naked by a gust of wind. And he shuddered in the paroxysm of lust as he recalled the sight of her naked body. And he knew that his free will and choice were as good as no will or choice.

He must have her.

He would have her.

On any condition.

'Yes,' he said hoarsely.

'I accept,' he added.

And then he moved towards her, and she towards him, in a blurring of emotion and flame.

And the rest was white satin bliss.

6

The next several months of Shantanu's life passed in that same blurring rush of lust and fire, hot seminal passion spent upon cool satin skin. His nameless wife, whom everyone addressed simply as 'Queen', 'Rani', or 'Your Highness' exchanged with him every manner of pleasure imaginable between man and woman. He had her whenever he desired, as often as he desired, with never a complaint, look of weariness, or gesture of denial. She was like a river in spate, always roaring with passion, brimming with desire, overflowing her banks with love. Her body undulated between his hands and his hips like water poured into a human vessel, seeming to take whatever shape he desired. And not merely the arts of love, she was equally immaculate in the arts of queenship: her conduct, behaviour, speech, generosity, social skills and royal bearing won the hearts of the entire court and the love of the people as well. Nobody could desire more in a queen, and even more amazingly, nobody did. Nor was she dominating or interfering: she let him have his way with the kingdom as he did with her, and somehow that only made him feel more responsible for his every action or word, more considered and just in his judgement, more exacting in his pursuance of dharma. They were golden days and they passed with the speed of a dolphin racing downriver. Even the kingdom flourished, for the rich alluvial plains of the kingdom, nourished by the Ganga and her sister rivers, seemed to pour bounty upon them, producing the most plentiful crop ever recorded, and the most bounteous quality of harvest.

When she gave him the news that she was to be the mother of his child, he was overjoyed. It was the diamond atop her tiara of accomplishments. He knew she would be a perfect mother just as she was perfect in all else she did. And she would give him the most beautiful, intelligent and capable child ever.

He sighed and lay back against the ornate golden rack of the enormous bedstead. They were lying in their bedchamber after a session of lovemaking. The moonlight was soft on the marbled floor, the wispy curtains fluttered in a cool night breeze, and somewhere a night bird was singing to its mate a song of sweet sad love. His life was perfect and about to be enhanced by the arrival of a new level of perfection: parenthood.

'How long?' he asked, smiling up at the curved ceiling, inlaid with precious stones and carvings.

'Soon,' she said.

He assumed she meant a few months. He had heard that women often did not 'show' their condition of motherhood until several months after conception. He did not know the exact numbers but he knew that the total gestation was about ten moon-months so he assumed she meant three or four or five months still to go.

'When our child is born,' he said, 'we shall have a grand celebration. I shall declare a feast day. There shall be...'

And he went on to describe all the wonderful things that would be done to mark the occasion of his first child. He did not even assume it would be a boy, merely that it would be his child, their child, and that was enough happiness for now. If it did indeed turn out to be a son, well, that would also satisfy the legal requirements of producing an heir and fell two deer with a single bow-shot. In which case, he would also... And he rambled on, spelling out the various things that he would be expected to do if it was a son and heir to the kingdom.

When he looked around, wondering why she had not spoken for a while or participated in his plans, he was surprised to see her gone from the chamber. Evidently, she had walked away while he was still speaking and he had no idea whether she had left a moment ago or several moments ago.

Puzzled, he rose and walked through their chambers, expecting to find her at any moment. His search took him all the way to the queen's apartments where he was surprised to find a flinty-faced old daii-maa barring his way.

'My apologies, your highness,' she said. 'The queen cannot receive you at this time.'

He frowned. 'I don't understand. She was with me only a short while ago.'

The old woman looked up at him with a strange inscrutable expression. 'It is her time, sire. She must be alone.'

He had no idea what she meant. 'Time? What time?'

She gazed up at him with the same infinitely patient look which all aging daii-maas seemed to reserve for princes and yuvarajas. 'A woman's time, my lord. Her confinement.'

He stared at her. 'Confinement?' He had heard that before. It meant... 'You mean to tell me that she is with child. Yes, I know this already. I wish to see her and have words with her.'

But she raised a hand as he tried to step around her. 'Please, sire, I dare not bar your way but she bade me tell you personally that if you enter her chambers now, you do so against her will and thereby break your promise.' The daii-maa swallowed nervously and joined her palms together. 'I am only repeating my mistress' message. Please, do not judge me harshly for it.'

'No, of course not,' he said, irritated by her obsequiousness and her sudden concern. He was not the sort of king who went about ordering the execution of daii-maas simply because they prevented him from... From what exactly? Bursting in on his own wife while she was pregnant with his child? He could not fathom how there could be anything objectionable in that. But he knew that the mysteries of women's bodies, especially those mysteries they chose to keep to themselves, were sacred and unassailable. And those words by the daii-maa—'if you enter her chambers now, you do so against her will and thereby break your promise'—had chilled him to the bone. So it had begun at last. The things that she chose to do which he would neither question, comment upon, criticize by word, deed, gesture or expression, and never stop her from doing herself. This was apparently the first. She intended to confine herself to her chambers for the duration of the pregnancy and only see him... when would she see him again? After the birth of their child? Months from now? He felt a surge of panic, as an addict of soma feels when told that there would be no further supply of his precious honey wine for an untold length of time. Months? He could not stay without her for months! Not like this, without even being able to see her, speak with her, touch her!

'How long do these things usually last?' he asked tentatively, not looking directly at the daii-maa because he was quite sure that she had been one of his many daii-maas in his infancy, which meant he had probably suckled at her wet teats at some time and it embarrassed him to be asking questions that reminded them both of that bond that linked them.

'In her state, your majesty,' he heard her reply with evident relief, 'no more than a day or three. Perhaps even hours, if the goddess wills it.'

He had a moment of disorientation wherein he was confused about whether, by the term 'goddess', she meant his wife. But the earlier part of her reply obfuscated that query altogether. 'You mean months, of course,' he said, certain that he must have heard her wrong. Of course she meant months. He had only just made love to his wife less than an hour earlier, her belly had been flat as ever. She could hardly conceive, gestate and produce a child within a few hours, at most a day or three! It was impossible.

Not to a goddess, he heard himself think. And you know she is no ordinary mortal woman.

He looked down at the daii-maa and saw her looking up at him strangely. 'Why, no, your highness. She is almost ready! I saw her only moments ago, before she sent me out here to await you and she was in the final stages of her labouring. The child has already turned and is coming soon. Perhaps even within the hour. The queen is blessed in her womanly perfection and it is possible she might deliver herself of your heir within—'

He turned on his heel and walked away, unable to listen to more.

Madness!

A woman who had made love to her husband only an hour earlier, then told him she was with child, then came to her chambers and summoned her daii-maas to her, and was now 'in the final stages of her labouring' and about to deliver herself of child 'within the hour'.

Impossible!

But not for a goddess.

He went to his throne room rather than his bedchamber, and sat in the vast empty hall, upon the great seat where his father and ancestors had sat before him, surrounded by the might and splendour of the Puru nation and the Bharata race.

And he waited.

It was all he could do.

7

'Your majesty!'

The old daii-maa's cry was cracked and heart-rending. She shambled in as quickly as she could, raising her arms in relief as she caught sight of the lone figure seated upon the throne at the far end of the hall.

'Come quickly!' she cried. 'Stop her!'

He rose at once from his seat, soma spilling from the goblet, running over his hand. He cast the goblet aside and ran from the throne chamber. The palace corridors were brightly lit and there seemed to be people clustered everywhere, speaking in whispers—the atmosphere was tense and curiously unnatural. The night on which the heir to the Bharata line was born ought to have been a bright, cheerful night, a night of feasting and revelry. But he sensed that the unusual circumstances of the birth had unnerved everyone, just as they had unnerved him. He caught fragments of conversation as he raced through the corridors, the footfalls of his mandatory king's guard echoing behind him: Yesterday…slender-waisted as a newly-wed…today delivered of child… Unnatural… Uncanny… Impossible… All his own anxieties and fears spoken aloud, the echoes of the whispers filling the endless corridors of the great house.

He burst into her chambers, startling the daii-maas, all of whom were sitting or standing around in a state of distress. Some cried out as if fearing the entrance of a rakshasa. They silenced themselves perforce when they saw it was their king. The sleeping chamber was in disarray, the usual evidence of childbirth—hot water vessels, towels and cloth, some blood and bodily fluids drying stickily on the bedding. All the things one might expect after a queen had birthed a child.

There was no sign of his wife or the newborn life she had just released from her body.

The daii-maas avoided his eyes, looking down as if in shame. 'Where is she?' he thundered.

One woman, nervous but strong, younger than the old wrinkled one who had come to him in the throne room—and who was no doubt still shuffling her old bones back here again—pointed to a doorway.

He leaped across the bed and went through the doorway.

Racing through antechambers, he found this led to the way out of the rear of the palace. He pounded down the rear steps of the palace where several of the bhojanalaya staff stood around, looking as unsettled and unsure as the daii-maas upstairs. He looked around, seeking her familiar feminine shape, the distinctive way she walked, swaying her hips, exactly like a queen of the world. There was no sign of her in the dark night.

'Which way?' he shouted.

A fat young man, probably a cook in the royal bhojanalaya, pointed.

Outside the palace compound? But that way led…out of the city! Why would a newly delivered mother take her newborn and leave her bed, her home, and walk out of the city itself? It was madness, all madness.

Suddenly, he understood the reason why his father had forewarned him. He had been too young then to understand, had only thought of pleasure, of taking, of getting, of enjoying. There was another side to those things, there always was. He had learned that painful lesson often as a king, a warrior and a commander of armies.

He was about to learn the same painful lesson now as a man.

He leaped on the first horse he saw, throwing off the man riding it. The man grunted in surprise as he fell, landing on his side with a thump, but recognized his king and bowed his head silently, joining his palms, making no complaint.

Shantanu rode through the city, startling the few citizens out and about at this late hour. Most appeared to be standing around in groups near the palace complex. The word had surely spread about the queen delivering a child as well as of the strange circumstances surrounding the event. He glimpsed nervous faces turned up towards him as he flashed past. Until today, everyone had accepted the queen as she was for what she was, her considerable charm, wit, intelligence, eloquence and numerous other skills negating the obvious lapses—Who was she? What was her family? Where was her homeland? What was her name? But now, everyone's unspoken doubts and suspicions had been proven true: the queen was no normal woman. She was something other than normal.

What that meant exactly, he knew he was about to find out.

From time to time, when people saw him coming and recognized him, they pointed out the way to go. Some even called out to each other: 'The king! The king! Show him where she went.' And others standing further on the road lifted their hands and pointed.

He left the city behind and rode through the darkness of a moonless night, finding his way by instinct. Once outside the city avenues, there were a dozen different ways to go, depending on one's destination. There were no citizens here to point the way—evidently none wished to follow the queen on her strange night errand. But he was certain he knew where she had gone.

The river.

The place where they had first met, or close by.

He burst through the thicket, the horse exhausted, and ran out towards the river. He wanted to call out her name but he had no name to call out. All the words that seemed so charming in the bedchamber—'Queen of my heart', 'Empress of passion', 'Sovereign of my body and soul'—he could hardly run about on the bank of the Ganga yelling such endearments.

He looked this way then that, harried, at his wits' end, unable to understand what she could be doing here in the dead of night. More than that, he found it hard to believe that a woman who had just been delivered of child could have walked this long distance so briskly. He feared that perhaps he had come to the wrong place after all. Perhaps she had gone some other way. To the city of his enemies perhaps... Then he saw her.

Exactly as she had been the day of their first encounter. Clad in the same white translucent flimsy garments that swirled around her like white mist—or like the white spray flung by cascading waves. She clutched the baby in her arms, gently, lovingly, exactly as a mother should. She appeared as slender as ever, and as strong, neither her outward form seeming altered nor her inner resilience reduced a whit, moving with that same sinuous grace that drove him mad with desire. Except that this time, it was not desire she evoked in him, but awe and terror.

For she was not standing on the bank of the river this time.

She was standing on the river itself.

Upon the cascading water, which seemed not to wash around her feet so much as worship them, like hands of water raised in praise and homage. Hands that bore her aloft as she stepped gracefully, as gracefully as if she were on solid firmament, until she stopped, in the middle of the vast concourse, between the banks.

She turned, facing towards him, northwards.

Somehow, despite the lack of moonlight, he found he could see her face as clearly as if in daylight. The river itself seemed to glow with energy, palpable power that exuded a luminescence that illuminated her from below. In that glaucous light, she appeared more beautiful than ever, but forbidding as well, like a woman far, far older than the young nubile nymph who shared his bed at nights, like much more than just a woman, a being of great age, energy, power and wisdom.

She raised the newborn babe in both hands, cradling

it gently upon her palms, holding it out above the rushing waters.

He broke out of his reverie and began racing towards her.

As he ran, it seemed as if the river itself raced alongside him, rushing downstream towards her. At first, he thought it was a blurring of his vision due to his emotional state, then he turned his head and saw that the river itself was rising up, to form a maw, a great open mouth of white water that roared towards her. He cried out and increased speed, pushing himself to the limit of his abilities. Yet he knew he could not win this race. These were forces far greater than he could possibly comprehend, let alone control. Still, he ran. For that was his son she was holding. If she did not care for him, he did. And if he had to wrest the child from her by force and violence, he would do so as well.

The maw of water grew until it resembled a great white serpent, and as it reached her, it released a bellow of such power and intensity, that the resulting blast of air and spray blasted Shantanu sideways and off his feet, raising him up in the air for several feet, to land with a cushioned thump on a midden of lavya grass. He lay there, winded, drenched, and stared at the incredible sight.

His wife, standing in mid-river, surrendered their newborn babe to a great serpent made of water. The serpent snatched the babe in its giant maw, roaring as it did so, and swept over and through and around his queen, overwhelming her.

Shantanu cried out in horror.

Then the cascade of water passed by, leaving behind a backwash that sloshed on both banks before falling back and settling.

And he made out the figure of his wife, walking back towards the shore on which he lay, stunned and breathless.

She stepped out of the river and onto the bank. He saw that the water clung to her with tentacles of longing, reluctant to release her. He saw also that her feet were not wholly human, they were something else, an amalgam of water and fish-tail that formed instantly into flesh, blood and bone, the perfect replica of human female feet, just as she stepped on solid land. Her form clarified, and she was the woman he knew again, the young eager loving wife who pleasured him and took pleasure with such intensity night after night. His beauty, his queen, his empress of desire, his sovereign of body and soul.

As she strode up the bank to where he lay, a smile playing on her lips, the wind whipped away her garments, snatching them with a single rough action, and she was left naked, perfect, flawless as ever, with no sign that she had ever been a mother, or that so much as a single day had passed since the first day he had met her here, in this very spot. Naked and undulating like water in human form, she came towards him, and despite the circumstances and his emotional turmoil, he was aghast to find his body aroused at the sight of her nudity.

Unable to stop himself, he raised his hands to greet her as she fell upon him, laughing with pleasure and desire. And despite himself, he found that he was smiling in response as well. Unable to prevent what was happening, he entered into love play and conjoined with her, the actions familiar and all the more pleasing for their familiarity. Men who seek comfort in the arms of new women each night are men who have not discovered the supreme pleasure of the perfect union. Those few, those lucky few, who are blessed with the perfect mate, achieve heights of pleasure that no grunting copulation between strangers can ever attain. For it is love which is the ultimate aphrodisiac and without that emotional bonding and joining of souls, the act itself is merely violence without weaponry. An act of rage rather than of pleasure. Shantanu's love and desire for his woman outweighed all else and he found himself unable to even speak out against what she had done—for he knew that the instant he spoke, all would be over between them. Those were the terms of their marriage and he had no doubt she would abide by them to the letter. So he kept his silence and took his pleasure and by morning, he was even able to pretend that nothing had happened at all, it had only been a bad dream. How could she have conceived, gestated and borne a child then killed it, all in one night? It was impossible of course. He had probably drunk too much soma the night before and suffered an impossible nightmare.

And like any nightmare, it was easy to push aside and pretend it had never occurred at all.

Until the next time.

8

In retrospect, it was extraordinary how easily life went back to the way it had been before. The events of that night might never have happened: the palace staff knew better than to spread tales openly and the citizens who heard the rumours quickly wondered at their veracity. After all, here was their queen, flat stomach and beauty intact, as winning as always. And the king beside her at all times, rarely apart for long, mooning over her as much as ever. The sight of them riding together in their royal vaahan, the ornamental bejewelled carriage, brought people running out of doors, leaving aside their work to watch the king and queen pass by. Shouts of joy were heard everywhere and those who possessed conch shells—or rather, those merchants and nobles rich enough to possess their own guard—ordered them to blow the conch shell trumpets heralding the approach of the royal couple. They were too dearly loved for the rumoured scandal of that one night to cast a shadow upon their reputation. People quickly dismissed it as an idle rumour and soon even the palace staff wondered if that had been the queen's newborn son she had walked out carrying that night, or merely a bundle of clothes. People even surmised their own explanations, assuming that in her homeland, wherever that mythical place was, they had such unusual customs as walking to the river and throwing in articles of clothing as a means of appeasing the gods and asking for the gift of an heir. This theory, that it was all an arcane ritual designed to obtain a son, was the most favoured, for it explained everything quite neatly.

Only the daii-maas who had been present in the queen's bedchambers when she gave birth to that beautiful, dark-hued, black-skinned prince of a child, knew the truth. And they were accustomed to keeping secrets and silencing rumours. They did so. For they understood that the king loved the queen and she loved him as well, madly. Whatever reason she had had for that extraordinary deed, or how in fact she had been able to produce a child within an hour of copulation and conception, were things they did not dwell on too long. They were superstitious women given to the wearing of amulets and sacred threads and chanting of shlokas designed to ward off evil eyes and spirits. They accepted supernatural impossibilities as a part of life.

Time passed, healing all hurts, annulling all hurtful memories. The human spirit survives by selective forgetting.

When a year had passed, on another night much like the first one, Shantanu and his queen were in their bedchamber, entwined in the grip of passion. When their ecstasy was spent, she looked at him in a certain way, rose, and left him. This time, he knew at once that something was amiss. He rose as well and followed her. He was just in time to see her enter her bedchambers. The daii-maas were already waiting with pans of steaming hot water and cloth. They looked at him sadly as they went into the chamber and shook their heads in commiseration before shutting him out.

After the child was born, he followed his wife once again, this time close on her heels.

On this occasion, the daii-maas had not informed anyone of the queen's impending delivery, even though she had asked them to make arrangements for it. They had thought it best to wait and see. If this was to be a normal birth—or as normal as an hour's gestation and delivery could be—then they would inform the whole city. Until then, it seemed best to keep their silence.

So the streets were empty and silent when Shantanu followed his wife. It was a long walk and he dearly wished he could offer her a ride on a horse or chariot or even a carriage if she preferred. But he dared not speak a word or delay her progress in any way for the terms of the agreement had been quite specific on those points. And so, he only followed at a discreet distance, going on foot this time as he felt ashamed to ride when his own wife could walk the distance.

Things went as they had the previous year. She reached the river, stepped out onto the water, then walked to the middle of the concourse. Raising her hands, she held the baby out. Shantanu felt a great piercing pain enter his chest and flood his being with sorrow. That was his son, their son! How could she do this? Why? Was it a sacrifice? For what? What deity could demand the sacrifice of one's own newborn child? And two sons in as many years? Why? But the terms of the agreement caused him to keep his silence. And he watched in silent anguish as the river came once again, roaring with deafening rage, and swept the child away as before. Once again, she walked back to the bank, stepped onto the ground and came towards him, growing visibly younger and more beautiful than ever. Once again, he succumbed to his love and lust and received her in his welcoming arms. As he held her tightly, feeling the stirring in his groin belie the sorrow in his heart, he shed a tear from each eye. Just the two. One for each lost son.

The next one, he promised himself silently. The next child she will keep. This is some ritual to ensure that the third child will be a great king of kings. It was the only explanation that appeased him and allowed him to accept her cruel actions as necessary in some fashion.

But of course, the next year, she did it again.

And again.

And yet again.

Seven times in all, over as many years, she threw his newborn sons into the river.

Finally, a day came when he could take it no longer.

The past eight years, he had wept silently, containing his grief within himself, keeping it all a secret between himself and the daii-maas. Nobody else suspected or knew, and those who heard the rumours dismissed them out of hand. One child might have been believable, for some arcane ritual. But eight children? Impossible! Even a rakshasi would not sacrifice eight of her newborn children for any reason.

On the eighth night when he followed her to the river, he broke down. 'Stop,' he cried out just as she stepped out onto the water. 'I beg of you, stop!'

She paused upon the water, standing as easily as if on an unseen rock beneath the surface. He knew she was not standing on any rocks for he could see the water rushing beneath her feet, even the occasional fish or turtle swimming beneath. She was standing upon the water itself, her feet melding with the fluid to become partly water as well.

He fell to his knees on the bank. 'Goddess, devi, demoness, whoever you are...' He pressed his palms together in supplication. 'I cannot stand by silently any more. Please. Do not kill our son.'

She looked back at him, her face still set in that resolute expression she always had during these nights, when she seemed older, wiser, more powerful than the woman he shared his bed with, and said, 'It is what he wants.'

It took him a moment to realize that she meant the child in her arms. 'He? How can he possibly know what he wants? He is a babe! Newborn! How can a newborn wish to commit suicide?'

She sighed and shook her head. 'It is for his own good.' There was a tone to her voice that suggested that he could still back away and let her continue, and she might not consider the agreement broken yet.'

But he no longer cared. 'Who are you? What sort of mother would kill her own newborn children? Eight years! Eight beautiful perfect young children. Sons! Why do you do this? Who are you?'

She paused and nodded. Turning around, she walked back to the bank and stopped just short of solid ground. Still on the water, she looked at him with the same loving expression he knew so well. 'Very well then. Since you have asked, I must tell you. For I cannot lie, nor can I conceal truth once it is demanded of me. I am transparent as clear water, as the glacial Himalayan ice from whence I come, and to do otherwise would be to dishonour my father. Therefore I shall tell you the truth as plainly as possible.'

He could not make head or tail of what she said, except that she was offering to answer his questions. His confusion only made him more belligerent. 'Tell me then. What sort of evil creature are you to do this terrible thing year after year? Answer me!'

A peculiar expression came over her face then, one that he had never seen, not even in her most vulnerable, naked moments. 'I am Ganga,' she said, 'daughter of Jahnu.'

He stared at her, then at the river, then at the place where they stood, upon the rushing water. And he knew she told the truth. Everything made perfect sense then. If she was indeed Ganga, the river-goddess, then it explained how she could appear and disappear at will on the banks of the river, how she could walk upon its waters—for she herself was water—how she could be so passionate and tempestuous, as the river was, and numerous other half-glimpsed, half-understood mysteries and doubts were cleared up at once. All save one.

'Then why do you do this terrible thing?' he asked. 'As Ganga, you are the most honoured of all maharishis, sacred river of the gods themselves. How can you commit such a heinous crime? How could you kill your own newborn sons?' She smiled. Tears sprang into her eyes and trickled down her face, and as she rolled down those smooth unblemished cheeks, he saw that the water was the reality and the flesh the illusion, for each teardrop erased the skin and body down which it ran. She was turning back to water again even as she spoke. 'These were the eight Vasus, great demi-gods from the heavenly realms. Due to a curse by Vasishtha, they were compelled to spend a year each on earth. They approached me and asked for my help. I agreed to take human form and give birth to them and to destroy each one at the time of his birth so that he could return at once to his true place in swargaloka. I was killing our sons, it is true, for I was destroying the physical bodies in which they took birth upon this plane. But by doing so, I was freeing their immortal souls which were never destined to remain here. If not by my hands, they would have died anyway. Better to throw them into my own waters for a quick merciful death, than for you and I to watch them grow for a full year only for them to die by some unimaginable unexpected method each time. Cruel as this was, and difficult for me to do—you cannot imagine how difficult—it still had to be done. It was the only way. Surely you can see that now, Shantanu, my love?'

He passed a hand across his face roughly. He was already drenched from the river's spray. His head swam with understanding and shock. A curse! A remedy. And each one a demi-god, herself a goddess. Then nothing was what it had seemed. All this was part of some cosmic plan that would have unfolded regardless. What she said was true: to live with each child for a full year and watch them grow, until their every action, expression, gesture and sound became intimately familiar, and then lose them...that would have been unthinkable. And to endure that eight times over? Impossible. He would have been driven insane, he was certain of it. There was a limit to how much anyone could endure.

He rose to his feet. 'I had no idea...'

She nodded. 'I know. But it was impossible to tell you. As a mortal, I could not share such knowledge with you. It is forbidden. Besides, it was necessary for things to proceed exactly in this manner, for even this was part of the plan.'

He looked around, stunned. 'You mean that even my protesting before the death of the eighth son was part of your intention?'

'Yes, my love. For I wished you to have the pleasure of raising one son from my womb. And by testing your patience all this while, I knew that you would eventually stop me. Thus, I am now entrusting to you your lawful son, born of our union. Take him now.'

She handed out the newborn to him. Shantanu took the bundle of warmth and softness, scarcely able to comprehend what was going on. The child began to wail and cry, dismaying him further.

'He will be a great man, a great king. He will do great
things and when he takes a vow, any vow, no matter how
terrible, it will be as rigid and unyielding as the sky and
the earth in resoluteness. He will do all he does for your
sake and the sake of your kingdom and your lineage. He
will do the Bharata race proud, and be a shining example
of the Puru line. This is my last, my only gift to you, my
beloved.'

And now her tears came faster and thicker, as her
lower body melted away, turning into a whirlpool of
raging water. Only her head and upper body remained
recognizable as the woman he had loved for so long.
In his arms, the child's crying grew more plaintive and
mournful.

'But I don't wish to lose you!' he cried. 'Now that I
understand everything, I forgive you! I didn't know, my
love. Do not blame me. Do not leave me.'

'I must,' she said, 'for that too was foretold.'

'Stay for the sake of our son,' he said. 'Stay and rear
him with me.'

'I cannot,' she said, 'stay another day in the world of
men. Once even a single mortal knows my true identity,
I must return to my original form. That is the dharma
that binds me.'

He shook his head and held out the child again to
her. 'Then take him with you. Raise him yourself. Raise
him like a god, a great being. His true place is with you,
not on this wretched mortal plane. Let him not suffer
the misfortunes of mortal living when he can live like a
god among gods!'

She hesitated then dipped her head. Already, he could see, the back of her head had turned to water, only the face and ears remained intact. Her arms were melting too. She reached out hands that were more water than flesh and accepted the child once more. She cradled him to her watery bosom, and he gurgled as if content and fell asleep again.

'I shall keep him and rear him as befits your son and heir,' she said. 'When he is ready, I shall send him to you again. Thereafter he must live out his time on earth. Indeed he shall live a great length of time, for he has taken his brothers' ages on earth upon himself as well. He shall live all their mortal lives in his own lifespan, and only by his own choice shall he eventually succumb to death, only when he has endured and suffered enough to atone for them all.'

Shantanu had nothing to say to that. He joined his palms together. 'I am honoured to have been your mate in this world. I have loved you as I can love no other woman ever again. I shall remain without a wife for the rest of my life henceforth. For no other woman can ever take your place in my heart.'

She smiled sadly, her face melting away even as she spoke her last words. 'Matters of the heart do not always turn out the way we plan, great Puru. As a man you may desire to live alone but as a king you owe it to your people to produce an heir. In time, you may learn to love again. Until then, remember, I am always here, always running beside you, as fast as you run, sharing in your every triumph and achievement. Come to me anytime you please. Except for that one limitation of the physical form, I shall always be your beloved Ganga.'

And with those terribly final words, she fell back into the river, the water spout that had been her body dissolving back into the body of fluid from whence it had come.

9

Shantanu grieved for his lost wife and sons. The official word given to the people was that the queen had dropped her child still-born and had taken her own life by flinging herself into the Ganga. This matched the rumours and gossip that had circulated for years and was in keeping with the queen's legendary love for the river. The people grieved with their king, for they had loved her dearly too. In time, they got over the loss and went on with their lives. There were enemies seeking to overthrow the might of the Purus and take over Hastinapura's territories, there were great swathes of newly conquered dominions to govern, and the countless other duties of any king. In time, Shantanu too got over the loss of his beloved Ganga. From time to time, he went to the spot by the river and sat upon the bank as his father had once done, but instead of meditating he talked to the river, confident that the steady roar would prevent his words from being heard by anyone within sight. He spoke of matters of kingship and governance, of palace intrigues and political manoeuvrings, of skirmishes and rebellions, fights and outbreaks, all the usual things that kings talk about to their wives at night behind closed doors. The river listened and in its steady relentless roar he often thought he heard an occasional word or phrase or sound of commiseration, sympathy or even, on rarer occasions, a few words of advice. Once, when discussing a certain noble and his daughter who were needlessly haranguing the ministers with constant demands, he was taken aback when a face appeared in the water below him. The face was exactly that of his former queen and wife, if it were to be formed of water. 'Beware. They mean to assassinate you,' she said in a watery gurgle that none but he could hear. Then smiled, pursed her lips in an action that resembled an affectionate kiss, shut her watery eyes, and melded back into the river. The following week, the noble and his daughter did indeed try to use a clever ruse as a cover for an assassination attempt—and failed because Shantanu had been having them watched constantly since the day by the river.

In time his visits grew less frequent as the empire grew and his responsibilities increased. He admittedly threw himself more completely into his work and vocation than he had before, as if conquering new territories or suppressing distant mlechchha rebellions in foreign lands could ever compensate for the loss of his beloved mate. They did not, of course, but they did help keep him from thinking as often of her. In his travels he found also that while the river was always benign to him—on more than one occasion, he was able to cross her in spate under impossible weather conditions, always to the astonishment of his own local allies in the region—the special bond he shared could only be explored in that particular spot on her bank, near his own capital city. At all other places, she would listen intently, but only here would she speak aloud or show herself in subtle, deliciously feminine ways: a wave of butterflies risen from the water itself, dissolving to a cloud of spray as they rose up in the air, a pack of dolphins mating in the water within sight of him, patterns in the water that defied the tide and made pleasing designs that reminded him of places they had been and things they had done in those places. These intimate secret communications kept his heart alive and kept love awake within him. Even though he had long since accepted that he could never have her back again, the sheer glorious intensity of their years and experiences together kept him emotionally afloat for another decade and a half. If nothing else, these platonic dalliances kept him from growing bitter and indrawn and from hating the sight and touch of all women.

In time, gradually, he began to form the idea that perhaps, just maybe, some day, he might learn to love again.

10

Shantanu dismounted from the small one-horse chariot he used for hunting and strode towards the river. The Ganga usually roared around this curve in full force at this time of year. Even at its lowest ebb during one drought-ridden summer, the river still flowed steadily, filling its concourse from shore to shore. Never had he seen a sight such as this before nor heard tell of it.

The river's flow had dwindled to a trickle. A gurgling brook dammed by logs of wood flowed with more force than this measly sluggish worm that gurgled along throatily. He could see fish flopping in their death throes, dolphins beached, and turtles lying on their backs, rotating their green stubby legs in dismay. These signs suggested that the damming had only just happened moments ago: those fish were all still alive. How was this possible? How could such a mighty river, as wide across as a lake, be slowed? Even if a few hundred logs were dropped into its concourse upstream, they would only flow downriver—indeed, this was how fresh timber meant for building was transported downriver from the Himalayan foothills to the cities and towns along the Ganga's enormous length. What then? An avalanche in the Himalayas?

He could think of nothing that could explain this sudden staying of the most powerful river in this part of the world.

The fish were starting to thrash desperately, clearly on the brink of death.

He looked around in helpless dismay, wishing there was something he could do to help. It was one thing to hunt down creatures for sport and food; it was wholly another to see countless innocent lives being squandered needlessly. A new thought struck him like a physical blow: the lives that would be squandered downriver would not be fish alone but human lives as well, for countless people depended on the river for their daily needs. His entire kingdom depended on her grace to survive.

Deva, help us, he prayed silently.

Almost at once, a great roar filled his ears, louder than anything he had heard before. He looked up from his joined palms to see an astonishing sight: the river unleashed again, roaring downstream! So great was its force that it was exceeding its banks. If he did not move aside in a moment, he would be swept away!

He ran then, up the bank, reaching the safety of the ridge on which he had left his chariot and horse just in time to escape the lashing whips of the raging water. Even so, he was partially drenched by the flood and as he sat on the bank beside his grazing horse, staring at the river roaring by in full spate once more, he shook his head in frustration, wondering what force could cause the river to cease and then restart its flow thus, within moments.

In any case, the fauna of the river would survive now,

he saw. The waters had reached them just in time to save their gasping lives.

His horse nuzzled his dripping hair and neck curiously, as if asking, what were you doing, great king, were you swimming in the river?

He smiled at the memory of the way he had scampered up the ridge. That flash flood had come by so suddenly, he had been genuinely afraid he would be washed away. So afraid, he had forgotten that he shared a deep bond with the river, especially at this place.

'You would never let your own waters harm me, would you, my love?' he asked quietly, not really expecting an answer.

As if in response to his query, the river's flow slowed, reduced by degrees, then returned to the sluggish muddy crawl he had seen earlier. It happened so abruptly, he blinked and rubbed his eyes to confirm that what he was seeing was real and not some illusion.

He rose to his feet and started down the ridge—the flood had dampened the soil, turning it slushy, and he slipped and slid the last yard or so, but regained his balance. Even before he reached the edge of the bank, he could hear the sounds of thousands of fish of all sizes, thrashing and flopping about on the wet muddy floor of the river. Dolphins cried out pitifully. There were creatures he knew no names for and did not recognize, creatures that spent their entire lives at the bottom of the river without being seen by human eyes, monstrosities with clicking claws and eyes extended on stalks, but he felt sorry for them as well, for they were clearly suffering and would die as well as their brethren if the river remained dry.

But this time, he did not panic or pray. He merely waited to see what would happen. And when the roaring resumed again a moment or two later, he was prepared for it and already starting back up the ridge. Even so, he only just made it before another flash flood came roaring past like all the elephants of the world stampeding in musth together. He frowned, placing his hands on his hips and stared down at the raging vigorous concourse that he knew so well. Something was amiss here.

This was no natural phenomenon. It could not be!

He mounted his chariot again, turned the head of his horse, and rode upriver. Whatever the source of the damming and the releasing, it had to be upriver. He stayed close enough to the river so he could hear its roaring passage, listening for any change in that familiar sound. Sure enough, it came.

The roar died down, leaving a deafening silence that was unnatural to anyone who had spent his childhood and youth playing by the banks of the great mother river, bringer of life and bounty. It made him wonder: what manner of being could be doing this? Who possesses power enough to stop Ganga herself at one of the fiercest parts of her journey, and restart her, at will? Surely it must be a god, or... He had no alternative to offer. He rode his chariot silently, listening. Once again, the roaring resumed within moments, again causing him to marvel. Clearly the being doing this remarkable thing knew exactly how long the stranded fauna could survive and was restarting the channel in time to ensure their survival. It was almost as if the being desired only to exercise his or her powers, and meant no creature actual harm. It also occurred to him that this could be the work of Ganga herself, for reasons known only to herself, but somehow he did not think it was so.

He had his answer soon enough. Tracking the source of the disruption, he found it surprisingly close by. Dismounting from the chariot to avoid warning whomever it might be, he went the last scores of yards on foot. He had his bow in hand, and he slipped an arrow expertly onto the string, ready to loose the instant he spied danger. For he had just thought of an alternative to this being the work of a god: it could be the work of an asura. He did not know why either a god or a demon might wish to play thus with the flow of the mightiest river, but it was best to be forearmed.

His first glimpse of the being was the back of a head and upper shoulders. From this angle, that was all he could see. The rest was concealed by the riverbank's curve. To see the perpetrator more clearly, he would have to step out of the treeline into the open—with all the risk that entailed. At first glance, all he could tell was that it appeared to be a very tall, powerfully built man. A mortal man. Although, after his experience with Ganga, he had learned the hard way that looks could be deceiving. Gods could assume mortal form and shape when they desired and shrug off those mortal garbs at will.

But not for nothing was he king of the Bharatas, lord of the Puru kingdom and the greatest civilized city in the known world. His prowess with archery was such that he felt confident he could strike even a killing blow to the stranger with only that little portion of his body visible, from this distance. He came to a decision quickly. He would give the stranger a single chance, for that was what honourable kshatriyas did, but if the man so much as looked at him crookedly, he would let loose.

The river had ebbed almost to a standstill again, its roar quietened to a trickling gasp. The bank was quiet enough for him to be heard even from this distance. He decided to make his move.

Staying behind the trunk of the tree, Shantanu shouted out: 'You! Drop your weapons and show your hands!'

The large head and powerful shoulders remained in view, neither ducking down in response, nor shying away. That in itself was reassuring. It suggested a man who was not afraid nor engaged in any activity for which he felt guilty.

Even so, the stranger had not raised his hands yet.

'I said raise your hands!' Shantanu shouted.

The stranger remained exactly as he was. Then, Shantanu's sharp sight saw the hint of movement on the man's right shoulder. A mere twitch, such as a warrior's shoulder muscle might produce when hefting or raising a weapon. It was all the warning he needed: he had killed men in similar circumstances for doing less.

He loosed his arrow, his fingers already reaching for the rig on his back to pull out a second arrow before the first had reached its target. He was hidden behind the tree trunk, the bow almost touching the trunk itself but not quite—contact would spoil the fineness of his aim, especially when making such a delicate shot. He knew his arrow would strike precisely where intended, unless the other man moved very quickly: at the sloping cord of muscle that joined the right side of the man's neck to the ball of his right shoulder. The tip should penetrate the muscle, and the arrow remain stuck there. It was a shot he used to warn his enemies and show them how easily he could do anything he pleased with his weapons.

The stranger's shoulder flexed a second time. He remained with his back to Shantanu, not having moved an inch other than those two flexes of his shoulder muscle. There was no way he could see Shantanu from that angle and distance. Even if he had turned and gazed directly at Shantanu, he would barely glimpse part of one eye and the line of shoulder and head, as well as the bow and arrow, almost completely hidden in the shade of the tree. Most likely, due to contrast between the brightness of the sunlight and the shadows of the trees, he would not see even that much, let alone be able to judge the precise trajectory of the arrow.

Yet, somehow, the second time he flexed his shoulder, it was just enough that the arrow passed over his shoulder. Shantanu thought he could almost hear the faint rasping of the arrowhead as it burred over the man's skin, but surely that was only his imagination. The main thing was, the arrow missed its mark.

No matter. He already had the second shot on the bow and lined up and this time he was aiming for the meaty part of the man's powerful neck. This shot would paralyse the stranger from the chest down, which was unfortunate—but necessary. Even those two shrugs were sufficiently threatening for Shantanu not to risk any further movement.

He loosed the second arrow, already reaching back for the third, when an odd thing occurred...

The second arrow simply fell at his feet.

Shantanu's feet.

It plopped down, landing in a heap of dried leaves, for it was early autumn, and the crinkling sound of its impact upon the leaves alerted him to its fall.

He blinked rapidly, unable to comprehend what had just happened.

How could an arrow loosed by his bow fall right here at his own feet? Unless... Unless.

He looked down at his bow, turning it sideways.

The string had been severed. It hung in two parts, dangling uselessly from either end of the bow.

Still, he could not understand how this had happened.

Had the string simply split? It was a perfectly good cord, wound by himself only an hour earlier. He always used fresh cords at every opportunity, knowing the importance of the string in the art of archery.

No.

The string had been cut.

By a sharply-honed metal point.

He looked around.

And saw the arrow sticking from the trunk of the tree behind him.

It was like no other arrow he had ever seen, the tube

of the missile gleaming as if made of metal, although that was absurd—no arrow could be made wholly of metal for no bowstring was strong enough to bear that much weight, nor could human strength power a metal missile over a long range.

Yet it looked very much like metal, although no metal he had ever seen. It glistened and glittered and reflected a rainbow range of hues, like…mercury.

Ridiculous!

An arrow could not be made of mercury. Mercury was liquid. That was why it was also called quicksilver because it flowed like liquid silver.

He stopped caring what the arrow was made of and tried to make sense of where it had come from. It took him only a turn of the head to calculate the angle of its trajectory and estimate that it had originated from…

'My apologies.'

Shantanu started, taking several steps back, his feet crushing the dried leaves underfoot and raising a loud crackling noise. He swung around, drawing the short dagger from his belt and crouching, ready to defend himself.

The stranger raised his palms in a gesture of surrender and appeasement. 'I mean no harm. I only cut your bowstring because it seemed the simplest way.'

'Who are you?' Shantanu said, circling around, eyes darting from side to side, alert in case the stranger had allies in arms. 'What were you doing by the riverbank?'

The stranger shrugged. Those powerful mounds of muscle flexed and Shantanu was left in no doubt: this was the same man who had been standing by the riverbank only a moment ago.

Impossible! He couldn't have covered this distance so quickly!

'Practising,' said the stranger.

Shantanu stared at him. 'Practising?'

The stranger nodded, then smiled in a manner that made Shantanu realize another thing with a sense of shock. He was no man at all, he was a mere boy. Only just come into manhood. It was his great height and immense size that belied his age.

But that smile, shy and uncertain, that was a boy's smile.

11

Shantanu watched warily from the bank of the river as the boy pointed. 'There,' he said. 'Do you see it?'

Shantanu looked down. All he could see was the raging current of the Ganga during the post-monsoon autumn season, with the usual flotsam and wet life that occupied it. 'What is it?'

'It's a...' the boy paused. He thought for a moment then shook his head. 'I do not know how to say it in your language.' 'So you are a foreigner then?' Shantanu asked with interest. 'Which part of the world are you from? Are you from this continent of Jambudwipa or...?'

'Of course!' The boy looked as if he had been asked if he was from another vishwa, a distant planet. 'This is my home.'

Shantanu wasn't sure what he meant. The boy had indicated the river, by which he probably meant here, this kingdom, this place. That seemed credible. The boy had the look of a Bharata about him, a Puru even. He had the same aquiline features, prominent nose, swept back ears and angular jaw, intense deep-set eyes beneath bushy brows, dark eyes and dark skin, crow-black hair, fine straight limbs and the posture of a man with enough muscle on his body to use weapons well yet not so much to hinder his movement in combat. Taller than most other people, tall even among kshatriyas—if anything, the boy was unusually tall, standing a good head above Shantanu's own height. Shantanu was not accustomed to looking up at a man and he found the effect disconcerting. Yet despite his considerable height, size, width, strength and evident skill, the boy was almost...bashful, shy, given to speaking with almost childish innocence and delight. At first, it made Shantanu suspicious, especially after the arrow that came unseen and the speed with which the boy himself had moved from the bank to the treeline, but as he came to understand that this was the boy's natural manner, his suspicion turned to amusement. What an odd fellow! Built like a giant warrior, skilled with a bow and arrow to rival Purandara himself, and yet he spoke, gesticulated and contorted his face in expressions that befitted an immature boy rather than a kshatriya of high breeding, which he obviously was.

'So what exactly did you do?' Shantanu asked again. They had walked to the riverbank together when the boy had explained that he had merely been 'practising'. Shantanu still had no idea what that practising entailed.

The boy looked at the river again, pointing. 'You see...' he stopped. 'No, of course, you cannot see. Nobody can.' He looked around, as if searching for something, then turned back. 'Do you know of—' He broke off abruptly, interrupting himself. 'No,' he said as if to himself, 'Pramaataamaha said I was not to speak of that to anyone. Anyone!'

'Did you say pramaataamaha?' Shantanu asked, curious. 'Is your great-grandfather from this region? What is his name? And your father's name?' He moved towards the boy, speaking gently. 'Where is your home, boy? Where do you come from?'

The boy looked at Shantanu again, as if seeing him suddenly for the first time. He shook his head and pointed again, as he had before. 'I do not know exactly but this is my home. This is where I come from. That is all I can tell you...in your language. If you wish to know more, you must ask my mother. She said I am forbidden to speak to people.' He looked around. 'I am not supposed to be here even. I was only practising.'

Shantanu could make neither head nor tail of this extraordinary young man. He decided to focus on something simple. 'What were you practising? Can you show me?'

The boy looked at him. 'Of course! I can show you! So much simpler than explaining and learning new languages. Although maatr says I must learn new things every day, for I am to be king and kings must know a great deal about the worlds they govern.'

Shantanu said nothing to this, merely watched as the boy stepped up to the edge of the ridge. He was a handsome young man, and something about the way he moved, that peculiar gait that certain very tall, muscular men favour, a graceful way of moving that came from their unusual height and strength of body, reminded him of someone else. But he could not place the person it reminded him of immediately.

The boy stood on the edge of the ridge, looking down at the river, silhouetted by the evening sky. It was not more than an hour or so to sunset and the colouring sky and distant mountain ridges behind him gave him the appearance of some prince in a royal portrait, the kind of portrayal that adorned the walls of the Hall of Ancestors in his palace in Hastinapura. He arched his back and shoulders in the exact stance of a bowman aiming downwards at a sharp angle and Shantanu frowned, for there was neither a bow nor an arrow—

A bow and arrow appeared in the boy's arms.

It was as if they had never existed before, and suddenly came into being at that precise instant. Out of thin air.

They were like no bow and arrow Shantanu had ever seen before.

He corrected himself: the bow was like no bow he had seen before.

The arrow he had seen a twin of only moments earlier. It resembled the arrow that had cleaved his bow-string and embedded itself in the tree trunk behind him. The arrow that gleamed and was rainbow-hued like a thing made of solid mercury or some fabulous liquid metal.

The arrow in the boy's hand was exactly like that, a liquid silver missile that caught the light of the evening sun and flashed in rainbow hues. Indeed, as Shantanu watched, the arrow's reflection created a small rainbow, just for an instant, curving around the boy's hand in mid-air.

The bow was like the arrow: quicksilver. Firm as metal. Reflective of light. Beautifully resplendent. It made a larger rainbow. The smaller rainbow of the arrow intersected the larger rainbow of the bow.

Shantanu never saw when exactly the boy loosed. Or the flight of the arrow as it left the bow.

All he saw was the twanging cord of the bow vibrating in the air.

Then the bow disappeared as suddenly as it had appeared.

Its work done, it returned to the invisible place from whence it had come.

The sound of the river, roaring magnificently, subsided abruptly.

Shantanu ran to the edge of the ridge and looked over.

He saw the quicksilver arrow shot by the boy, fixed in the ground of the riverbed, standing straight. From the arrow emerged a wall of silvery light that extended from bank to bank, translucent, shimmering with rainbow hues, reflecting the sky and trees and landscape. This wall of shimmering silver light barred the passage of the river as effectively as a dam built of solid rock. A mountain could hardly dam the river more effectively!

All this from a single arrow.

Downriver of the arrow, the river's flow had turned into a muddy trickle. The same as he had seen earlier. Fish flopped on the riverbed, dolphins cried out in outrage, turtles moved their limbs helplessly, and weeds and undergrowth hung limp and immobile on the muddy naked riverbed.

Shantanu turned and looked at the boy in disbelief.

The boy beamed at him, pleased at what he had done.

It was the grin of a boy who had shot his first bird from the sky perhaps, or ridden his horse over a chasm for the first time. Shy, proud, yet guileless and utterly innocent.

Then, as he saw Shantanu's expression, the boyish grin faded.

And turned to one of trepidation.

'You needn't worry about the wet-ones. I would never harm them. They are my bhraatr. I only tease them this way sometimes. In sport.'

Shantanu stepped closer to the boy, examining him as if for the first time. He caught hold of him by the shoulders—he had to stretch out his own arms to reach those two wide muscled trunks—and said, 'I know who you are. You are the eighth son! Her eighth son!'

The boy looked at him with total incomprehension. Then suddenly, he glanced over Shantanu's shoulder and reacted to the sight of something else.

'Maatr!' he cried out, with the childish alarm of a boy caught doing a mischievous prank he has been forbidden to play many times before. 'I was only showing the nice mortal how—'

'SILENCE!'

The word was a crashing no less than thunder.

Shantanu spun around to see the river break through the barrier of the arrow, splitting the arrow's shaft into countless slivers, each as beautifully reflective and metallic as the arrow itself—it was like watching crystal explode—and roar along its concourse again, stronger than ever. The waters boiled and seethed, throwing up a spout that hung in mid-air several yards high.

From the angry spout, a figure was sculpted.

It was the figure of his former wife, his queen, the only woman he had ever loved.

'Gangey,' he said softly, altering the last syllable of her name to the affectionate 'ey' sound as only a spouse could do.

'Then this is…'

'My son,' said the angry goddess of the river, moving across the surface of her waters with a great churning energy. 'I have forbidden you from playing these games. Indeed, you have been forbidden from stepping out onto land unsupervised, have you not?'

The giant of a boy hung his head. 'Yes, maatr,' he said miserably, 'but I was only—'

'Silence! Not a sound from you!' she said, and there were teeth in her watery mouth, Shantanu saw, long white teeth as sharp as any predator's. 'I wish to have words with the dry-one…with this man.'

The boy stood by silently.

Ganga turned to face Shantanu.

He joined his hands before her. 'Mother river,' he said, 'it is such a pleasure to see you again.'

'And you, my husband,' she said gently. She assumed the form he had known her by, partially, just the face and a suggestion of the upper body, while still retaining her river aspect. It was enough to make his heart ache for all that they had shared, for the companion he had lost. 'I see you still remain single, still wifeless.'

'None but you,' he said simply. 'You know this well. If you wish me to be loved and to love again, then come back to me. Come back now.'

She smiled and laughed a throaty watery chuckle. 'Would that I could. But my time on the mortal plain is past. It can never be again.'

He sighed, feeling the pain of their parting as freshly as if it had been only yesterday. 'Then I remain wifeless forever.' 'No, do not say that,' she whispered. 'For to remain wifeless is to remain childless. And that is not ordained.'

He was about to ask her what she meant. For he remembered her saying something similar fifteen years ago, when they had parted. But before he could speak, she gestured to the boy standing beside him.

'You were right. This is he. The eighth child. The one I did not drown, but took away with me.'

He nodded slowly. 'It took me some time, for somehow...' He passed a hand across his face. 'Somehow I had forgotten! Forgive me for that lapse.'

She shook her head in commiseration. 'The mind forgets what it cannot bear to remember. If only the heart could forget so easily.'

'Exactly. My mind had forgotten about the last child, but my heart recognized him somehow...' He gestured towards the boy, still standing contritely, watching and listening to them with a curious look on his innocent handsome face. 'He has your aspect about him...and clearly your supernatural powers.'

She smiled proudly. 'He has great abilities and profound knowledge. He will do you proud. He will be the greatest son you could ever desire. It is he who will ensure the survival of your kingdom through its darkest days...until...'

Shantanu frowned. 'Until?'

She shook her head, water droplets flying hither and thither. 'I cannot say more, I have said too much already. Only know this, he is your son and a great being. His name is Devavrata.'

'Devavrata,' Shantanu repeated approvingly, 'God's vow. A fine name.'

'But he is accustomed to being called Gangeya. If it pleases you, call him that as well, sometimes. It will remind you of me and keep my name upon your lips.'

And now she was already moving back into the water, dissolving, descending...

'No,' he cried. 'Wait! There is so much I wish to say to you! To ask you! Please stay.'

She joined her palms together in supplication as he had at first sight of her. 'Henceforth, you may say and ask all of Devavrata Gangeya. He shall answer and advise you perfectly in all matters. He has been groomed for this purpose. Love him as well as he shall learn to love you, and use his powers wisely, for he is greatly gifted and no mere mortal.'

And then she was one with the water and the waves enveloped her and she merged with them and was gone.

Shantanu sat for a long moment, crouched by the riverside, staring down at the place where Ganga had emerged from and returned to again.

If there is one pain that can equal the pain of grief and parting with our most dearly loved one, it is the pain of seeing that dearly loved one again, years later, long after one has finally forgotten, and to be reminded once again, if only for a fleeting moment, of all that was, could have been, should have been, but can now never be again. Who among us can know the pain that Shantanu felt at that moment, to have seen his beloved wife again, if only for a few moments, and to know that she was always here within reach, yet always out of reach to him.

And the Ganga flowed on by. And the greatest love he had ever known, might ever know even in years to come, was gone forever. Like a poet's lyric spoken into a storm. Like a reed-flute's song drowned by a hurricane. Like a love story written on water.

Finally, as the sun was setting, he felt strong arms with a gentle touch upon his shoulders.

'Father,' said a gentle voice behind him. 'Let us go home now.'

And Shantanu permitted his son to help him to his feet and together they walked back towards the city of his ancestors.

SATYAVATI AND SHANTANU

1

When Shantanu returned to his capital city, a great host was waiting to receive him. After the passing of his wife Ganga, all the people had mourned the loss of their dearly loved queen and shared his grief and loss. But of late, they had begun to grow concerned for their king's well-being. No man could mourn forever, no heart could grieve indefinitely. These were hard and dangerous times. Many feared that his rivals and enemies might take advantage of Shantanu's distraction and disaster would befall them.

When the king had disappeared unannounced for days without any word, anxiety rose high. At the sight of him returning, in good health and sound of body, a resounding cheer rose to the skies. When he paused to introduce the youth beside him as the son of his late wife Queen Ganga, their joy was replaced by shock and consternation for a moment. But only a moment. Explanations be damned. If their king said this was his lawful son by his late wife, that was good enough for them. This meant that the kingdom finally had an heir! The celebrations began at once.

The nation greeted Devavrata with great warmth and approval. They were told the truth: that he was the son of their late queen, that she had had to leave them unexpectedly before delivering him, and his nurture and education had been accomplished by the most renowned sages possible. Now that he was of age, he had returned to aid his father in administering to the needs of the kingdom. Shantanu waited a respectable time before officially announcing Devavrata as his heir apparent. During this period, the young prince won hearts and dazzled even the most sceptical minds with his natural boyish charm, incredible mastery of weapons and unmatched valour. Soon, there seemed to be nothing Devavrata could not do, and do with charm, grace and the gentle manner of all truly strong men. By the time Shantanu installed him as crown prince and Devavrata became Yuvaraja Devavrata, he was already the most beloved man to rule Hastinapura.

In four short years, the young boy Shantanu had encountered by the river had grown to become an admirable young man. His innocence had been honed away through exposure to the daily politics of statecraft, and replaced by a canny understanding, insight into human nature and ambition. Yet he never succumbed to shrewdness, grew wily or resorted to manipulations in order to have his way. He proved himself a much more resourceful player than all those who stooped to such petty trickery. He was a gentleman of the game of thrones, a master of the art of kingship, and his natural innocence and boyish charms belied a keen and insightful knowledge of every aspect of governance. He routinely shocked opponents by turning the tables on them just when they were certain of success, or thwarting their designs by the simplest and most obvious of methods.

Yet even in his moments of triumph, he never rubbed salt into their wounds or pressed their snouts into the foulness of their mistakes, choosing instead to smile with a twinkle in his eye and a friendly pat on the back. This won over more rivals and opponents than outright conflict, and in time, even those who had resented him the most began to ease their efforts to unseat him or thwart him, choosing instead to ally and benefit from his rise and governance. Many became his disciples in all but name, studying his moves and choices, marvelling at the way he handled delicate matters, learning his methods—yet even they came to realize in time that his store of wisdom was far deeper than they could fathom in one lifetime. He had no set methods or approach; it was as if he knew precisely how to deal with each individual problem on its own merits. The only thing they truly learned from him was that they could never govern as wisely as he did.

In four years, everyone who knew him came to love, respect, admire and rely on Devavrata. Even those who had hated him grudgingly accepted his superiority and allied with him for their own benefit; little realizing that it was he who was wise enough to let them stay alive and in power so that he might know, monitor and control his enemies. Even at that tender age, he was still wise enough to know that a powerful king always had enemies. It was best to keep them close to oneself and watch them closely, rather than foolishly waste one's efforts battling and chasing them constantly. This way, it was in his enemies' interest to see Hastinapura prosper and the Puru empire grow in strength and wealth, so that some day, when the time was right, they could reap the rewards of all these decades of sowing.

Shantanu watched with constant amazement as his son took over the reins of kingship so effortlessly that it soon seemed as if Devavrata had always ruled and would always rule. He was like a force of nature: immutable, constant, dependable, perfect in his judgement and knowledge, just in his choices, merciful in his sentencing, and wise beyond measure in foresight and foreknowledge. Even Shantanu found himself learning from him rather than teaching him. He recalled Ganga's words that their son had been well schooled by the greatest of gurus and he marvelled at how much had been taught to the young man in so short a time. He had no way of knowing, of course, that Devavrata had spent not merely fifteen years in study but fifteen hundred! For in the ocean of stories, time flowed at a different pace and their young son had imbibed all the collective knowledge of all the Puru and Bharata kings of his line, learned from their mistakes and successes, and gained wisdom that no ordinary mortal could hope to acquire in his lifetime. There were many advantages to being the son of a goddess and the reincarnation of a demi-god; this was one of them.

The other great advantage was his prowess at war. In a sense, it was this formidable ability, coupled with his keen political acumen, that forced his enemies to resort to quietude and alliance to survive.

For Devavrata could not be beaten in battle. This

premise was tested frequently at first, then rarely, then almost never, for there comes a time when such a man's fame itself becomes his most powerful weapon. Any challenger to the Puru dominance had only to be told the single word: 'Devavrata' and he would pale and put down his weapon and go home to his cookfire. For the whole wide world soon came to know that the son of Shantanu could not be bested in any form of combat: single, melee, or pitched battle. Or for that matter, in the use of any weapon.

Still, there were some who were foolish enough to test this reputation. They rarely survived long enough to realize their own folly.

After four years had passed, Shantanu was satisfied that his son's authority and governance were secure and would endure even without his presence. Indeed, he had deliberately chosen to take a back seat and let Devavrata take on more power and responsibility with each passing year. He began to withdraw from the daily tasks of a king and began to prepare for an early retirement. Yet he was still young, too young to go into the forest and spend the rest of his life pursuing austerities. As his responsibilities decreased and his mind had more time to turn to other matters, the loneliness that had engulfed him those many years ago returned, gradually at first, then with an overwhelming rush that threatened to overpower and incapacitate him. The very sight and sound of Devavrata reminded him constantly of his lost love. He loved his son dearly but that intense love only made him long for his wife all the more. He lamented the fact that they could not be together as one united family, enjoying one another's company and love. But he also longed for a woman to love and be loved by once more. For having known true love once, the heart can never accept the solitary state as anything but a lesser condition.

In time he ceased his visits to the riverside that he had loved for so long. He had accepted the cruel sentence that fate had condemned him to and knew that Ganga could never return to him. Seeing her watery aspect, however remote that might seem from the living, breathing, flesh-and-blood woman he had held in his arms, kissed and loved, only served to aggravate his heartache. He took to travelling by different routes, hunting in different forests. Since being within reach of a river was essential and inevitable on his travels, he made sure that it was any river but the Ganga. Little did he realize that all rivers are sisters and Ganga watched over him no matter where he went, whether through her sister Yamuna or others, and not a day went by when she did not miss him as much as he missed her. If anything, her heartache was greater for she could see him anytime she wished and so she was constantly reminded of the love and companionship she had lost forever.

2

Not coincidentally, it was while walking by the Yamuna that the course of his life took another turn. Listless and unable to enjoy the pleasure of the hunt as he once had, he was wandering the banks of the river, lost in his own thoughts. After a while, he grew aware of an exceptionally sweet floral fragrance that enveloped him on all sides. The sweetness of the odour was the more remarkable because it was not the season for such aromatic flowers to blossom and try as he might he could find none in sight. Using the same skills that served him so well as a hunter, he tracked the fragrance to its source. When he saw a boat pulled up by the bank and a woman seated within it, an oar in hand, he was struck by her beauty. She rose at the sight of the stranger, assuming him to be a passenger. He stood before her, staring unabashedly, unable to believe that she was the source of the powerful aroma. Embarrassed by his stare, she lowered her eyelashes demurely and waited for him to board her boat.

Understanding that she was a ferry woman, Shantanu climbed aboard her craft. She reached out a hand to help him aboard and as she touched him, he felt his skin ignite with a fiery sensation he had never felt before.

He jerked back his hand, seating himself heavily and setting the boat sloshing to and fro. She steadied it with the use of the oar, her shoulders and arms displaying considerable strength coupled with feminine grace. He could not help but watch her back and shoulder muscles move as she worked the oars, turning the head of the boat around to push it off shore. He could see her shapely legs beneath her garment and they were strong yet perfectly shaped as well. Her physical beauty captivated him, her aromatic body odour aroused him, and the intelligence and intuitiveness he glimpsed in her eyes caused him to respect her as well. He could not recall the last time he had been so overwhelmed by any woman. Except of course, Ganga herself. He was simultaneously surprised and a little guilty at the stirring in his loins and attempted to look away, staring out across the river as they commenced the long, slow crossing. The tide was relentless if steady and it took considerable skill and effort as well as a keen knowledge of the currents for her to steer and row the boat in a reasonably straight line across the river. Lesser boatmen would have offloaded their fare half a mile downriver, given the width of the river and the strength of the current. He found another reason to desire her, for he admired great prowess in any person, no matter what his varna or vocation. He could see that she was a highly-skilled ferry woman, apart from her extraordinary beauty and allure. That awareness of her skill only made him desire her all the more greatly.

Still, being a king and a widower he tried his very best to contain his passion. It would not be right for him to simply throw himself at a ferry woman thus. She could well be married and a mother herself for all he knew. And so firmly had he put all thoughts of loving or marrying again out of his mind that it was difficult to even contemplate the thought of broaching the matter.

But the heart wants what the heart wants and by the time the beautiful ferry woman had rowed Shantanu across the river to the far bank of the Yamuna, he could not bear to leave her company without at least speaking with her briefly. He had his opportunity when she brought the boat to rest on the south bank and waited quietly, keeping her eyes lowered to the rippling wash.

'How much do I owe you, beautiful lady?' he asked.

She started at the compliment. This pleased him for it indicated that she had not been complimented too often. With her extraordinary beauty that could only mean that she was too young to have met enough men, for he had no doubt that were she to go out into the world, there would be a rainstorm of such compliments showered down upon her daily. But then she spoke and her voice thrilled him, sending a flurry of unwanted emotions surging through his being like a sudden current under the surface of the river. 'I am but a fisherman's daughter, sire. You may pay me what you can. My father says that it is our dharma to help those who wish to cross and how can one put a price on dharma?'

He was pleased at her response as well. It indicated good breeding and learning. But that voice! And that beauty. It was beyond his tolerance now to ignore how he felt.

He was a king and kings did not carry coin or items of trade. He tugged off the first ring that came to hand and held it out to her.

She was demure and innocent enough that she accepted it without a glance. But as her palm opened to receive the payment, he enfolded her hand in his own, tightly. She gasped at the sudden contact and her eyes instantly went to his face. As her beautiful black eyes stared directly at him, he felt a rush of pleasure such as he had not experienced since...since too long. His entire body was ablaze, his skin tingling from the contact of their open palms. He moved closer to her, close enough that he could inhale her body's scent, deliciously aromatic and irresistible. He had never known any woman whose scent alone could provoke such arousal. The way she sought to pull her hand back, the way her back arched, her lips parted, her dark skin and coal-black complexion, her dusky aspect and perfectly shaped features, her musical voice, every single thing about her pleased him greatly. He knew then and there that if he were to ever find happiness again with any woman, she was that woman. He might search the world over and not find another like her. She could never replace his Ganga. No woman could, for Ganga was a goddess and the first great love of his life, possibly the greatest. But she would very well. Very well indeed!

'My lord,' she said, 'Why do you take my hand thus? What is it you desire?'

He looked into her eyes and inhaled her anxiety and her excitement, and saw that there were indications of arousal in her as well. She was flushed and blushing, a thin layer of sweat had appeared on her upper lip, and while she had attempted to pull her hand free, her body was arched towards, not away from him.

'I desire you, lady,' he said gently, unable to stop himself. 'I would have you row me through the journey of life.'

She stared at him uncomprehendingly for a moment then understanding dawned slowly. Now she blushed even more profusely and he was thrilled to see the change in hue of her dark complexion as her excitement showed itself. Yes, she was not disgusted or dismayed by his proposal; she was aroused. That meant that she either desired him as well or at least found him pleasing enough to accept as a mate.

She dropped her gaze to the river again, no longer struggling to break free. Her free hand stayed on the oar, holding the boat in place, and it would occur to him later that any fisherman's daughter strong enough to row a boat across the Yamuna at one of its widest points could surely have struck him down and beaten him off with that same oar had she desired. There was no doubt at all about it: strong enough to defend herself, she nevertheless chose to let her hand—and possibly her heart—be captured by Shantanu.

'I cannot speak of such things,' she said, keeping her eyes averted from his face. 'You must speak to my father if you have such intentions.'

He nodded. 'Very well then. Tell me your name and your father's name that I may do so.'

She glanced up at him in shock. 'You have only known me a short hour!'

'And I now wish to know you for the rest of your days.'

Her throat worked as she stared at him a moment longer, wide-eyed. She saw something in his intensity and determination that had a profound effect on her. She looked down again but not before smiling briefly this time. It was the smile of a woman who has just been paid the highest compliment and is overwhelmed with delight. 'I was born Kali but came to be called Satyavati,' she said softly, her voice a lyric song pitched against the Yamuna's background chorals. 'My father is the chief of the Manchodri fishermen.'

Shantanu frowned. 'Manchodri...'

'It is the region known by the name Panchmani to travellers.'

He nodded. He knew the territory of which she spoke—it was a patch of forested land on the vast north-central plain through which the Yamuna mysteriously chose to take a westward turn, doubling back upon its own course for reasons that nobody had been able to fathom. It was taken as one of many such signs marking the greatness of the Puru empire and the Bharata race, for it was one of several borders that marked the limits of the territories won by his ancestor King Sudas in the legendary and crucial Dasarajna battle which first established the race of the son of Shakuntala and Dushyanta upon this subcontinent. The bend in the river, if imagined from a bird's eye view—or god's eye view, if one wished—could be interpreted as a finger pointing to Hastinapura, the seat of his dynasty. This part of the river was in that same region.

She looked up at him bashfully again, and he saw her gaze flit across his person from head to toe, taking in his attire, his jewels, his bow and rig, seeing him with a frank curiosity he found refreshingly direct. 'Clearly, you are a great lord, sire.'

He smiled. 'I asked your name and about your father. You have every right to ask mine as well.'

She smiled and kept her eyes lowered to the level of his chest, saying nothing.

'I am Raja Shantanu, son of Pratipa, lord of the Purus.'

Her eyes widened but her gaze remained fixed on his chest. 'Samrat of the Bharatas,' she said, wonderingly, 'Master of Nagapura.'

He bowed his head. 'Nagapura, Hastinapura, Kurukshetra, Puru rajya, Bharata-varsha, Puruvansha... call it what you will.'

And he raised her hand to his lips and kissed her palm. He kept his lips parted and moist, tasting her hand as much as kissing it.

She gasped with pleasure, as if he had put his open mouth upon her body not merely her palm. 'I am eternally your servant,' he said.

Her gaze shot up to his face, her eyes startled, yet still displaying signs of obvious pleasure. 'Nay, my lord,' she said, 'I am but a humble fisherman's daughter. You are the greatest emperor of our age. I am always in your service.'

He shook his head. 'You do not know me yet, Satyavati. Once you come to know me well, you shall understand that love is the greatest kingdom of all, and she who rules the kingdom of love is the most powerful emperor. I have given my heart in tribute to you, now it remains only for your father to accept my offer, and put me in eternal subjugation to you.'

She stared at him directly, her breathing hastened, her face flushed. Drops of perspiration were visible on her bare shoulders and upper chest.

He kissed her palm again, then released her hand at last. 'I now take your leave. I shall go to your father in state and ask for your hand in marriage. Then I shall come and take you to Hastinapura where you shall rule as the empress of my heart, queen of my nation, mistress of my race.'

He turned and walked away, not because he was in any hurry to go but because he knew that if he dallied any longer, he would not be able to resist his desires and would commit an indiscretion. His heart sang as he walked along the bank of the Yamuna and it was all he could do not to dance and sing in joy, for it felt as if a great cloud that had been lurking over his head for years had suddenly passed on by, permitting the sun to shine down and bathe him in golden warmth. All he desired was to return home and arrange for an entourage to visit her father with due pomp and ceremony as soon as physically possible.

It took him the better part of an hour of brisk walking before he realized he was on the wrong side of the river and he would now have to travel a further two yojanas out of his way to return home!

3

Satyavati heard the commotion outside and knew it must have something to do with her suitor Shantanu. She had made an excuse to be let off ferry duty for a few days and had stayed home, rarely venturing away. Her father had found this odd since Satyavati hated being cloistered at home and was always out doing something or other even when she was not ferrying. His concern for her behaviour manifested itself in various puzzled glances and sounds of curiosity but since she made no move to explain herself he did not press her further. But now, when the entire fishing village of Panchmani seemed to be in an uproar, she knew her patience had been rewarded. Her suitor had come as he had promised!

Several people burst into their house, chattering excitedly. 'Chief! The great emperor himself comes to grace your house! He has come with a fabulous procession, in full state and finery!' 'Chariots!' cried another man.

'Elephants!' someone else said.

'Jewelled crowns!'

'Soldiers on horses in fine uniforms!'

'Banners and flags on lances!'

And from the sounds of the conch shells, elephants

lowing and horses neighing and clip-clopping, it was evident that the procession had now arrived at the doorstep of the chief.

Her father shushed his people and told them to make way if the great lord wished to enter. Then he glanced at her, frowning as if wondering whether this unexpected event had something to do with her being at home.

She blushed and looked away.

When she glanced back again, he was grinning shrewdly, a knowing look on his face. He nodded to her, still grinning, and twirled his moustaches as if to say: I knew it! I knew you were hiding some secret!

She blinked her eyes at him affectionately and smiled back.

Then the royal crier was at the door, calling out the name and titles of the visiting royal, while soldiers clattered into the house and formed a corridor for their liege to walk through safely. Her friends and neighbours and relatives all stared and gawked between the soldier's raised spears and swords, even bending to peek under their armpits for a better look. Nothing like this had ever happened in Panchmani before. A king! Visiting here! The emperor of the Puru empire no less. The air was electric with excitement, like the crisp air on the high mountains before a thunderstorm, just before lightning began to fall from the sky.

The sight of Shantanu took her breath away. The day she had met him, she had been vaguely aware that he must be someone important but she had never dreamed he could be a king, let alone the king. He had been bedraggled from long travel, listless, and looked like a rich nobleman fallen on hard times. Why would a king be wandering through that remote region alone? She was still curious to know the reason but it hardly mattered now. The main thing was the way she had felt when he had expressed his desire for her. She'd known, earlier, that even when Sage Parashara had wanted to cohabit, it had been simple bodily desire. With Shantanu she had seen something else: he was a man capable of great love. His words, his manner, his gestures, the way he had taken her hand, the way he had kissed it...she had felt a sense of something impossible. Something she had never expected to feel in her life. To be loved so madly and by a great emperor? It was hardly the fate in store for every fisherman's daughter! Yet it also felt perfectly right. As if it was meant to be. She had felt her own being stir when he held her hand and they exchanged glances. She could love this man. She could bear his children. She could spend her life with him. She knew these things implicitly even without having spent more than a brief time with him, most of it spent in silence as she rowed him across the river. A few such moments can be worth an entire lifetime. Most lifetimes pass by without a single such moment. Satyavati knew enough about Shantanu and her feelings for him to stake her life on this union. The rest was a gift from the gods.

She watched as the initial formalities dragged on with excruciating slowness. The visit of a king could not be treated like a neighbour dropping by for a drink of local brew. As chief of the fishermen, her father had to show respect for the king of the land, and to display his own status too. The formalities went on for ages. Finally, when the time came to speak of the things that truly mattered, Shantanu and her father went into the inner chamber and spoke privately. Satyavati waited in agonizing anxiety.

She had no doubt her father would agree to the match—why would a fisherman refuse a king as a son-in-law? But she still feared some hitch, something unexpected. Surely it could not be this simple? A king appeared one day, fell instantly in love with her and asked her father for her hand in marriage? Why not, she asked, defiantly. Even fairy tales and legends grew out of some truth. Reality did not always have to be harsh and unforgiving.

But there was a secret dread in her heart that she could not dispel. It was the knowledge of her own indiscretion with Sage Parashara. She had cohabited with a man, had borne his child. She was a mother. It did not matter if nobody else knew or could ever know, it did not matter if her virginity had been restored and her body returned to its virginal state in every respect, as if her womb had never been filled with child, her hips had never parted to birth a babe. She knew. That was all that mattered. And though she knew that what had happened was more in the nature of a supernatural aberration than a typical everyday occurrence, she nevertheless felt guilty about it. She had mated with another man. She had experienced the bliss of physical union. She had watched her own belly swell with child then undergone the wonderful trauma of birth. She had held her newborn babe in her arms, slippery, and beautiful. Whatever else had occurred, however bizarre and extraordinary, was beside the point. These things had happened and were real. She could never change that fact. Even the brahman power of Parashara could not undo her memories, her feelings, her experiences.

That guilt made her fear that perhaps, just maybe, she did not deserve to be loved by such a man—not without him knowing the truth about her past, and naturally, she could never tell him that truth. For regardless of how much he loved her, it would change everything. She would not be what he had perceived her to be, she had kept a great thing secret, and that act of secrecy was what made her feel guilty.

And yet.

Keeping that secret was the only reason the king of Hastinapura was in her house now, asking her father for her hand in marriage.

And as for the guilt and her deserving this, yes, she did deserve it. For whatever had happened in the past, she was genuinely attracted to Shantanu, felt a powerful connection. Surely he too must have experienced love before now. She knew he had been married, had a son, and there were mysterious rumours surrounding the late queen's demise in childbirth. Something scandalous that nobody knew about fully. So he was no virginal innocent either. He must have his secrets too.

If he loves me and I love him then that is all that matters. Today we begin our life together. And it is our life together that matters.

She smiled, straightening her head, releasing the dread

that had been clouding her heart at unexpected moments these past days as she had waited.

We all deserve love. No matter what went before, no matter what might come later. Today belongs to us, today we stand naked and true before one another, and today is all that matters.

Satyavati waited for Shantanu to emerge and for her new life to begin.

4

Shantanu liked the chief. He was a man rarely seen in royal circles. A man unconcerned with appearances and protocol beyond the bare necessity required for social nicety. His oiled moustaches, bulging belly, hairy chest and arms unabashedly exposed in his simple fisherman's vastras, the simplicity of his house and belongings, all represented a man who was exactly what he appeared to be. Honest, hardworking, tough, yet soft-hearted, fair, decent, and a servant of dharma in his own right. Such men were the backbone of a nation. Nobles postured, traders cared only for profit, soldiers protected and expanded the nation, brahmins guarded the precious light of learning, but it was men like Panchmani who did the work that actually enabled a nation to prosper, grow and progress. Farmers, fishermen, workers. They built, maintained, fed and clothed the nation. Citizens. Praja. It made him proud to be Prajapati, lord of the people, when the people he ruled were of the mettle of Panchmani. Even his name, simply an appellation referring to the region and tribe he administered to, was a demonstration of his true nature. The individual man and the chief of the people who worked alongside them daily were one and the same.

When Shantanu spoke to him he felt as if he were speaking
to all of Panchmani and as if all of Panchmani listened.
That might have something to do with the fact that the
whole population of the region was gathered outside the
chief's house, waiting eagerly to know why the king of
the Purus was visiting but it was also indicative of the
grassroots power such men possessed. They were the land,
and like the trees, fruit and other things of that land, the
land and they grew, prospered or fell together.

Right now, all Shantanu wanted was for Panchmani
to agree to his proposal. He had said what he had to say.
The chief had listened with an impassive face, his broad
coarse features displaying no clear emotion. Now he was
stroking and twirling his moustaches, a gesture Shantanu
was familiar with. From the odour in the room, it was
evident the chief used fish oil to lubricate and maintain
his considerable facial hair. But the stench of fish did
not bother Shantanu overmuch; not when the sweet,
unmistakable fragrance of Satyavati wafted in from the
very next room. Gandhavati, she had been dubbed because
of the unusual sweet odour. Yojanavati even. And that
fragrance overpowered all the fish smell in this entire
village. But even had it not, it would take far, far more
than the stench of fish to dissuade Shantanu.

Yet there was a sense of something in the chief's
manner, the heavy-lidded gaze with which he observed
Shantanu, the way he kept sighing again and again, a
sense of something troubling. Shantanu felt a curious
foreboding. He had a good instinct for how his proposals
or ideas would be received, the result of a lifetime spent

in political deal-making. He sensed that for reasons he could not fathom, this proposal was about to be rejected. Impossible though it seemed, a fisherman was about to refuse a king as a son-in-law!

In a sense, he was right as well as wrong.

'King of the Purus,' said Panchmani in a rough voice, 'I am a simple man of plain mind. Therefore forgive me for speaking plainly.'

Shantanu said nothing but dipped his chin in acknowledgement.

'What father would not want you for a son-in-law?' Panchmani said, gesturing as if to indicate the whole world. 'It would be a father's dream to see his daughter marry such as you.'

And yet... The caution was implicit in his tone. Shantanu waited with pounding heart and sweating palms. He had not felt this anxious before major strategic battles. Yet here he was in a fisherman's hut, waiting as if his life depended on it. And it does, for I must have Satyavati, she is the only chance I have to find love and hope and happiness again in life.

'I would be proud to call myself your father-in-law,' the fisher king said. 'You know this and I know this, the whole world knows this for it is sense. All I ask is that you pledge one thing to me. If you pledge this thing, you may marry my daughter at this very moment if you so desire. I shall bless both of you with all my heart. I shall even throw a lavish wedding that all of Panchmani will recall for a hundred years.' He paused, thinking as he stroked his oiled beard into curls. 'Perhaps not lavish by Hastinapura standards. But the most lavish that this little hamlet has ever seen or will see again. I will see to it that nothing and nobody prevents you and my daughter from spending the rest of your lives together in blissful harmony—'

'Speak then,' Shantanu said, almost stepping on Panchmani's last words. 'I am a direct man too. But I cannot pledge something unless I know what it is. Name your condition and I shall grant it if it is within my means.' Now it was his turn to pause thoughtfully, 'And as you can well imagine, there is little in this world that is not within my means to possess, gift or grant.'

Panchmani sighed. 'Her son.'

Shantanu frowned. 'Her son?'

'Her son by you. Whenever a son is born to the both of you.'

Shantanu felt a glimmer of hope. 'Then you consent to our marriage?'

'On condition that as and when she bears you a son...'

'Yes?' Shantanu leaned forward, eager now, anxious, a spark of joy igniting in his heart. 'When we have a son, yes...?'

'You must pledge that he and he alone will inherit the throne.'

Shantanu blinked, absorbing the meaning of the chief's words. 'Of course. Any son of mine will inherit...' He stopped. '...will inherit the throne, in order of succession. Naturally. That is dharma.'

Panchmani sighed again. 'I know this. And you already have a son. And he is already acting regent and a good one at that. He is loved, popular, efficient, a great warrior, a formidable emperor...he has no flaws, lacks nothing. He is healthy and robust and indomitable in battle or combat. He might well outlive us both!'

Shantanu was silent. The spark that had flared was already flickering out, the glimmer fading.

'So long as Devavrata lives, he is the rightful heir to your throne and legacy. I know this already. That is why my heart cries. It cries like the female wet-one who loses her partner, for the dolphins of the river are like wolves and hawks, they mate for life.' Panchmani spread his large hairy hands wide. 'What can I say? I ask only that you pledge that when you and my daughter have a son, it shall be that son who inherits, not Yuvaraja Devavrata. I have no animosity towards Devavrata. I hear he is a fine king. But as a father-in-law, I wish to see my line continue as well. I need to ensure that my grandson should have his fair share in life. If he is a fisherman's son, then he should inherit his father's boat and nets and fishing sticks and other belongings. If he is a king...'

Panchmani gestured as if the rest was obvious.

It was.

5

Satyavati almost cried out with excitement when she saw Shantanu emerge. Several in the crowd did cry out and the cry was taken up and carried out throughout the village and perhaps the whole region, from the sound of it. But she saw Shantanu's face and her heart caught, like a fish trapped in a hook that would rip its life out if struggled against. And she knew without having to ask that something had gone wrong.

She pushed her way forward through the crowd of well-meaning relatives and neighbours, all the women eager to see and be seen by the king. Shantanu caught sight of her and his eyes softened for a second, but then they filled with a look of such pain, her heart went out to him. Then he shook his head once, slowly, and walked past her. His gait was as heavy and forlorn as if he were attending a funeral rather than a potential marriage. He had not looked so sad even on the day she had first met him wandering on the banks of the Yamuna. He looked utterly lost and heartbroken now.

6

Devavrata knew something was seriously amiss. He had been aware of his father's gradual withdrawal from matters of state and governance. That was something he himself had encouraged over the past four years, assuring Shantanu that he would take care of whatever needed doing. And it was a matter of pride that he had lived up to his assurances: Shantanu himself had embraced him warmly on more than one occasion and congratulated him on how well he was managing the affairs of the kingdom. He had even admitted that for the first time in his life he felt able to take time off for himself without the constant sense of anxiety that had always plagued him earlier. Devavrata had encouraged him to do as he wished, going hunting for weeks on end if he desired, or travelling to remote places he had always wished to see incognito, unburdened by the military and royal entourage a king had perforce to take along. The past year, he had taken to coming to court only occasionally, dropping by unexpectedly just to observe and listen in on the sabha sessions, often without saying a word the entire time.

What a contrast this was to the king who had rarely slept a full night and was constantly on edge dealing with one political crisis after another all day long, day after day, during the first several weeks after Devavrata had come to live with him. So much so that he had rarely found time or leisure enough to do the things he dearly wished to do with Devavrata. Each time they were out visiting some site of pilgrimage, or viewing the actual field where great battles had taken place, or observing wildlife in its natural habitat, the ubiquitous messenger would invariably turn up with an urgent summons to return to the city. It had become such a predictable pattern. Yet Shantanu had made the effort and clearly enjoyed that time away immensely: Devavrata was young and innocent by mortal standards but he was in fact older and wiser than anyone else around and knew how much his father pined for his mother and that lost companionship. A king has no real friends. His only true friend is an understanding spouse or son or daughter. Devavrata was all Shantanu had now and he poured his heart out to him often, not by bursting into long monologues, but through the subtle way he said or did things, communicating more through pauses and sighs than by eloquent explication. Over time, this burden of sadness reduced considerably as he found genuine companionship and support in Devavrata's company and came to rely on his judgement not only as a statesman but also as a friend and confidant.

Over the course of these four years, their relationship had developed to the point where Devavrata would see his father looking troubled over some issue of a border dispute or political complication and put his hand on his shoulder, smiling. That was enough for Shantanu to lose his wrinkles and smile back, then pat his son on his shoulder in return before walking away, confident that Devavrata would handle the problem, whatever it might be. And Devavrata had handled it—had handled everything that came his way these past four years, to the point where those wrinkles rarely appeared on Shantanu's forehead and his father actually began to look younger and healthier. It was amazing what a difference the simple removal of daily stress could affect on a person. Shantanu had become fitter, leaner, more confident, less given to outbursts and dark depressions, drank less, slept more soundly, ate sensibly, and indulged himself in leisurely pursuits that he would never have dreamed of just a score of months ago: he painted from time to time, played musical instruments, taught children their alphabets, and did things because they pleased him not because they were expected of him as a king. And in the past several months he had begun to go off on trips frequently, returning with a spring in his step and a sharpness in his eye. At night when he told Devavrata of his experiences in the wild, Gangeya felt a great sense of joy and satisfaction, for he knew that he had helped make this possible. Had he not come to Hastinapura, had he not taken the reins of the kingdom from Shantanu so efficaciously, Shantanu would never be this happy and relaxed today.

It pleased Devavrata to see this dramatic change. He looked forward to those times when his father and he would sit and sip freshly squeezed pomegranate juice and he would listen as his father regaled him with stories and anecdotes gleaned on his travels.

But in the past several days, something had gone amiss. He knew this because Shantanu had not spoken with him for several days, had in fact been avoiding him in the palace and at various occasions. This was not unusual in itself but there were the reports from various sources that said the king was looking like his old gloomy self again, that reported that Shantanu was drinking again, had cloistered himself in his palace and was not seeing anyone or venturing forth, had given up his activities and pursuits and sent everyone away. All this had happened after Shantanu returned from a trip which he had made with a full royal entourage. Since all matters of state were overseen by Devavrata himself, he had been curious as to the nature of this state visit. Shantanu had laughed and said that it was a secret he would share with Devavrata if the trip was successful, but in any case it was not a matter of state, it was a matter concerning the state of his heart! Devavrata had laughed at the pun and wondered if this meant his father had found a woman he desired. His mother had told him that this day might come and when it did, he was to encourage his father in every way, and do whatever was required to ensure that his father found happiness in the new match. He had been a little surprised at her insistence on her own husband finding happiness with another woman but after he had come here he had understood how bereft Shantanu was. As he knew that Ganga was never coming back, he had resolved to do exactly as his mother had instructed. Shantanu deserved happiness again. So when he had received word that his father had returned from the visit of state—or state of the heart, as Shantanu had wittily put it—he waited eagerly to hear the good news. But it had never come. And then Shantanu had avoided him for all these days. And then these disturbing reports came to his ears of his father's lapse into the old, gloomy depressive ways...

Now, he entered his father's palace with only one goal in mind: To find the source of Shantanu's sorrow and resolve it.

He was shocked at the sight of his father.

Shantanu lay sprawled on a couch, his hair, face and garments unkempt, dishevelled, uncared for, eyes red-rimmed from lack of sleep and too much wine, the discarded goblets around him testifying to his lapse into the old over-indulgent habits. But more than these things, it was the look on Shantanu's face that alarmed and dismayed Devavrata. Shantanu looked as if he had aged a decade in as many days. He had not looked this haggard and miserable even during the worst crisis of the first several months after Devavrata's arrival.

Devavrata sat beside him, waiting for Shantanu to speak first. That was always their way. Devavrata simply sat beside his father and waited and eventually Shantanu spoke, confiding in him, speaking his mind—and his heart—and Devavrata listened and replied and advised.

But this time, Shantanu said nothing. There was only silence between them. Silence and a sense of something dark and dismal that hung over them like a foetid pallor.

Finally, Devavrata took the initiative and spoke.

'Father? All is well with the kingdom. The last peace pact with the border rebels was sealed three days ago.

The foreign envoys returned home to their respective distant nations with our gifts, beaming with pleasure, and promising to tell their nations of our great hospitality and rich resources. Within the sabha, the feuding over the sudra-vaisya land disagreement has settled as well. We have reached a mutual compromise that is more than acceptable to all concerned. There is no fear of rioting any longer. Things are very well. They are as close to perfect as possible. Yet you sit here all day, quaffing copious quantities of soma, alone and in darkness, seeing no one, speaking with nobody, uncaring for your own appearance and well-being. What ails you, father? Tell me.'

Still, Shantanu was silent. As Devavrata had begun to speak, he had covered his face with his hand, as if closing his eyes for a moment, and the hand remained there even now, masking his features and expression.

Devavrata tried again. 'Father, in the time since I came to live with you, you have confided everything to me. Have I ever betrayed your trust? Have I ever given you reason to regret having confided so much? Have I disappointed you somehow without being aware of my lapse? If I have offended you in any way, then forgive me at once and tell me how I may atone for my mistake. For I cannot bear to have you angry with me and refusing to speak with me. A day without hearing your voice speaking affectionately and feeling your arm upon my shoulder is like a day when the sun has failed to rise.'

At this emotional appeal, Shantanu removed the hand covering his face, revealing eyes filled with tears. He reached out and took hold of Devavrata's forearm. 'Nay, my son. Nay! You have done nothing to offend me. Do not blame yourself. You are the perfect son. No father since the beginning of time has been blessed with a son as fine as you. In every respect, you are perfect. Do not question your own merits or blame yourself for anything.'

'Then what is it, father?' Devavrata asked earnestly. 'What ails you? I have not seen you this troubled since I first came here and you were sad over the loss of my mother. I know you well, father. I know something is eating at your heart, destroying you from within. Confide in me. Tell me. Maybe I can help you.'

Shantanu shook his head vehemently. 'No, Gangeya,' he said emotionally. 'I cannot tell you this. It has nothing to do with you. It is only the misery of my own dark soul. I have to bear this myself and I shall. Go about your life as usual. Do not worry on my account.'

'How can I ignore my father's sadness? How can I smile and live my life happily if you are not happy? What is a son if not his father in a new life? How can a part of you go on living as normal when you are suffering some inner turmoil?' But still Shantanu would not confide in Devavrata. He spoke in elliptical riddles, referring to various ancient texts that advised men to have more than one son, or that elaborated the merits of having many sons. He lapsed into a discussion on whether or not a man should take a new wife, what the reasons were for such an act, and spoke on this for a while. He spoke also of his lineage, of the uncertainties of life, of war and the risks a king faced, of fearing for Devavrata's early demise in battle... But then he mused that Devavrata's prowess

at arms was so formidable that it was his enemies who
should fear losing their lives, not he. So it went for a
length of time, Shantanu speaking round and around the
subject without clearly stating what was on his mind, and
Devavrata understanding much without understanding
fully.

Eventually, Shantanu was exhausted, emotionally
and physically, and Devavrata put him to bed tenderly.
Watching his father fall into uneasy sleep, he vowed to
find the source of this misery and end it at once.

Whatever it takes, he told himself.

He went in search of the old guard.

Not literally guards, these were aging kshatriyas who
had fought and seen great conflicts of yesteryear. Now,
they were ailing or aging and unable to take part in active
combat but they gathered daily in a garden adjoining the
royal palace and talked robustly of old wars and battles
and enemies. Shantanu had brought Devavrata here to
listen to them, then later to speak a little only if he was
spoken to, in order to learn about the art of war from
those who had actually waged war. 'This score of old
kshatriyas,' he had told Devavrata fondly, 'when taken
together, represent close to two millennia of fighting
knowledge and experience. No guru can possibly tell you
all they know. You can learn more simply by listening
to their arguments than from most masters of weapons
and pundits of strategy.'

Devavrata did not tell him that in fifteen hundred
years he had seen, experienced and learned possibly

far more than these twenty old warriors had in their combined lifetimes, indeed, he possibly knew the same battles and conflicts they spoke of as intimately as they did, for he had watched many of those wars when they were waged, through his supernatural abilities under his great-grandfather's guidance, and then been taught what was done rightly or wrongly and how it could or could not have been done better. But he listened. And he learned a great deal. And in time, gradually, he began to share his own observations as well. At first, the old guard were suspicious, even hostile to this upstart young boy who dared to speak of conflicts waged when he was not even born. But they soon realized that he was no mere self-important prince airing his half-baked views, he was a prodigy who somehow knew crucial details and elements that even they lacked full knowledge of, and spoke of battles with an authority that suggested that he had actually been present there.

The old guard began to use a term to describe this extraordinary perceptiveness that Devavrata displayed: they termed it blood memory. 'His blood is the blood of his Puru ancestors,' said one of them, 'and that rich blood carries with it the knowledge of all the deeds and experiences. Somehow, young Devavrata is able to access that vast store of knowledge and speak of it.' And the others all dipped their white heads and beards and agreed solemnly, 'It is in his blood. His blood speaks.' And in time, they began to respect his deep insights and formidable store of knowledge and even picked his brain. Whenever any two or more of them reached an impasse in an argument over some detail of some battle or campaign, they would eventually turn to Devavrata and sigh, 'Yuvaraja, settle it!' And he would always provide the crucial missing link of information or detail that would enable them to resolve the argument, without actually taking any one's side.

He came to them now. They greeted him with warmth for since his duties of kingship had increased, he did not have as much time to spend with them as before. But they did not resent this. They were old warriors. They knew their place in the world. They felt proud that he came to them at all, deferred to them and treated them with such respect. They were even wise enough to refer to him jokingly as their 'guru'.

'Guru!' they cried out as he entered their corner of the garden. An argument over the Dasarajna battle and whether or not Indra had actually descended to aid Sudas against the Anu was raging; it died down as they saw Devavrata enter and greeted him warmly. Then they quietened down, seeing from his face that he had come not simply to chat but on some important matter. They were kshatriyas, they believed in coming straight to the point.

He told them what was troubling him. 'My father,' he said simply. 'What is it that ails him? Do you know?'

They looked at each other as if they had been expecting him to come and ask this very question, then looked at him again and nodded. He sighed and sat down. 'Tell me,' he said.

They told him.

When they were done, he thought for a moment, then

said, 'Very well. Will you come with me…to Panchmani?'

They looked at each other and grinned toothless grins. They were old warriors. Nobody asked them to go anywhere. They went nowhere. Now the emperor of the Bharata race was asking their help in a crucial matter.

'Of course!' they said, raising their walking staffs like weapons of war and waving them in the air.

7

Panchmani was holding a meeting of the fishermen when Gangeya arrived. He received Devavrata with great respect and proper protocol. Once again the word went out that the king of the Purus had returned to see Satyavati's father. This time, Satyavati herself was away, ferrying her boat across the Yamuna as usual. Heartbroken after Shantanu's proposal had failed, she had overcome her own despair and reluctantly gone back to her old routine. But where she had often sung sweet songs while ferrying passengers across, she now sang melancholy songs that brought a tear to the eyes of those she ferried. She did not hear of the news of Devavrata's visit until later that evening, and even then, she did not allow herself to raise her hopes once again. What was to be would be, nothing she did could change that now. She loved her father too dearly to ever go against his wishes. And much as she had come to love Shantanu, or at least the idea of marrying Shantanu, she had always known that their union was a highly unlikely one. It did not make the disappointment any easier but it did make it seem more logical and inevitable. How could a fisherman's daughter marry a king! It was quite absurd of course. And yet, when she sang of Shakuntala and

Dushyanta, and of how Shakuntala had pleaded for hours in full court, and been repeatedly humiliated and insulted by her own lover and husband, father of her child, her voice had such pain in it that even the kraunchya birds on the shore cried out in commiseration.

'Yuvaraja,' said Panchmani warmly. 'How may I serve you?'

Devavrata leaned forward. He gestured to the old guard that had accompanied him. Except for them, he was alone. He had elected not to bring the whole royal and military entourage as it would have required time to prepare them, and he did not waste time. 'It has come to my notice that my father, King Shantanu, proposed to marry your daughter. And yet you refused.'

Panchmani paled at Devavrata's words. 'Nay, prince! Who am I to refuse the king of Purus? Even Indra himself could not refuse such a match for his daughter. Besides, Satyavati was born from the seed of a great raj-kshatriya. She is not an ordinary fisherman's daughter. I have always known that her future lay in palaces with kings, not ferrying a boat across the Yamuna and cooking river fish for one of us! So when Samrat Shantanu came to see me, it was the fulfilment of all my dreams and expectations. Where is the question of refusal?'

Devavrata looked around. 'And yet, I see no signs of preparation for a marriage. I see no festivities. No indication that you are expecting a bridegroom's procession to arrive, much less a royal one!'

Panchmani cleared his throat. 'I cannot dispute what you say, great one. Your reputation as a master of governance is a formidable one, outmatched only by your reputation as an indomitable warrior. Who would dare argue with anything you say? But I did not refuse the proposal of Shantanu. I merely laid out a condition. Should he promise to uphold that condition, I shall be happy to make the arrangements at once!'

The other fisherman all nodded vigorously, lending their chief support and encouragement. Devavrata saw the anxiety and genuine concern on their faces. They desired to see a daughter from their village marry a king of the Purus.

There was no ulterior motive here or secret agenda. All was as it seemed. He could even sense Satyavati's sorrow as she rowed her boat and sang her sad song, for the Yamuna was his maternal aunt and he was privy to her knowledge as well. 'Your condition is that your grandson, Satyavati's son, should inherit the throne of the Purus from my father, is it not?'

Panchmani glanced at his fellow fishermen. That glance communicated the fisher king's own concern and doubts. As the obvious heir and already crowned yuvaraja, Panchmani's condition affected Devavrata far more than it affected Shantanu. There could only be one reason why Devavrata had come to confront Panchmani personally: he must resent anyone asking that he be set aside in favour of a future step-son of his father.

Devavrata knew that fishermen across the village were secretly preparing to take up arms and attack him if need be—not because they were violent or aggressive but because they feared his motives for coming here. He could glimpse the taking up of hooks and fish-spears around him.

He held up his hands and turned a full circle, addressing the village at large. 'I am not here to make war on you. Look at my companions.'

He indicated the old guard. The toothless white-haired men waved and grinned at the fisherman who stared at them curiously.

'Does this look like an attack party? I deliberately brought only my father's oldest advisors in order to show you that I have only peaceful intentions here. Had I meant you harm, I would have brought an army and you would all already be dead.' He did not need to add that even an army would have been overkill; he could have massacred the entire community singlehandedly if he had desired, and still could. But he meant what he said, and had no desire to do harm to anyone here. These people were relatives of his father's chosen beloved, therefore they were related to him as well, or would be soon.

Being fishermen, they were also close to the river and that affinity gave him a sense of greater understanding of their ways and attitudes. He knew such men well enough to know that they had their own sense of pride as well. They might not live in palaces and their homes and clothes may always smell of fish but in their own way, they were kings and queens and princes of the earth.

'You are kings of the river,' he said to them, and at once saw a change come over their faces. 'You are no less masters of the world than my father or his illustrious ancestors. The goddess of the river is herself your patron and she watches over you in all you do or say. I bow to her, mighty Yamuna-devi, and in her sacred presence, I ask you sincerely: What can I do to make this marriage possible? I love my father deeply and desire his happiness more than anything else in the world. Tell me what I must do to ensure his marriage to your daughter and I shall see that it is done. You have my word as yuvaraja of the Puru kingdom and leader of the Bharatas.' Chief Panchmani stared up wordlessly for a moment then rose suddenly and raised his hairy arms to Devavrata in a gesture of acknowledgement. 'Great one, what they say about you is true. You are a great, great yuvaraja and someday shall be a great king. You are capable of defeating your enemies with a single blow yet you choose to use conciliatory words and kindness instead. But I fear there is nothing you can do here. I have told your father my only condition for this marriage. If he cannot fulfil that condition, then what can you do?'

'The condition is that only your daughter's son shall inherit and rule in my father's stead, is it not?' Devavrata asked.

Panchmani nodded, gesturing broadly again.

'Aye. So it is. For it is the dharma of a girl's father to ensure that she is always treated well by her husband and I know that if Satyavati were assured that her son would inherit then she shall be queen mother in time and guaranteed life-long security and status.'

'She shall be guaranteed all that in any case,' Devavrata said, 'but if it is this assurance you desire, then I shall give it to you right here and now. Your daughter's son shall inherit the throne, not I. I give you my word in this matter.'

Panchmani stared at Devavrata in wonderment, then turned to look at his companions, who also raised their eyebrows and gestured as well. 'What a great being! He offers to step down as heir apparent and surrender his rightful inheritance in order to secure his father's happiness! What son would do this for his father? Truly he is a great one.'

'Aye!' said the other fisherfolk. Even the old guard joined in heartily.

Panchmani paused, bent over in thought, his back to Devavrata.

Devavrata waited a moment then, when there was no further word from the fisher king, he said, 'Is it agreed then? You will make the arrangements for the marriage?'

Panchmani turned suddenly and stared at him. 'Would that it could be so, Yuvaraja! Would that it could.'

Devavrata frowned. 'I fail to understand. I have agreed to your condition. You have the assurance you desire. Now what prevents this marriage from taking place?'

Panchmani sighed heavily. 'Alas, young prince. Your assurances are honourable and I have no doubt you shall keep your word from now to the end of your days. I know you would never violate your oath once given. But...' 'But...?' asked Devavrata.

'But what of your sons?' the fisher chief said, looking up at Devavrata. 'Your future sons by one or more wives you may take in years to come?'

Devavrata frowned, listening.

Panchmani went on, gesturing as he explained. 'You are a virile young man. Handsome. Powerful. Wealthy. Even if you step down as heir apparent, you shall always remain prince of the Puru empire. You shall have no dearth of wives or lovers. You shall love them in time and produce sons of your own. You will adhere by your vow, of that I have no doubt. But will they? What about after you have passed on or died in combat? They may well rise up and claim the throne, one or more of them? My grandson's place will be jeopardized. The people love you dearly, I have heard. They may well support one of your sons over my daughter's son. What then?'

Devavrata listened silently. He looked at the faces of the old guard. They had finally stopped smiling and were shaking their white heads in commiseration. The other fisherfolk were looking down as well, for they did not wish to spurn a king's offer, nor miss the opportunity to align their tribe with the most powerful one in the world. Yet what Panchmani said was true: any assurance that Devavrata might give was useless because he could not predict what his sons might do in future. And by law, regardless of whatever he promised, it was his rightful claim to be king of Hastinapura, and by extension, his sons could inherit that throne. This was indisputable.

'Therefore, great one,' Panchmani was saying sadly, 'I fear we still face the same dilemma. Even if you swear the most powerful oath on earth, it will not prevent your future heirs from rightfully staking a claim to the kingdom and that will disinherit my daughter's line, which is unacceptable to me and my people.'

Devavrata held up his hand. 'I shall take a greater vow.'

Panchmani shook his head, sighing again. 'No vow can suffice, Yuvaraja.'

Devavrata looked at him. 'Hear the vow first, then decide. As of this moment, I relinquish all rights to the kingdom. I divest myself of the title and status of yuvaraja. I am neither prince nor heir to the Puru throne. This I say in presence of my father's oldest advisors and most wise in the knowledge of kshatriya dharma.' He held his hand out to indicate the old guard, who dipped their heads soberly to acknowledge his words.

'They will assure you that such a pronouncement is akin to a writ of law as I speak with the full authority of the position bestowed upon me—even as I divest myself of that very authority and position! Confirm that my words are truth, wise ones.'

And the old guard nodded and said as one, 'Devavrata speaks truth!'

Panchmani looked stunned. 'You disinherit yourself? But for what purpose? I have already told you, it will not suffice to appease my fear that—'

'Your fear is that I may someday, knowingly or even unknowingly, sire one or more sons who will lay claim to the throne, thereby preventing your future grandsons from inheriting, am I right?'

Panchmani nodded, looking around at the gathering as if asking if they saw and heard this extraordinary debate. All raised their voices in agreement, speaking for Panchmani. 'Aye!'

Devavrata raised his fist, clenching it tightly, and

held it to his chest. 'Then let me remove that last fear from your heart, king of the Yamuna. Now that I am no longer yuvaraja of Hastinapura, my dharma to my people has ended. Therefore I am merely an individual and may choose to do as I please with my life and body. I am not required to produce heirs for the sake of the continuance of my lineage. Therefore, from this moment on, I swear the oath of brahmacharya. I am a virgin and have never known the pleasures of woman until today and never shall I know those pleasures. I shall remain celibate as I am now for the duration of my life on earth.'

A great outcry rose from across the village. Even the old guard rose to their feet, astonished and shaking their heads in dismay. Every single fisherman and woman cried out in horror and shock. Panchmani himself staggered back, as if struck a heavy blow.

Devavrata continued: 'Panchmani, king of the Yamuna! I have fulfilled your condition! As I am now a brahmachari, and incapable of fathering children, the throne of Hastinapura has no heir. Only by wedding your daughter and siring a son upon her can Shantanu produce an heir. So what say you now? Do you consent to marrying your daughter to my father?'

Panchmani fell to his knees. 'Yes! Yes! Of course. But this vow you have taken…it is too terrible! It is bhishma, monstrous!'

Devavrata lowered his hand at last, uncoiling his fist. 'It is what I had to do in order to ensure my father's happiness. And his joy is my only goal.'

He reached out the hand, open now and offered as

a gesture of friendship. 'I have your word, then? This marriage shall take place at the earliest?'

'YES!' Panchmani said. 'As Yamuna is my witness, yes!' He was crying now, tears rolling down his face. It was impossible to say whether they were tears of joy for his daughter's impending happiness or tears of shock at Devavrata's extraordinary sacrifice.

Devavrata gestured to the old guard. They came towards him, their faces pale and shocked, gazing up at him as if seeing him for the first time. He turned to the chief one last time. 'I shall go and make arrangements. When next I return, it shall be as my father's charioteer, bringing him as a groom to collect your daughter. Ensure that all is in readiness. You are about to be allied with the House of Puru and join your fortunes to the Bharata nation.'

And he turned on his heel and walked out through the village. As he went, people crowded close to get a better look at his face, his aspect, his eyes. From behind, he heard the chief call out again, 'Bhishma! The most terrible vow ever!' The fisherfolk took up the chorus: 'Bhishma! Bhishma! Bhishma!'

Overhead the skies growled thunderously as if echoing the same word.

The old guard struggled to keep pace with him but caught up by the time he reached his chariot. They looked up at him, spreading their hands in plea. 'This vow,' they said, 'how could you take such a vow? To give up your life, your own future, your happiness, all for your father's sake? It is too much! What the chief said is true, this is

a monstrous oath. Bhishma! Never before have we heard
of any kshatriya swearing to a life of brahmacharya for
his father's sake.'

Devavrata shrugged. 'It is what had to be done. It
is done.'

He climbed aboard the chariot and clicked his tongue
at the horses.

One of the old guard was saying to the others, 'He
shall henceforth be known by the vow he took here today.
It shall make him legendary!'

Behind him, the fisher tribe of Panchmani roared
with one voice: 'Bhishma!'

8

Shantanu wept when he heard of Devavrata's terrible vow. But the old guard informed him that the vow was already taken and in effect. His son would not take it back under any circumstances. Therefore, they argued, Shantanu must go ahead and wed the fisher king's daughter now. 'He sacrificed his happiness for you,' they said, 'we have never seen or heard the like of it before. Accept it. This is a gift from the gods!'

Shantanu embraced Devavrata, still weeping. Devavrata held his father upright, embracing him fiercely as well. 'Gangeya,' he called him in his moment of extreme emotion. 'What have you done?'

'What any son would have.'

'No,' Shantanu said, shaking his head. 'No other son but you. I shall honour your sacrifice. Satyavati's son shall be king of Hastinapura in time. But you shall be king among all sons everywhere, from now to the end of time.' He cried profusely and said, 'If the gods are listening then I pray they hear me now: Any boon you desire is yours to have. Ask me anything. You have given up your inheritance, your throne, your status. What shall I give you in return, my son?'

Devavrata bowed his head. 'I desire only your blessings, father. But if you wish to grant me a boon, then grant me this one gift: give me permission to die only when I will it. Not a moment before, regardless of my wounds or condition.'

'It is done!' Shantanu cried.

As word spread through the city and the kingdom, people began to gather and talk in crowds, then cry out in lamentation and wonder at the great sacrifice of their yuvaraja. Soon all knew of the terrible vow he had taken and of the word the Panchmani fisherfolk had shouted as he left.

And from that day onwards, Devavrata came to be known as Bhishma. Taker of the terrible vow.

Shantanu and Satyavati lived together in great happiness. With his second wife, Shantanu found all the fulfilment he desired. Even more than with Ganga, he experienced the full spectrum of mortal companionship, for Satyavati was mortal and had no secrets to hide, nor any hidden agenda. In fact, it was for the ways in which she differed from Ganga that Ganga herself had chosen her as Shantanu's second mate, guiding him unknowingly towards her boat on that blessed day of their first encounter. And Bhishma, with the taking of his terrible vow, had been the hand that knowingly fulfilled her wish that her husband find a soul-mate again. So it was that love engendered love.

AMBA AND BHISHMA

1

Shantanu, king of the Puru dynasty, had married a second time. His wife was Satyavati, a fisher chief's daughter. From his previous marriage to the river-goddess, Ganga, he had a son, Devavrata, who came to be known as Bhishma due to the terrible vow he took in order to ensure his father's happiness.

Shantanu and Satyavati lived together in great happiness. With his second wife, Shantanu found all the fulfilment he desired. In time, he filled her womb with child and she gave birth to a beautiful son. They named him Chitrangada. From the very outset he was fond of sports and games of valour and it was evident he would turn out to be a brave and famous kshatriya. Soon after, Satyavati gave birth to a second son, whom they named Vichitravirya. While unable to keep up with his elder brother in sports, Vichitravirya discovered that he was superior with the bow and concentrated his efforts on mastering that weapon. Soon he was one of the best young archers in the city.

But their happiness did not last. The malaise of dynasty that had plagued the Bharata since the origin of their race continued to take its toll upon the Puru race as well.

Before his sons could attain maturity, Shantanu succumbed to a fatal condition. Before he died, he instated his elder son Chitrangada as heir apparent. Chitrangada took his position and his father's loss very seriously—perhaps too seriously. At a young age, he accepted the challenge of a powerful gandharva. Unable to draw the legendary Bhishma into battle, the gandharva saw his opportunity to best a Puru king by provoking Chitrangada. Against Bhishma's advice, the young king joined combat with the notorious rascal. On the banks of the river Hiranyavati they met one day and began to fight. Days later, they were still fighting and a camp had to be set up nearby to provide for them and their supporters. That duel continued for three long years, with neither champion able to prove himself superior. Finally, resorting to trickery, the gandharva used asura maya—the power of illusion—to delude the young Puru king, turning himself into a mirror image of Chitrangada himself. His ploy was successful: unnerved by facing himself in combat, Chitrangada hesitated and the gandharva struck a fatal blow. But even as Chitrangada fell, he struck back, slaying his opponent. Both Chitrangadas died together, equal in death as they had been in life.

After this tragedy, Bhishma installed Satyavati's younger son Vichitravirya as the king of Hastinapura. Vichitravirya was still but a boy and sensible enough to know that Bhishma Pitama, as he called him, was the real force behind the governance and administration of the empire. He did as his step-brother advised and the kingdom ran as efficiently as ever, for the people and the enemies of the kingdom all knew that so long as Bhishma stood by the throne, none could challenge it successfully.

2

Unlike his over-eager brother, Vichitravirya had no appetite for war or combat. Perhaps it was the result of being in his brother's shadow during his formative years, watching the elder one achieve such mastery at such a young age and knowing he could not match that level of achievement or talent. And then, later, to see that same valorous brother whom he had come to think of as indomitable and invulnerable killed in combat. Perhaps the shock was too great or perhaps he simply lacked as great a desire to do battle, but Vichitravirya was careful to choose his fights wisely and engage in violence only when he had no other resort. When he did fight he did so bravely and fiercely and none could question his ability or his courage. But with Bhishma Pitama as his champion and protector, he rarely had occasion to lift a sword or put an arrow to a bow-string. And this perhaps was the real reason why Vichitravirya never had a chance to acquire the fame of a kshatriya as his brother and so many others in their line had before him. Who could emerge from the shadow of Bhishma Pitama—and why would Bhishma Pitama ever let his ward face any real danger? Bhishma was twice as protective of Vichitravirya now that Chitrangada was gone, leaving this slender and quiet young man the sole heir to the throne of Hastinapura. He went to great lengths to ensure that the young prince was never put in the path of danger for any reason.

This became most evident when Vichitravirya became an adult and of marriageable age. Bhishma and his step-mother Satyavati both knew that it was imperative that Vichitravirya marry soon and sire children in order to further the dynasty. It was rare for there to be only one Puru male extant; if anything were to happen to Vichitravirya, the dynasty would end abruptly. That would be the greatest tragedy of all. Bhishma assured Satyavati that he would not let such a tragedy come to pass.

So when he heard that the king of Kashi was seeking suitable husbands for his three daughters, each of whom were famed for their beauty and talents, he resolved that he would marry at least one of them to Vichitravirya. Now, the lord of Kashi had arranged a swayamvara and invited all the kings of the land to come and prove their prowess at arms in order to claim the attention of his daughters, each of whom would then choose her husband from among the victors. The expected thing would have been for Vichitravirya to attend the swayamvara and compete for the hand of the princesses. But Bhishma knew the level of competition was high, far higher than his ward was capable of matching. At best, Vichitravirya might fare as well as some of the others in archery. At worst, he would be hopelessly humiliated and stand no chance of winning even one of the girls. Vichitravirya had grown up in the shadow of first his brother and then Bhishma, and this over-protectiveness had made him softer and less aggressive than most. Bhishma knew the kings who would attend the swayamvara: they were lions and hyenas and would happily tear one another apart with their bare hands just to prove their masculine superiority. With three beautiful princesses at stake, they would do anything. Vichitravirya would be lucky to return home unscathed and alive.

Bhishma knew what he had to do. He informed neither Vichitravirya nor Satyavati of the swayamvara, nor of his plan. He had a single large chariot prepared for himself and set out for Kashi. Arriving at the tournament pavilion, he observed the thousands gathered there. There were hundreds of participants alone: all kings of larger or lesser kingdoms, each a champion in his own right. Tens of thousands of Kosalans had come to view the competition. Upon the great dais sat Raja Kashya after whom the capital city of Kosala was named. Beside him were three young women of such breathtaking beauty that even Bhishma Pitama, brahmachari though he was, knew that he could not find a better wife for Vichitravirya if he were to search the entire kingdom.

Swayamvaras were elaborate affairs and Raja Kashya intended to make the swayamvara of his daughters the grandest ever. There were endless formal gestures and protocols, culminating in a lengthy, laborious recitation of the long list of participants, with suitable introductions for each of the kings present. This itself went on for an hour or more and it was while the recitation was at its most boring point, with even the kings themselves eager for the contest to be underway, that Bhishma made his move.

Striding onto the dais, he walked right up to the bejewelled thrones on which the three princesses sat. They looked up at the unexpected stranger, puzzled at his appearance. Bhishma smiled at them, then bent down and grasped their wrists. His hand was large enough to clutch two of them in one fist, and he caught hold of the third princess' arm with the other hand. Forcing them to their feet, he began walking off the dais with them in tow. At first the princesses were too shocked to react. They stumbled after him, not fully comprehending what was going on. It was their father the king who, seeing the tall black-bearded man leading his daughters away, rose to his feet, stunned.

'Halt!' cried Kashya. 'Unhand my daughters! Who are you? How dare you lay hands on my princesses?'

Bhishma continued walking without bothering to respond.

'Guards,' cried the king. 'Stop that man!'

There were thousands of guards present at the event and all of them were alerted by the king's cries. The announcer who had been droning out his recitation of the names of the participants, ceased speaking and by degrees everyone present began to grow aware of the commotion on the royal dais. Several scores of soldiers began surrounding the dais, blocking Bhishma's path. With drawn swords, spears and bows, they threatened him on every side.

In response, Bhishma pushed one princess towards her two sisters and grasped hold of all three wrists in his left hand. Then, with his right hand he drew his sword and held it to their throats, or close enough that he could stab them with a quick jab if he wished.

At once, the king cried out in dismay. 'Please! Do not harm them! They are the jewels of my life. Tell me what it is you desire.'

Bhishma indicated the soldiers with a jerk of his head. 'Ask your soldiers to withdraw. Let no one threaten me or your daughters may fare the worse for it. I will not leave without a fight, and if we fight, these three jewels will surely be reduced to precious dust.'

King Kashya swiftly gave orders for the soldiers to back away. Bhishma saw that his request was being obeyed and waited for a pathway to be cleared so he could leave with the princesses. Meanwhile, they had begun to struggle against his grip. Amba, the eldest, struggled most fiercely, and when she found herself unable to break free of her captor's iron grip, she said to her sisters, 'He must be too cowardly to take part in the swayamvara and win us by fair means, therefore he manhandles us and steals us away by force!'

Bhishma grinned at her words and turned to her father, the king. 'Kashya! Your daughter calls me a coward. Do you think me one as well?'

The king was too diplomatic to answer aloud but stared balefully back at the abductor of his daughters.

It was Ambika, the second sister, who spoke up. She said spitefully, 'What else can we think of a man

who behaves in this barbaric fashion? If not a coward,
a mlechchha!'

Bhishma laughed long and hard. The other watching
kings, now aware of what was going on, also stared
balefully at the man who was attempting to steal away the
women they had dreamed of making their wives. 'Listen
to me, all of you! My name is Bhishma Devavrata, son
of Shantanu. Do you know who I am?'

At the mention of his name, everybody reacted.
Champions and warriors all, they each knew who he was
and what he was capable of doing on the battlefield. 'Do
you think me a coward?' he asked. 'Or a mlechchha?'

They shook their heads, many speaking aloud to say
'Nay.'

The king of Kashi knew who Bhishma Devavrata was
too. He decided to chance speaking: 'Then why do you
do this deed? You are a legendary warrior from one of
the greatest dynasties. If you desire one of my daughters
as your wife, win her hand fairly. If the legends are true,
you are capable of besting all the kings present here!'

'I am,' Bhishma said, completely without arrogance
for he knew this to be a simple fact, 'And that is precisely
why I assert my right to take your daughters home today.
I do not need to participate in this week-long contest to
prove my superiority at arms. But I wish you to know that
I do not do this for myself. For I have taken a lifelong
vow of brahmacharya. I am taking them to Hastinapura
to be wives to my ward, Vichitravirya. Take comfort in
the fact that they shall be queens of Hastinapura, Kashi-
naresh. Surely you would take pride in that?'

Kashya had to admit that the thought of being allied to the House of Puru was a fine one. The Bharata nation was more powerful than any of the others represented here. He was silenced by Bhishma's words.

But his daughters were not. 'What of our choice?' cried Ambalika, the third sister. 'In a swayamvara, we have the right to choose our husbands from among the victors. This violates our right to choose!'

Bhishma nodded. 'I cannot argue with that. But under dharma, this form of marriage is equally acceptable. It is one of the eight known forms. And as your father and many others here will attest, it is a long time-honoured tradition to take brides by force. If any here is brave enough to stop me, I shall face him in combat and prove my worth. If not, then I assert my right to win these princesses for my ward Vichitravirya!'

And with these words, he began walking again, dragging the princesses past the cordon of guards that stood and watched powerlessly as he went up to his chariot. Lashing the girls to the rein post so they could not escape while he drove, he started the chariot and began riding away at great speed. He had asked his sarathis to harness the strongest and fastest horses in the royal stable, and the chariot raced away from Kashi with the speed of lightning. At once, each of the kings present began wearing his armour and calling for his chariot or horse in order to give pursuit. A few were wary enough of Bhishma's reputation to decide to abstain from any direct conflict, but they were willing to follow to view the encounter.

The king of Kashi's chief minister asked him if the army was to be sent out to follow after the princesses.

King Kashya watched the hundreds of kings who had come to participate in the swayamvara clambering aboard their chariots and mounting their horses, clad in full armour, each accompanied by their retinue of personal guards, all wheeling and turning to leave the city, giving chase to the kidnapped princesses. 'How many armies shall we send?' he asked. 'Besides, these were the men who were to compete for their hands in marriage. Let this be their test.'

The chief minister was an old man and he saw the wisdom in the king's words. In older times, this was in fact what a swayamvara meant: a melee in which all suitors fought to the death. Once the dust and bloodspatter settled, the women chose their husbands from among those left standing. All Bhishma Devavrata had done was to cut short the ceremonial pomp and regress the event to its older, more brutal origins. Now, all that remained was to wait and see who 'won'.

3

They were less than a yojana out of Kashi when Amba called out triumphantly: 'Here they come!' Her sisters cried out with matching enthusiasm. Bhishma glanced back over his shoulder. Driving an eight-horse team required constant adjustment and a single error of judgement could bring down the entire team, most likely hobbling or crippling several of the horses. The journey to Hastinapura was a long one and he needed all eight to carry the combined weight of the chariot and four persons. It was the reason why he had not brought even a sarathi, preferring to take on this task alone rather than rely on anyone. Alone was how he fought best. He allowed himself a single glance back.

They had pursuers.

An unfurling cloud of dust was visible on the horizon, perhaps half a yojana behind them. At that rate, they would catch up with Bhishma's chariot very quickly. He had expected that. He didn't know the territory here too well, otherwise he would have picked a suitable vantage point and waited for them to come to him. He could still do that: this was a hilly region and there were any number of high spots which made suitable defensive sites. But he discarded that option in an instant: he had no desire to prolong this fight. Stopping and picking a spot could easily turn into a long siege. His pursuers had only to surround him and keep overwhelming him with force of numbers. He would not lose in the end but the princesses would likely end up dead as a result, if not from the crossfire then from starvation, thirst or exposure.

So he chose to ride on, increasing speed and forcing the enemy to come to him and fight him on the run. Few kshatriyas could fight well from a chariot and it would weed out the ineffectual and incompetent. Those that remained would have to use their best efforts right away or risk being outpaced. This way, he would force the fight to begin and end quickly, reducing the risk to the princesses to a minimum.

The princesses took his increase of speed to mean the exact opposite, as of course, they would.

'See, Ambika, Ambalika,' said the eldest one with the sharp tongue. 'He is too cowardly to stand and fight, so he tries to run away. He does not realize that Shalva will catch him no matter how fast he rides!'

Bhishma wondered who this Shalva might be, but knew better than to speak just then. He focused his attention on steering the team across a rocky path, trying as best as he could to avoid the fist-sized rocks that lay strewn about everywhere.

They took his silence to mean fear as well. 'You speak truly, Amba,' said the third sister, Ambalika. 'It will not be long now before we are saved and can return home.'

Bhishma smiled at that. He finished negotiating the

rocky path and saw that the way ahead was clear for a good few miles. 'Is that what you wish?' he asked, speaking loudly enough to be heard above the sound of the horses and the chariot and the wind. 'To return home...and continue the swayamvara?'

'Yes!' said Ambika, the middle one. 'For that way we have pride of choice and dignity!'

Bhishma laughed at her pomposity and naiveté. 'You foolish girl! If you really wish to have pride and dignity, you would not have a swayamvara at all. You would simply choose your man and marry him. That is true freedom of choice.'

They exclaimed at the absurdity of this suggestion. 'How would we know if he is the best at arms or not?' asked the eldest again, her beautiful brown eyes flashing angrily.

Bhishma had to admit she was the most attractive of the three, if also the most shrewish. 'Why should a man only be best at arms to be a suitable husband? Can he not simply be a good man? A loving, caring, sensitive, educated, intelligent man?' He was describing Vichitravirya although she did not know it.

She wrinkled her nose at him as if he had suggested she marry a bird or a fish instead of a man. 'A man who cannot best others at arms to prove his love is not fit to be my husband,' she said haughtily. 'Or the husband of either one of my sisters!'

Bhishma laughed long and hard at that. She did not understand why he laughed and turned away, after shooting him a last smouldering look of fury. He was surprised to find himself provoked, perhaps even a little aroused by that look. But he had long since mastered his senses and desires and his arousal was more by way of a faint memory of what arousal had once been rather than the actual sensation. Still, it took him by surprise, to encounter a woman who evoked even the memory of that feeling within him. He thought it would be a fine thing to see this one, Amba, eat her words and accept that she was wrong. And he also thought that she would be a difficult but strong wife for Vichitravirya.

Their pursuers caught up with them after another yojana. Bhishma felt them coming by the change in the vibrations from the chariot. There were at least a hundred of them in the first group itself, with others forced to follow only due to the limitations of the terrain. He felt also that several would be taking different routes to try to cut them off at various points, some to lay ambushes ahead. He grinned to himself. It would be an interesting journey home, that was certain.

He bent to pick up his bow, to string it, and sensed one of the princesses watching him balefully. He glanced at her: it was Amba, of course. She turned her eyes away when he caught her looking and he sensed that she had been sizing him up, evaluating him as a warrior. And perhaps something more.

'Who is Shalva?' he asked casually as he strung the bow. The effort didn't exert him at all, and he noted the way her eyes narrowed at the ease with which he bent the longbow and strung it deftly.

She did not answer at once. He waited, not pressing her, acting as if the question hardly mattered to him, which in fact it did not.

'He is the one who would have won me,' she said shortly, then looked away as if regretting having answered. But something occurred to her and she turned back almost at once. 'And will do so even now,' she asserted vehemently.

'He shall certainly have his chance,' Bhishma replied jovially. 'But do not judge him too harshly if he fails. Winning at arms is not the only victory.'

She stared at him as if he had spoken a foreign language instead of common Sanskrit. 'Of course it is!' she said indignantly. 'You only say that because you are afraid you will lose and be killed!'

He smiled sadly at her. 'There is much you do not know about the world, princess Amba,' he said. 'And I am one of those things.'

She stared at him in complete incomprehension. Then, frustrated, she turned away again and ignored him. She spoke to her sisters and all three of them looked back and watched as the dust cloud following them coalesced into recognizable forms.

Bhishma counted at least four score chariots hard on his heels. Of them, about two handfuls would reach arrow range in moments. And one of them, a bright, shining, gold-inlaid chariot that reflected the late morning sun's rays like a mirror, was far ahead of the pack, already within arrow range and gaining fast. He wondered why that forerunner had not started firing arrows yet then realized the reason: *he is afraid of hitting the princesses by mistake.*

He smiled to himself. That was one of the things he had hoped for when he had decided upon this plan. *At least for now, the desire to prove themselves superior warriors was still outweighed by their desire to gain wives. It was when that balance shifted to the former desire that the real fighting would commence.*

The forerunner drew closer and as he approached, the two younger sisters exclaimed and turned to their elder sister, smiling. 'There he comes! We knew he would come!'

Out the corner of his eye, Bhishma saw Amba smile. She sensed him watching her covertly and glanced at him. He turned to look at her and she turned away at once, but not before he had seen the uncertainty clouding her beautiful brown eyes. *She is intelligent enough to know that this will not be as simple as she would like it to be. Or else I would not have been able to abduct her and her sisters in the first place, from under the very aquiline noses of several thousand armed men in the heart of her own homeland.*

Yes, he thought, smiling inwardly, *this one would make a very good wife for Vichitravirya! He only hoped that Vichitravirya would be able to keep her in control.*

The thundering of chariot wheels other than his own grew steadily until the forerunner was only a few score yards behind. When the distance between them had reduced to three score yards, Bhishma saw sunlight flash on something metallic as it left the chariot and rose into the air in a bowing arc. 'Keep your heads down,' he told the three princesses matter-of-factly. 'And don't get in my way.' He looked at each of them in turn, making sure their eyes met and he communicated his seriousness. 'Don't even try,' he said, his voice steely. 'Even if one of you survives the trip, that will be acceptable to me.'

He saw their eyes widen as they realized what he meant. All their lives they had encountered only men who obeyed their every command or desired them intensely enough to do as they wished. He was probably the first man who didn't care if any of them lived or died.

The javelin was beautifully launched, taking into consideration the respective speeds of both chariots, the wind factor and the precise location of the target. Bhishma estimated that it would land precisely on his back, punching a hole through his rib cage and bursting his lungs, to explode out of his chest. The wound would be a mortal one, instantly fatal. There would be no escaping it. And due to the nature of the road, he could neither swerve the chariot to avoid it, for fear of striking against one of the many large boulders bordering the road on either side, nor leave the reins for fear of the horses veering slightly off path and the chariot striking the same boulders. Every team has a leader who tends to pull the team in its direction slightly. Bhishma's team leader was on the foremost row, on the extreme left corner. If he left the reins untended, the chariot would move to the left slowly but surely.

So he did the only thing he could. Waiting until the last instant, judging the trajectory of the falling javelin exactly as the thrower himself had done, he reached out at precisely the right instant, and snatched the falling missile out of the air. The sound of the heavy wood slapping hard into his palm was shockingly loud, even above the thundering of the horse hooves and chariot wheels. And the force of the impact was enough to jar him to his heels. But he caught it perfectly, the deadly metal-coated point barely inches from his back.

He lowered the chariot and turned to glance at the princesses. They were gaping wide-eyed at his hand, the one holding the javelin.

'Sisters, did you see…?' asked the youngest one.

They nodded dumbly, too stunned to speak.

Bhishma grinned at them, then turning from the waist without leaving the reins, he sent the javelin flying back the way it had come, but at a direct trajectory. The missile flew back as straight as an arrow shot from a bow, and passed within a hair's breadth of the lead pair of horses drawing the forerunner's chariot, startling them into loud whinnies, to embed itself in the front armour plate of the chariot. The chariot shook with the impact and the man driving it stared down with eyes that showed white even at this distance, realizing what Bhishma intended him to realize: that he had deliberately thrown the weapon to warn away, not injure or kill.

'The next one will go through your chest,' Bhishma murmured, and turned back to mind his horses. He had only taken his eyes off the road for a few moments and already the team leader had begun dragging them leftwards. He straightened them out as he heard a familiar whistling sound that could mean only one thing. 'Arrow shower,' he sighed.

He raised his bow and without even turning back this time, loosed a single arrow, firing up into the air.

Then he continued driving the chariot without looking back.

4

Amba had never seen a warrior like the man who called himself Bhishma Devavrata. What sort of name was that, anyway? Bhishma? Terrible one? Well, it certainly fit him. He was terrible, monstrous, awful. The nerve of the man, to storm into her father's city and abduct her sisters and her while every suitor who desired them watched helplessly! What audacity! And the way he had spoken to her father—she had seen her father's face change when he announced his name and dynasty. She knew of the Puru dynasty and the Bharata race too. In a sense, they were the mother race of all who lived upon the subcontinent. Even she, a Kaushalya, was a Bharata. But the Purus were the core tribe of the original Bharatas, the descendants of Sudas via Bharata, son of the legendary Shakuntala and Dushyanta. And their nation was one of the most powerful, widest, and richest. Had their name been called during the recitation of suitors participating, she would have felt a thrill of excitement at being desired as the wife of such a great House. But to be abducted like this was humiliating and degrading! She had prayed for Shalva, her beloved, to come and slaughter this impudent bearded giant and cut off his head...or worse.

But then she had seen the way he caught the javelin. She had never witnessed anything remotely like that before. She had seen a man catch a javelin once, but that had been on an open field, the man had been able to watch for the javelin's approach and adjust his body to catch it. This Bhishma fellow had been driving a chariot team of eight horses, looking ahead, and he had simply stuck out his hand and caught the javelin as it fell on his back. How was such a thing even possible? How could he have seen and judged its approach so perfectly, and how much strength did it take to stop a flung javelin like that? She could hardly imagine. It was a godlike feat, the kind written about in the fables one read in the puranas and itihasas. Something that Indra once did, or Varuna or Vayu.

Now, she watched with wide eyes as he shot a single arrow upwards, this time not even glancing back to judge the trajectory, wind speed and direction or any of the myriad factors involved in a precise bow shot.

What impudence! How could anyone possibly aim an arrow without seeing? By sound alone? What if he misjudged? There were so many factors to consider, it was not remotely possible that he could hit his mark. Even if he didn't care whether or not he hit—even if he was simply shooting blindly to dissuade the pursuer—what about the arrows shot by Shalva that were now falling towards him, only an instant away from killing him?

Yes, arrows. Plural.

For Shalva had loosed his legendary astra, the Hailstorm, as he called it. A single thick arrow that split open during flight to divide into numerous smaller darts, each deadly enough to punch through armour and deal a serious injury if not a mortal blow. It took great strength to simply loose such an arrow, and a special bow that required three men's strength to bend and string. And once shot, Shalva had claimed, it never failed. He had downed entire companies of enemy soldiers with that arrow. He had even demonstrated it once to her, showering an area three yards square with scores of tiny deadly black darts.

Amba had never expected to see the same weapon deployed at her.

If even one of those strikes me or my sisters in a vital organ, she thought as she watched the hail of missiles descend towards her, we will surely die.

She realized that Shalva must know that. Which meant that he had chosen to loose it anyway, risking her life and the lives of her sisters, in order to stop their abductor from getting away.

Stupid man, she wanted to scream.

But then Bhishma had loosed his single arrow.

And as it shot up, she found herself unable to take her eyes off it, even though the Hailstorm would strike down in an instant.

Bhishma's arrow rose up and burst into a hundred fragments.

Each of the fragments flew sideways, parallel to the surface of the earth, like a flock of birds that rise upwards then suddenly split off to go their separate ways.

The fragments of Bhishma's arrows sliced through the Hailstorm.

Amba watched in disbelief as the fragments cut each of the several black missiles into half, rendering them harmless as well as halting their progress.

The chariot thundered on, and the pieces of Shalva's fabled Hailstorm clattered to the dusty road behind the chariot, useless pieces of metal and wood.

'How—?' she started to ask, then stopped.

Bhishma's face had turned as dark as a stormcloud.

'He meant to kill you as well!' he roared. She recoiled at the sound of his voice. It was louder than any voice she had heard before. She had heard men bellowing before but never so loudly. She had not thought it possible for any man's voice to be this loud! 'He was able to judge my ability from that single catch and counter strike and because of my reputation he assumes that he will not be able to defeat me fairly. Therefore he continues to strike from behind in violation of kshatriya dharma and attempts to slay you innocents as well! This is unacceptable!'

Amba felt her sisters clutch her arms for comfort, frightened by the anger and intensity of Bhishma's roaring. Amba herself was more frightened by the knowledge that he was right: Shalva had meant to kill them, or else he would never have used the Hailstorm.

'Kill him then,' she heard herself say, her voice barely a croak lost in the thundering of hooves and wheels.

Bhishma turned his head towards her and she had a moment when she felt as if he would surely strike out at her. He possessed the power and rage to do it. But she saw his eyes and they were not filled with hatred for her, only curiosity.

'Kill him then!' she repeated, loud enough that he could hear her clearly. 'He has already forfeited me by targeting my sisters and myself. So do what you must to save us. I will never accept him as my husband now.'

Bhishma's face cleared as suddenly as it had clouded. It reminded her of a time when she was younger and had been looking down at her reflection in a lotus pond, wondering if she really was as beautiful as everyone said she was. A cloud had passed across the sun just then and she had been startled, thinking something had changed in her face, then realized it was only a passing cloud. The way her own reflection had clouded then cleared as the cloud moved across the sun was exactly the way Bhishma's face clouded and cleared. He is as transparent as water itself if you know how to gauge him, she thought, and the insight moved her deeply for some reason.

Bhishma smiled at her. 'I did not ask for nor need your permission, milady,' he said, in a tone that mocked her lightly. At once her anger flared again and she hated him once more.

But she watched with renewed interest as he raised his bow again, shut his eyes, and loosed another arrow.

She watched the arrow rise at the same instant as Shalva loosed another arrow as well. Because she was watching so intently, she knew that Bhishma had loosed his own arrow a fraction of an instant before Shalva had loosed his. She knew also that Bhishma had his eyes shut and was facing forward, one hand still gripping the reins even as it gripped the bow—another impossible feat she would not have thought possible if she had not witnessed it herself—and so he could not possibly have seen Shalva loose his arrow.

Yet when she looked back she realized that Bhishma must have known Shalva was about to fire and that he was about to use that precise arrow at that instant. For he had performed the perfect counterattack.

Shalva's arrow rose at a sharp angle, as if climbing a mountain gradient rather than sketching a rainbow curve. She knew what that meant as well. It was Acidfire: the arrow that passed directly above its intended target, showering droplets of powerful acid as it went. Even a single drop of that acid was toxic enough to burn through skin, flesh and bone itself, causing unbearable agony. If it fell on a delicate organ or area such as the face or eyes, it would mean the end of the targeted enemy.

But because Bhishma's arrow had been loosed an instant earlier, it arrived while Shalva's arrow was still rising sharply, at its slowest point, before the ventricles had opened to release the acid. Bhishma's arrow burgeoned like a sheet hung to dry on a windy day, spreading outwards in all directions to completely envelope Shalva's arrow.

Shalva's arrow struck the enveloping folds of cloth and instead of ripping through, was enfolded in the fabric and plummeted groundwards. It fell with a useless plop to the ground and was trampled underfoot by Shalva's own team of horses.

Amba gazed at Bhishma in amazement. He grinned at her. 'A good warrior always knows the enemy's next move.'

Then his face darkened again. 'This time he meant you not merely to die, but to suffer.'

Her heart was chilled by the knowledge that once again, he was right. The Acidfire was an arrow Shalva would only use if he felt personal animosity towards the enemy. She looked back with sudden growing hatred at the chariot of the man she had been prepared to marry that very day. 'How could you, Shalva?' she shouted, shaking her fist at the pursuing chariot.

In response, Shalva loosed another arrow. This one aimed directly at them, not at an angle. She watched in horror as the missile sped towards them at the speed of wind, and reacted to the sight of it splintering to a score of tiny metal fletches, each sharp enough to tear through flesh and cause great pain and damage.

Before the shower of metal fletches could reach their chariot, an arrow shot from beside her raced to meet them, splitting itself into as many pieces, each of these pieces obstructing the fletches and dropping them harmlessly to the ground. She turned back to stare at Bhishma, who was lowering his bow, still looking ahead to watch the road. She understood that his aim had been perfect but how could the metal pieces in his arrow have perfectly blocked every single fletch coming at them? Could anyone loose an arrow with such a precise degree of skill?

That was when she first began to realize that Bhishma was no mere mortal. And when she first fell in love with him.

Bhishma grew steadily angrier with Shalva as the suitor continued pursuing them and continued to loose deadly arrows at them, each more ingenious and malevolent than the one before. He dealt with each missile in turn, shooting back a suitable counterattack, but after this had progressed for a while he began to resent the attack. It was now no longer a question of escaping with the princesses, it was a matter of Puru pride. He could keep this up all day, and counter everything Shalva threw at them, but it would encourage the other kings following and give the impression that Shalva harried him all the way to Hastinapura. It was important that he prove his superiority once and for all and end this game. He was incensed by Shalva's repeated attempts to kill the princesses rather than merely stop Bhishma. This was a direct challenge to Bhishma's manhood and family pride: Shalva was effectively saying that he would rather see the girls dead than married to his ward and what the devil was Bhishma going to do about that, hey?

The first chance Bhishma got, finding an open area with dry baked earth and almost no foliage or tree cover, he turned the chariot around. He did not bother with a wide wheeling arc and a genial approach. He slowed his team, then executed a smart turning manoeuvre, then coaxed them back up to speed and charged directly at Shalva. Before he did this, he had gained a good mile or so on the forerunner. This gave him an excellent approach and he picked up speed as he drove towards his pursuer. He was pleased to see Shalva's chariot slow as the suitor reacted to the sight of his prey turning upon him, and behind the fore chariot, he saw the other pursuers arriving in quick succession, drawing up their chariots and horses and fanning out in a wide arc to enable a better view of the coming duel. He knew that none of them would interfere since Shalva had taken first strike and was entitled to the first duel as well. That too was a matter of kshatriya dharma. So long as two champions fought single-handedly, none other could interfere, no matter what the outcome. Entire armies sat and watched and waited until champions finished their bout, leaving one dead and the other victorious, and often these duels lasted for hours or days, or even longer—as in the case of poor Chitrangada who fought his opponent for three years! Bhishma had no intention of letting this bout last more than a few minutes.

He saw that Shalva had opted to remain standing while Bhishma approached. It was a sensible move. This way, Shalva would presumably have better aim and stability while Bhishma, having made the first move, was entitled to take his best shot. Shalva intended to survive this shot and then make his own counterattack against Bhishma, this time using the closer range to finish off his targets. Bhishma would not give him that chance.

But as Bhishma had expected, Shalva deviated from custom. Instead of letting Bhishma have the first shot as was traditional in such a situation, he loosed first. This time, he used the advantage of stillness and stability to unleash what must be one of his most powerful weapons.

The princesses screamed in alarm as the javelin-thick arrow shot by Shalva burst into a veritable cloud of arrows. It seemed as if the arrow split and split again and continued to divide itself infinitely, producing an impossible number of missiles that filled the air and darkened the sky itself! Bhishma knew that Shalva had used a cannon-bow, an oversized bow fixed to the chariot itself that loosed a container missile as thick as a pole. Within this container missile were the individual barbed arrows, released in stages as the pole split apart at different times during its short flight. Due to the power of the cannon-bow and the relatively lengthy flight time, Shalva was able to loose a second and a third container missile in quick succession, and now, even before the first shower of arrows arrived at its destination, he was letting loose a fourth.

A great roar of approval rose from the gathered crowd of princes and kings. Naturally their support was for Shalva who was fighting for all of them. In Bhishma's view that made all of them equally culpable for his actions and transgression of the norms of combat. Even now, what Shalva was doing was unethical in the extreme: it was one thing to use such weapons against superior forces such as a larger army, but to do so against a single kshatriya enemy, with innocents in harm's way, that was unacceptable.

'Bhishma!' cried the eldest daughter of Kashya, appealing to him. She was staring up at the approaching cloud of arrows with abject horror. He saw that she expected to die this time. For how could he possibly counter such an attack? Even if he loosed an arrow to stop the first barrage, the second barrage was already following close after—and the third and the fourth and the fifth... and Shalva would continue to rain down arrows until his goal was accomplished. It was impossible to escape such an attack in theory and impossible in practice as well, for any mortal warrior.

Bhishma had adjusted the pace of his charge to match the trajectory of the approaching arrows. He only desired that his horses escape unhurt. They were most innocent of all in this conflict and did not deserve to be injured or killed. He rode until he was certain that the team had passed ahead of the shower of death that rained down from above, then released the reins and turned to the princesses. It did not matter if the team went off course slightly, there were no impediments or obstructions here to fear. The princesses were his only concern now.

Bhishma threw himself over all three girls, embracing them tightly, wrapping his arms and legs over them, ensuring that every inch of their bodies was covered by his own. They squealed in shock, unaccustomed to any man coming into physical contact with them, then somehow implicitly realized he sought only to protect them, and grew still.

The arrows rained down.

Bhishma felt them land. They struck the ground, the

chariot, and his body. Dozens, scores, hundreds, then, it seemed, thousands.

The barrage continued endlessly. The clattering and thudding of arrows as they struck the ground and embedded their metal heads in the packed earth, or the wood of the chariot or the flesh of his body, along with a variety of related sounds that rang out like a death rattle, played a ghastly dirge.

It seemed to go on forever.

Then, as suddenly as it had begun, the rain of arrows ended.

No doubt, Bhishma mused through the fog of pain and sensation, Shalva had run out of container missiles. There was a limit to how many he would have been carrying in the limited space of his chariot.

He estimated that Shalva would have loosed at least ten or twelve barrages in all. Perhaps ten or twelve thousand individual missiles. Most of them would have fallen around the chariot. Perhaps a tenth of that number would have fallen on the chariot itself. And of that number perhaps a third would have struck Bhishma.

He unwrapped his body from the princesses, regaining his feet. He stumbled and had to reach out for support. He saw Amba's face as she looked up, opening her eyes and staring at him in astonishment. She was staring at his back, his arms, the rear of his neck, his legs... She exclaimed in horror, clapping a hand to her mouth. Her sisters simply stared silently in mute disbelief.

Bhishma felt as if his back had been set ablaze. He could feel a thousand pinpricks of fire burning into his skin, boring through his flesh, some reaching all the way into his organs, touching upon his bones, penetrating his joints, cracking his spine, his neck, piercing his lungs, his heart, even punching through the soft area at the back of his neck to penetrate his brain-case at two points. It felt like nothing he had ever experienced before: to call it pain would be to understate it woefully. To call it agony would be merely a word. The actual sensation was indescribable, and yet it was also much as the reality suggested. He had been pierced by hundreds of tiny barbed arrows. He knew from the wetness that drenched his back, pouring down the rear of his legs, collecting in a puddle on the floor of the chariot, that he was mortally wounded...by mortal standards. In fact, he was probably mortally wounded several score times over! Yet he could still stand, with great effort.

He looked at the face of the eldest daughter of the king of Kashi. Amba lowered her hand from her mouth, still staring at him in utter disbelief, yet assimilating the fact that he still stood, despite his terrible wounds. He saw in her eyes an understanding, an awareness that he could not possibly survive such wounds, no man could, and yet, if he did, then it meant something. It meant he was more than just a man. He saw also that she understood the most important thing: that he had done this to protect her and her sisters. He could have let them die and saved himself—or even if he could not save himself, he still did not need to protect them by using his own body as a shield. Yet by doing so, he had proved one thing beyond dispute: he deserved to decide

their fate far more than that treacherous rat of a suitor
Shalva, who intended to murder his own beloved rather
than let her wed another man.

He saw also that she now desired him, Bhishma. She
was in awe of him. The way she looked at him at that
instant was the way he had seen his mother's followers
gaze at her, reverentially, adoringly, devotionally. She
looked at him as if he were a god. And she wished to
give herself to him.

He shook his head once, silently denying her. She
blinked, startled. He did not speak or explain.

This was not the time nor the place.

He turned, hearing the gasps of horror from the
princesses as they saw his back now and viewed the full
extent of his injuries. He knew his back must resemble
a porcupine, bristling with arrows. Except that he did
not possess the power to simply shoot these arrows from
his own body and assault his enemy. He would have to
remove them the hard way, by tearing out his own flesh
and skin and organ tissue. But that was for later, after he
finished the task at hand. For now, he had to deliver a
rejoinder to King Shalva, one that he would never forget
so long as he lived.

Bhishma was relieved to see that the horses were
unharmed. He had used those precious seconds to ensure
their safety and then the safety of the princesses. He had
not cared about himself. He could survive this. He could
survive far worse than this, he knew. Although at this
instant, with arrows piercing every part of his body, he
could not imagine what could be worse.

He coaxed the team into starting forward. They smelled his blood and whinnied angrily, upset. Animals responded well to him, sensing his affinity. He knew they could still smell the river in him, even if mortals could not. It was not a fish smell, but something deeper. An atavistic link to other animals of all species that bonded them at the deepest level.

'Ride,' he urged the beautiful Kambhoja mares, great powerful glossy giants all of them. 'Ride, my beauties! And trust in me.'

They did trust in him. They would ride off the face of a cliff if he commanded them—because he never commanded, merely coaxed, urged, requested, asked lovingly. It was sufficient. When there is a bond of love, even selfish mortal men lay down their lives for one another. Animals? They are born loyal. Dying for one another is part of life for them.

The cheers and roars of approval from the large gathering of watching kings had continued all this while, celebrating what they believed was the extinction of the impudent Puru abductor and the saving of their honour. It died down now as they saw his chariot pick up speed, resuming its charge directly at the chariot of Shalva. They watched with surprise and renewed interest. He saw many hands raised to point and many voices raised in consternation as they saw the brindled fur coat of arrows he had sprouted.

'Today you face Bhishma in battle,' he roared, loudly enough to be heard by even the farthest pursuer, still half a mile distant and approaching steadily. 'Those of you that survive, go home and tell them this tale!'

He saw many of them look at one another in panic, some taking up weapons, others reaching for their reins then dropping them as they realized that flight was useless: they were gathered too closely together to escape easily. Easier to stand and fight. Shalva too was raising a weapon, his longbow again. No doubt he intended to demonstrate some new ingenious kind of arrow.

Bhishma uttered the mantras he had learned when still a boy, the ones he had been taught in the heart of the deepest ocean, where the sun had not shone for aeons and where only one deva ruled supreme. Varuna. It had been Varuna-Tau himself who had taught Bhishma the mantra, back when he was still Gangeya to all his family, friends and gurus. Varuna had taught him the arts of war in watery environments, arts which Bhishma later realized he might never have occasion to put into practice during his life as a mortal on dry earth. But some of what Varuna taught him was applicable on land or sea or sky, like this mantra, and he used it now.

In response to the mantra, a bow appeared instantly in his hands. The moment it appeared a thunderclap sounded in the clear sky, deafeningly loud. The bow itself was immense, the size of a lance from tip to tip, and the only way it could be held was by standing it on the floor of the chariot. Even so, it towered above him. The texture of the bow itself was not wood but water, for it was made of water held in solid form; not ice, but simply water held rigid by the power of the mantra. The arrow that appeared, accompanied by a flash of lightning was white as a vajra. It was made of densely packed ocean salt, as hard as lohitwood and as heavy. Hard enough to penetrate armour and bone and punch through flesh with the same impact as any wooden missile. Yet when it penetrated flesh, it would dissolve to its natural state, filling the wound with pungent ocean saline.

He was within a hundred yards of Shalva's chariot now and could see Shalva berating his sarathi. The charioteer was panicking, and in the confusion, their horses were rolling their eyes and whickering restlessly, unnerved by the thunderclaps and Bhishma's chariot, which was bearing down on them at relentless speed. Bhishma loosed the first arrow from Varuna's bow and watched it slash through the reins and rigging of the team. Freed of their harnessing, the horses milled about for a moment, then realized they were free and began to race away.

The chariot itself settled to the ground with a rude thump, spilling the sarathi out and onto the ground where he sprawled.

Shalva shouted with anger and raised his bow again to fire back at Bhishma. He loosed an arrow which spread into a wall of fire that raged towards Bhishma's horses. The team whinnied, unable to control their natural terror of fire, but Bhishma's next arrow turned to water, dousing the wall of fire before it could come close enough to harm his horses.

What followed then was a humiliation and a rout.

Bhishma snapped Shalva's bow with his next shot. Then he shattered his chariot wheels.

Turning around Shalva's chariot, he rode in a circle, firing inwards at the suitor, demolishing his chariot piece

by piece. Each time Shalva attempted to raise a weapon—
an axe, a sword, a spear, a javelin, another bow—Bhishma
destroyed it with a single shot.

Soon, Shalva lay on the ground, the ruins of his chariot
around him. He beat his chest and slapped his arms in
anger, challenging Bhishma to do his worst.

Bhishma ripped his clothes off, rendering him naked
for all to see.

Then he sliced off his moustaches and hair, turning
him bald-faced and bare-headed.

Then, unleashing an arrow that turned in mid-flight
into a storm of tiny birds, he pinned Shalva down on
the ground, arms and legs spread akimbo, naked and
bald, helpless.

The suitor of Amba cried out in shame and humiliation
and begged Bhishma to kill him.

Bhishma turned on the watching kings instead. They
had stayed to watch Shalva's humiliation, unable to look
away from the denigration of one of their own rivals. The
truth was, while they had cheered Shalva on earlier, he
had been the prime contender at the swayamvara and
most likely to have his pick of the princesses, which had
earned him a great deal of animosity. So long as he was
victorious, they cheered him. Now, they jeered instead.
And applauded Bhishma's skill at arms and extraordinary
ability.

But their jeers did not last long.

When Bhishma turned his bow on them, they quailed
with fear. At once, those that were expecting this, loosed
their own volley of arrows. Another storm of missiles

shot towards Bhishma. But this time, he had time enough to counter it. He shot a single arrow that exploded with a blinding blue flash in mid-air. So powerful was the explosion, the hail of arrows was shattered into fragments which were in turn driven back at the kings who had loosed the arrows. Thrice each king was pierced by his own arrows, and cried out in agony as he fell to the ground or to the floor of his chariot, clutching his wounds.

Those who remained unharmed applauded Bhishma's skill nervously, hoping they would be spared his wrath. They were. Bhishma did not harm those who did not attempt to harm him.

Then Bhishma turned the heads of his horse team and rode away, heading towards Hastinapura.

This time, he was not followed.

6

After travelling for the rest of that day, they stopped to make camp for the night. The princesses had been silent after the battle with their suitors, although they held one another close and averted their eyes from Bhishma's wounds. Bhishma's terrible wounds, bhishma wounds.

Once they had a fire going and had eaten the game Bhishma hunted down for them, and the horses had been watered, fed and groomed, he asked Amba's help in removing the arrows from his body. She agreed readily. It was a long and painful process, the worse for him of course, but no less for her, because she could feel the pulling and tearing of each barbed head as she teased and worked it free of his flesh. His wounds began to bleed again and soon the grass beneath his body was soaked with his blood. She began to weep then, unable to help herself. He turned his head to look at her but did not say anything at that time. After a brief respite, she regained control of her emotions and resumed her work. It was late, the night was quiet, the moon was high, and her sisters were asleep when she finished. The pile of arrows lying on the ground was half a yard high. It was impossible to imagine that they had all been embedded in his flesh only hours earlier.

And yet, even as she washed the last of his wounds clean under his direction, she saw that the first ones, from which she had first removed the arrows, were already closed and starting to heal. It was remarkable. She had never seen the like before. Clearly, his ability to endure pain and injury and to recover successfully from them was beyond human measure. The fact that he could still sit, stand, move and talk was in itself a miracle.

He thanked her quietly and was about to turn over and sleep when she spoke.

'Great Puru,' she said, still too self-conscious of his stature to call him by his name directly. She was a princess born and raised, she could not overlook protocol and etiquette, even under the circumstances. Besides, for all his actions, he was still very much a gentleman and a royal, as was she. 'I had already chosen the king of Saubha as my husband to be. He had accepted me and made his desire known to my father. It also pleased my father to have him as his son-in-law. Once he excelled at the swayamvara, I would have declared him as my choice of husband. But now, I can never do so. This is your doing. You appear to be a man who knows dharma. Therefore decide what is the right course of action for me to follow under dharma.'

So saying, she went to bed beside her sisters.

But she did not fall asleep at once. Instead, she lay awake, hoping that Bhishma would come to her and answer her proposal in words or deed, or both.

Bhishma lay on his pallet of grass and thought long and hard on her words. He knew what she meant but could not say directly. You have defeated the man whom I intended to marry. By defeating him and proving yourself the better man, you earn the right to claim my hand. It would not displease me if you declare your intention to marry me.

He knew that she was awake yet, sighing and turning from side to side in order to let him know that she waited for his answer. He knew she meant for him to come and claim her, as was his right under dharma. She desired him and wanted him to desire her as his wife.

In another life, at another time, perhaps he would have done as she wished. Perhaps he would have wished the same.

But in this life, he was foresworn from marriage, cohabitation, love, sex...and that meant he could not allow himself even to feel such desires for a woman, let alone express them. To him, the line between brahmacharya and grihastha was not a fine one. It was clearly etched, large and bold. And he could not approach it even from afar, let alone broach it.

Moments later, he woke Amba with a hand on her shoulder.

She started awake at once, beaming with pleasure. For she thought he had come to steal her away into the shadows to demonstrate his desire for her. She was excited and awaiting it eagerly. Never before had she desired a man as she desired Bhishma. Even Shalva's proposal and her infatuation for him seemed juvenile and puerile now in retrospect. This was a real man, and real love. And under the circumstances, what could be more thrilling than to give herself under the stars to a prince of the Puru empire after being abducted from her own swayamvara? It was like being the heroine of her own puranic fable.

What she failed to remember was that the heroines of puranic fables almost always found their stories ending tragically.

Bhishma took her around the trees to where the horses were tethered. Her heart was pounding and she found her breath catching in her throat as she prepared to receive the touch of her first lover. She was surprised to see that he had separated a horse from the team and had saddled and harnessed it for individual riding. She was even more surprised when he turned to her and said, 'This horse will carry you to your destination. Ride southwards and westwards and you will find your way.'

She stared at him blankly. Southwards and westwards? What did he mean? Then she remembered what kingdom lay in that direction.

'Saubha?' she asked. 'You are sending me to Saubha?'

It was impossible to see his face clearly in the shadows of the tree. 'It is what you desire, is it not? You were all but betrothed to King Shalva of Saubha. I am doing the right thing under dharma, as you requested. Your two sisters will continue to Hastinapura with me, to be married to my ward, Vichitravirya. They shall be treated as princesses deserve and shall be as happy with him as they could ever desire. He is a handsome young man and a good king. They will not lack for anything and shall live as queens of the earth.'

She was still trying to get over the shock of disappointment. 'But...you do not wish me to go as well...to Hastinapura?'

'Two wives are good,' he said. 'And yes, had you not asked me to release you, I would wish you to go to Hastinapura as well. To wed Vichitravirya. But since you asked for my mercy, I am granting you this reprieve. I wish I could let your sisters go as well, but trust me when I say, I am sure they will do far better with Vichitravirya than with any of those dolts at your swayamvara!' She did not know what to say. This was an unexpected turn of events. Clearly, he had misunderstood her, or... Or he had deliberately rejected her overture and invitation, spurning her. Why else would he send her to that naked, blubbering fool? That coward who had tried to kill her and her sisters to prove his own valour as a warrior and had then proved himself utterly incompetent before a real warrior like Bhishma! She didn't want to go to Shalva now! She had no desire to see Shalva ever again. Yet she seemed to have no choice. She could not refuse to go now, for it would be humiliating to beg him and be rejected again.

She made one last attempt. He was turning to go and she reached out and caught his arm. He stopped and looked down at her hand holding his forearm.

'Will you not take me yet?' she asked, leaving it open for him to interpret in any way he pleased. To say more would be to say too much, and that would mean a loss of dignity. For a princess raised as she had been, dignity was more important than anything else.

He reached down and removed her hand from his forearm, gently.

'Goodbye, princess,' he said softly.

And walked away.

She left in tears, riding hard.

He stood, listening to the sound of the hooves fading into the night, then turned and walked away.

DEVAYANI, SHARMISHTHA
AND YAYATI

1

The ancient enmity of the devas and asuras had flared into a new rage. This time they fought for the dominion of the three worlds, as well as the natural riches and resources of each one. Determined to win, the devas appointed Brihaspati, son of Angirasa, as their preceptor, to officiate over their yagnas. Not to be outdone, the asuras appointed Kavya, son of Kavi, the Wise One, also known as Shukra, Shukracharya or Ushanas.

Now, Kavya Ushanas and Brihaspati were bitter rivals. Though both were brahmins and possessed of great spiritual power, each had different abilities and strengths. Immensely knowledgeable Brihaspati was able to guide the gods time and again to secure victory in battle, so much so that the result was almost always a foregone conclusion. Each time they joined battle, the devas massacred the asuras. But Kavya Ushanas possessed something that Brihaspati did not: he had the legendary sanjivani. This arcane science enabled him to restore the dead to life. Each time the devas joined battle with the asuras and slaughtered them on the battlefield, their guru applied his formidable craft and resurrected each one, as strong and virile as before.

After several such battles, the gods grew miserable. What good was their superiority in war, their immense feats of valour and daring, their bold assaults and brilliant strategies, their sacrifices and preparations, their relentless campaigns? Each time they wiped out their enemy forces, the preceptor of the asuras was able to revive them and things went back to the way they had been before! There could be no end to the conflict if this went on.

Finally, in desperation, the gods devised a plan. They met with their guru's eldest son, Kacha, and appealed to him for help. 'Kavya Ushanas has a daughter named Devayani of whom he is most fond. You are of an age to be attractive to her. Insinuate yourself into her graces, use generosity, charm, impressive deeds, mellifluous words and all your virtues to steal her heart. Your mission is to convince her to get her father to reveal the secret of the sanjivani. Once we possess that secret knowledge, no longer will the asuras have this unfair advantage.'

Brihaspati's son Kacha considered their proposal carefully and agreed that there was no other way to accomplish their aim. He consented to undertake the mission and left immediately for Vrishaparva, capital city of the kingdom of the asuras and abode of Shukracharya.

Presenting himself to Kavya Ushanas, he offered his services as a disciple. He introduced himself honestly, for there was no point in trying to delude a man of such great wisdom. 'Mahadev, I am Kacha, son of Brihaspati, grandson of Angirasa. If you do me the supreme honour of accepting me as your shishya, I shall practise brahmacharya for one thousand years.'

Irrespective of the differences between himself and Kacha's father, as a brahmin Shukra could not deny Kacha's request. It was the dharma of a brahmin to accept suitable disciples to his fold and he could find no fault with Kacha. Even if he was the son of his enemy, the fact remained that Angirasa himself had been Kavya Ushanas's own guru at one time. How could he now refuse to teach the grandson of his own teacher? He welcomed his rival's son with respect and warmth. 'Kacha, you are welcome to reside here and learn what you can for as long as you desire. Your father's reputation earns you that right. By asking me to be your guru, you show me immense respect. In turn, I too shall treat you with the same respect. In doing so, Brihaspati is also honoured.'

Under Shukra Ushanas's guidance, Kacha took his vows, swearing allegiance to his new guru for the formidable duration he had himself imposed. Then began the thousand years of Kacha's apprenticeship. He devoted himself to his allotted tasks with full diligence and devotion. But in every spare moment, he wooed the guru's daughter, Devayani, with the same dedication and determination. He sang, played musical instruments, danced, made offerings of fruit and flowers, praised her beauty at every opportunity, and melted away her resolve and reserve. Yet while he charmed and won Devayani's heart without question, whiling away every free moment with her, Kacha never broke his vows or strayed from his chosen path as a celibate disciple. Devayani respected him the more for this resoluteness, and as time passed, began to love him dearly. They sported together and were lovers in all but the physical sense, and sang and danced away, intoxicated in each other's company. Five hundred years passed in this manner.

Romancing the daughter of the preceptor of the asuras in the heart of their own domain was not something that could escape the attention of the demons. Assuming that Kacha was merely a disciple of their guru, they did not concern themselves much with the matter. But one day, quite by accident, the danavas came to know that Kacha was the son of Brihaspati, none other than the preceptor of the devas, their mortal enemies. When this knowledge spread through their ranks, the danavas were outraged. They debated whether to let the rest of their allied asura races know this shocking truth, but decided to keep it a secret for the time being. The truth could prove embarrassing and humiliating for the asuras, for their enemy had been cavorting with their own guru's daughter under their very noses for half a millennium! Not speaking a word of what they knew, the danavas decided to solve the problem themselves, quietly and discreetly. Waylaying Kacha in the forest one day, they killed him. Chopping his body into pieces as tiny as sesame seeds, they fed his remains to the wild jackals and wolves of the forest. Then they departed, pleased at how they had handled the problem and avenged the shame visited upon their guru.

Kacha had been with the cows that day, overseeing them as they grazed. That evening, when the cows returned home without their cowherd, Devayani's heart skipped a beat. She waited until sundown, hoping beyond hope that he was merely delayed for some reason. But when the sun had set and dusk had fallen over her father's ashram, there was still no sign of Kacha. Perturbed, she went to her father. 'Pitr, it was Kacha's task to light the agnihotra fire after he returned home with the cows. The cows have all come home on their own, the sun has set and still the sacred fire has not been kindled. My heart tells me that something terrible must have happened to him.'

Her father considered the facts and mused that it was not like Kacha to forego his duties. Not once before had the loyal disciple ever failed to carry out a given chore on time, and failing to light the agnihotra fire before sundown was a major lapse. He agreed with his daughter; something must surely have happened to Kacha in the deep woods. The sage's first thought was that perhaps some wild animal had killed and eaten his disciple, although he did not say so aloud, for his daughter was already agitated. Devayani persisted. 'Father, you possess the knowledge to revive even the dead. I am convinced Kacha must be dead, otherwise he would never fail his chores. I beg you, use the power of the sanjivani and resurrect him. I cannot live a day without him!' When Kavya Ushanas saw that his daughter meant every word she said, he did not hesitate further. If Kacha was not harmed, the sanjivani would have no effect; if indeed his disciple was dead, as both Devayani and he feared, then resurrecting him was a simple enough matter. He used his secret knowledge to summon Kacha.

To the great relief of his guru and the delight of the guru's daughter, Kacha appeared soon afterwards, looking much the way he had looked before. When asked what had happened, he told them the truth: all he could recall was herding the cows through the pasture that afternoon, when someone struck him from behind, rendering him unconscious. The next thing he knew, he was awake and lying on the leafy forest ground far from the pasture, and night had fallen. For some reason he was naked, although shreds of his garments still clung to his skin in fragments. Curiously enough, the bodies of several dead wolves and jackals lay all around him, their bodies ripped and torn apart as if their bellies had exploded. Fashioning a temporary covering from bark, leaves and vines, he had found his way back through the woods to the ashram. That was all he recalled. Devayani was thrilled beyond words to have her beloved back home safe. It was assumed that Kacha had been killed by the wolves and jackals and that the use of the sanjivani had compelled his digested remains to tear their way out of the bellies of the beasts, to reform magically into a living whole. The only facts available suggested such a conclusion.

Things went back to normal at once. Devayani and Kacha resumed their mutual adoration, and Brihaspati's eldest son continued serving his guru faithfully and adhered rigidly to his vows, pleasing Shukracharya greatly with his devotion and austerity. Soon, the danavas came to know that Kacha was still alive and learned what had happened. They resolved to kill Kacha again, but this time they would ensure that even their great preceptor would not be able to resurrect his pupil. They waited impatiently for a suitable opportunity and found one soon enough.

Devayani had sent Kacha into a remote region of the forest to fetch a particular variety of flower she wanted. The danavas were waiting and waylaid him, killing him instantly. This time, instead of chopping his body to pieces, they burnt it first. Once it was charred and reduced to ashes, they pounded every last fragment of bone into fine powdery dust. This residue they mixed with soma, which their preceptor was partial to, on occasion. Kavya Ushanas drank the soma given by the danavas, unaware that he was consuming the remains of his shishya. Elated at their success and certain that their enemy could not be resurrected this time, the danavas went away to celebrate by indulging in some wine-drinking of their own.

A little later that same evening, Devayani grew convinced that some mishap had befallen Kacha again. She went to her father who was resting languorously after consuming the soma. 'Father, Kacha left this morning to collect flowers but has still not returned. Again the agnihotra fire is not lit and the cows remain unpenned. Surely something has happened to him again. Please use your sanjivani knowledge to locate and restore him.'

Shukra meditated briefly and immediately understood the extraordinary fate that had befallen Kacha. He opened his eyes and sorrowfully explained to his daughter, 'My girl, Kacha has been killed again but this time I cannot revive him. We must let him proceed to the land of the dead. After all, he is mortal and all mortals must die someday. Today was his day to die. Accept it and let him go.'

But Devayani would not be appeased. She cried and grieved and wailed her anguish, straining her father's heart. 'What wrong has Kacha done that he should die so young? He was your most attentive and obedient pupil. He always served you immaculately. He performed every chore allotted to him and fulfilled his dharma. Even when I desired more than mere friendship, he stuck to his brahmacharya vows and remained austere and celibate. He is a great man, son of a great rishi and grandson of a great rishi as well. I could not ask for a finer life-companion. I love him too dearly to accept his loss and continue living. If you cannot revive him, then accept the knowledge that I too intend to kill myself. I shall go with him to the land of the dead and live there with him in the hereafter.'

By this time, his daughter's anguish and the realization of what had befallen Kacha had removed all trace of intoxication from Shukracharya's senses. He was upset by the foul murder of his pupil. The danavas had had no right to slay a pupil under his own guidance. 'This is the murder of a brahmin, a terrible, unforgiveable sin under any circumstances. What Devayani says is not wrong. Kacha was innocent and pure. He did nothing to warrant such a heinous end. This is pure evil. How dare the danavas slaughter my own pupil? I shall not let this stand.'

Spurred by his daughter's tears and angered by what his followers had done without consulting him, Maharishi Ushanas once again used the sanjivani to summon Kacha.

By the power of the arcane art of resurrection, Kacha's consciousness returned to life. His body began to form and reassemble itself. But almost immediately, he became aware of his surroundings and understood where he was. Willing his own being to stop the process of reconstruction, he spoke to his guru from within his mind. 'Gurudev, if you bring me back fully to life as I was before, it will cost you your own life! I am within your own belly.'

Even Maharishi Ushanas was taken aback at this revelation. 'How did this come to pass, Kacha?'

This time, through the teachings of his guru, Kacha had been able to retain the memory of what transpired even after he was killed. He recounted everything that had been done to him. When Kavya Ushanas came to know that his own followers had not just committed the crime of brahmin-hatya, but had also desecrated their own guru's body by tricking him into consuming another living being, he was deeply upset.

Devayani knew nothing of the conversation that had transpired between the disembodied Kacha and her father. She asked him tearfully why Kacha had still not returned. 'Have you deployed the sanjivani yet, father?' she asked.

'This time, even my secret knowledge will not avail us, daughter,' he said sadly. 'For even though I dearly wish to restore your beloved Kacha to you, I cannot do so without ending my own life.'

Devayani could not follow her father's meaning. So he explained further, touching his belly. 'He is in my stomach. Only by tearing me apart can he live again. If you still wish me to do so, I shall deploy the sanjivani, but you will regain your beloved only to lose your father. Is that what you wish?'

Devayani's heart was rent with pain yet again. 'Of course not, father! How can I want you to die? That is too great a price to pay for Kacha's resurrection.' But having said this, she could not discern what to do next. Losing Kacha was the end of her life, while the price of losing her father was too great to pay.

Kavya Ushanas saw her pain and confusion and came to a decision. Without troubling Devayani further, he sent her away with the assurance that all would soon be well. Trusting her father implicitly, she left him alone.

Shukracharya addressed Kacha directly through the power of his mind. 'Heed my words well, shishya. Today is the day that you graduate from my gurukul, for I am about to do that which I have not done for any student before you in countless years. I am about to grant you knowledge of the secret and potent sanjivani. Through the use of this arcane craft you will possess the power to bring the dead back to life.'

The unformed Kacha was overjoyed when he heard this for it meant that his mission was about to be successful. 'But why do you do me this great honour, master?'

'My daughter loves you as dearly as she loves me. That is clear. Otherwise she would not be confused and

would only grieve for you. But even though she knows
now that restoring you to life would end my own life,
she is unable to tell me plainly to let you remain dead.
This proves to me that her love is genuine and enduring.
I cannot see her pine her youth and life away, therefore
I have decided to restore you to life.'

'But it will kill you, Gurudev!' cried Kacha in alarm.
For though he desired the success of his mission he
respected his guru and did not wish to bring him harm.

'That is why I am teaching you the secret of sanjivani.
I shall use it first to restore you fully to life. This will
result in you bursting out of my belly and cause my own
death. Thereafter, you shall use the knowledge to restore
me to life again! I have considered all possibilities and this
is the only way for us both to live and for Devayani to
have both a husband and a father.' Kacha was humbled by
his guru's great wisdom and trust. 'You are great beyond
description, Gurudev,' he said.

Ushanas nodded in response and said silently: 'Act
in accordance with dharma.'

Then the preceptor of the asuras administered the
sanjivani in full, and Kacha was instantly restored to his
full bodied form. He emerged from the guru's right side,
as radiant with life as the full moon in shuklapaksha, and
stood before his master's mangled corpse. He looked down
at the torn organs and gore and mused at the supreme
trust his guru had placed in him by sacrificing his own
life to save his future son-in-law. Not for an instant did
the thought of treachery ever cross Kacha's mind. Acting
with speed and exactly as he had been instructed, the son

of Brihaspati used the same knowledge that had just saved his own life to resurrect his guru. Before his marvelling eyes, the body of Ushanas reformed itself, leaving not a trace of blood or a single spare bit of flesh. A moment later, Maharishi Kavya Ushanas stood before his pupil. Pleased at his work, the guru blessed his student even as Kacha prostrated himself on the ground and paid homage to the great one.

Kacha said, 'Not for nothing is the guru–shishya parampara the cornerstone of our civilization. Not for nothing is the guru regarded a god in human form and equally deserving of worship and devotion as the thirty-three devas. For the guru is the giver of knowledge and the guardian of the fount of wisdom. Without the guru, future generations would become directionless and lose their way in the world. Of all precious objects in the world, nothing is more precious than knowledge, and the guru, as caretaker of knowledge, is the most precious of all things on earth. You may search the four cardinal directions without finding anyone or anything of greater value than a good guru. To fail to acknowledge the guru's greatness is to inevitably descend into the hellish realms.'

Moved powerfully by Kacha's words and devotion, Shukracharya was keenly aware that though this was the son of his greatest enemy, he had honourably and diligently followed dharma, fulfilled his guru's given task, and upheld the sacred tie of guru and shishya. Once given knowledge of the sanjivani method and restored to life, Kacha could easily have left this place, taking Devayani with him if he pleased, and returned to his father and his allies, the devas, his mission successfully completed. For by dint of his having ingested and digested Kacha, Shukra now knew everything about the young man. There were quite literally no secrets left between them. And he was profoundly moved by what he had learned. Not only had Kacha done exactly as instructed, he had then professed his love and devotion to his guru in such a passionate, eloquent outpouring that Ushanas was moved to the core. In contrast, consider the heinous nature of his own followers. Look at what the danavas had done! They had committed sacrilege, desecrating their own guru's body by feeding a dead corpse to him! Outrageous and unacceptable behaviour such as this could not go unpunished. Moreover, they had duped him by plying him with soma, knowing he had a fondness for the honey wine. And as for the supreme sin of killing a brahmin—that too an innocent who had committed no harm or transgression against anyone—his brain seethed with anger.

But first he must address his own weakness. The failing that had enabled the wily danavas to succeed in this ploy must be eliminated. Not only in himself, but in all brahmins henceforth. For as a preceptor to the race of asuras, he had a responsibility to lay down tenets of dharma that would benefit future generations to come as well.

Kavya rose in anger, even Kacha stepping back wide-eyed as he saw the resoluteness shining on that ancient face, made powerful and dazzling by the blue sheen of brahman that exuded from his being.

'Hear me now,' said Kavya Ushanas, 'it was my own stupidity in drinking soma that brought about this pass. Had I not been self-indulgent, the danavas could not have plied me with this polluted wine and made me too drunk to know what I was doing. Had I not drunk, Kacha would not have been subsumed into my body, nor would I have had to reveal to him the sanjivani method to restore him to life. Therefore, I start by pronouncing an eternal ban on the consumption of wine by brahmins. Should any brahmin be stupid enough to drink wine, he will be deemed to have committed a crime no less than that of killing a fellow brahmin and shall be hated by everyone. For the consumption of wine is but another form of murder. I, Kavya Ushanas Shukra, lay down this dharma for brahmins in all the worlds, in all time.'

Then did the preceptor of the asuras roar with power and use his brahmanic energies to summon the foolish ones who had attempted to dupe him. Ripped from reality wherever they were, in the midst of doing whatever they were doing, the danavas who had slain Kacha and fed him to their guru in the soma were dragged by unseen forces and hurled across the sky. Screaming and wailing in fear, they came flying through the air like rotted tree stumps flung helter-skelter by a cyclone. They landed hard, their bones cracking loudly as they fell to the ground before Maharishi Ushanas. At the sight of their guru, his face masked with anger and shining with immense power, they trembled and cringed in fear. Prostrating themselves before him, they pled for mercy and admitted their crimes unconditionally.

'Danavas,' said Kavya. 'You thought you were shrewd and tactful. You thought that by murdering the ally of the devas you would kill a spy and prevent our secret of resurrection from being stolen by the enemy. But in fact, by your own efforts and folly, you have ensured that Kacha now possesses the very secret you sought to protect!'

At this, the danavas moaned and cried out with self-recrimination and were miserable at the error of their ways. They pleaded with their guru to forgive them and to take back the knowledge he had given Kacha.

But Ushanas was firm. 'This knowledge was not stolen by Kacha nor was it obtained by him through any ruse or deceptive means. He was performing his duties as a shishya diligently and had served me immaculately for five hundred years. Your devious actions brought about this crisis. I wished to restore Kacha to life but could not do so without killing myself. Therefore I willingly and happily entrusted him with the sanjivani and requested him to use the knowledge to restore me in turn once he was revived. He fulfilled his dharma and acted more honourably than you, my own followers! Let him now stand as an example of the greatness of a brahmin when he adheres to his given path without compromise. Due to his actions, words and unstinting adherence to dharma, I pronounce Kacha to be as powerful as Brahma himself!'

At this the danavas were filled with a great fear for they had accomplished the exact opposite of what they had sought to accomplish. Instead of killing the spy and depriving the enemy of the secret knowledge, they had handed it over on a platter and in addition had rewarded the spy with the ultimate blessing any brahmin could attain. Humbled and ashamed, they crawled and carried one another away from the guru's ashram before he could turn his wrath upon them for their part in the mishap. Disgusted, his anger spent, Shukracharya let them leave unharmed, knowing that what they had already done was punishment enough.

2

The remainder of Kacha's apprenticeship to Guru Shukracharya passed uneventfully. When the full thousand years had ended, Kacha asked his preceptor's permission to depart and received it with warmth and blessings.

While he was preparing to leave, Devayani heard the news and came rushing to his humble dwelling place. She was breathless, heaving with excitement, her face flushed and reddened. 'My love, what is this I hear? Tell me it is not true? You cannot be leaving here without even saying goodbye to me?'

Kacha continued putting things in order as he had been doing. He wished to leave everything exactly as it had been before he came, as surely another disciple would take his place in this humble spot. He spoke to Devayani as he worked. 'I shall say goodbye now then, Devayani. I am leaving now. I shall not return. My apprenticeship is done and Mahaguru has given me his blessing to go home.'

Devayani stared at him. 'But what of our love? Our long wait for this very day? So many times we have talked of how you would complete your apprenticeship and receive my father's blessings to go home. Then you would be free to become a grihastha and take a wife.

And now that day has come at last! Surely we shall now do what we have planned for so long, Kacha, my love?'

Kacha finished setting the little corner of the thatched hut in order and looked up at Devayani. 'Beautiful Devayani, it is true we have spoken of this and many other things during the time I was here. But now I wish to return home to pursue my dharma. I came here with a goal in mind, to learn the sanjivani secret. That goal has been accomplished. Now I must return home and pass on the secret to my father's followers that they may use it profitably in the war against the asuras. That is my dharma and I cannot deviate from it.'

So saying, Kacha turned his back on the guru's daughter and exited the hut. As he emerged into the sunshine of the bright, cheerful morning, and began to walk through the ashram, filled with sweet air and the euphonious songs of birds, Devayani came rushing out behind him, her anga-vastra, hair and kohl in disarray from weeping and beating her chest. 'Stop!' she cried out, eyes flashing. 'As your preceptor's daughter, I command you! Halt!'

Kacha indeed stopped but remained facing in the direction of departure, not even turning his head back to look at Devayani. For despite his intense resolve and self-discipline, the son of Angirasa's heart was not made of stone. He felt the pain and anguish of being parted from Devayani no less than she did. It was breaking his heart to walk away thus from his great love, with whom he had spent a thousand years of his youth in anticipation of this very day when he would be considered ready to assume the mantle of a married man and householder. His soul wept to deny her—and to deny himself—that pleasure, and instead to stick to the original plan for which he had been sent here, sacrificing his own desires and love so that he might fulfil his dharma. The other denizens of the ashram paused in their chores to observe this unfolding drama. All of them already knew what was unfolding and it was only her naive innocence and unswaying love for Kacha that had blinded Devayani to this inevitable outcome. Their hearts also ached for the two young lovers and this tragic end to their love story.

Approaching Kacha, Devayani raised a hand, pointed a finger at him, and shook it violently in his face. 'You are my father's pupil. You have exchanged words with me. I now demand that you act upon those words! Take me as your wife!'

When Kacha did not respond at once, she softened, perhaps hearing the tone of her own voice. 'Kacha, I love you! I know that you love me too. Why do you deny our love now? I am not asking that you take me away stealthily. I am certain my father will give his blessings to our union. We can be married with all rites and ceremony.'

Kacha looked at her sorrowfully, his wan face revealing the anguish he held contained within himself. 'Devayani, you are greatly beloved to me and shall always be. But you are my guru's daughter. I must honour you no less than I honour him. Therefore, according to dharma, I cannot accept you as my wife. This union is not possible. It is best if you forget me completely and continue with your own life.'

He made a move forward but Devayani blocked him physically with her own body. 'Kacha, Kacha, listen to me! There is no question of violating dharma! I am my father's daughter. I would never do anything against dharma either! If you were my father's son, that would be a different matter. But you are only the son of his preceptor. While I admit that does make you akin to his son in a sense, it is not a biological fact!'

Kacha said gently, 'Devayani, what you want can never happen. Let me pass.'

But still she persisted. 'Have you forgotten that it was I who urged my father to revive you when the danavas first killed you in the forest? And the second time as well, when you were in my own father's body, even then I wished him to revive you and could not bear losing you forever? If not for me, you would not exist today! You owe me your life, Kacha!'

He bowed his head. 'That I do, and for that I am eternally gratefully. I shall worship you no less than I worship your father. But I cannot marry you.'

'Why not?' she cried. 'What do I lack? What do you find wanting in me? Is it beauty? Is it my body, my face, my eyes? At least tell me why you spurn me so cruelly? I have never loved anyone but you. And for a thousand years I believed you had never loved anyone before me.'

'It is so,' he admitted. 'I did not. And to answer your question, no, it is not that I find anything wanting in you.' He reached out, touching her face one last time, stroking her smooth cheek, her delicate jawline, her soft upper chin. 'Your eyes, your face, your beauty, everything

pleased me more than I can express in words. If I sought
a wife now I would not seek anyone else. But I have a
dharma to uphold and to marry you would be to violate
that dharma.'

She started to speak again and he shushed her with
his finger, gently.

'Hear me out,' he said softly. 'For there is a very valid
reason under dharma why I cannot wed you. It pains me
as much as it pains you but it is a fact that cannot be
disputed.' Her eyes asked the silent question: WHAT?

He took a deep breath, released it, then said: 'When
I was killed by the danavas the second time, my body
cremated, then crushed to fine powdery ash, mixed with
soma wine, and fed to your father surreptitiously, his
body ingested and digested me.'

She nodded slowly. 'Yes, I know this already. So?'

'By the time your father sobered sufficiently to decide
what to do to revive me, he had already digested me almost
completely. I had become a part of his body, mingling
with his blood, his flesh, his bones, his hair, his nails...
there was no part of him with which my body had not
intermingled.'

She frowned but was silent, considering this. Even
though she had been aware that Kacha was in her father's
belly, she had never thought through the implications of
that fact. Her beautiful forehead creased in thought as
she listened to Kacha's words.

'When he revived me, it was not possible to perfectly
separate every cell of my body from his own. Therefore, I
was reconstituted from parts that could only be described

as a hybrid of his and my bodies. In short, I was created from your father's own body, no less than you yourself were created from a part of his own body.'

Devayani's eyes widened as she finally understood what Kacha meant to tell her. She began to shake her head from side to side in denial, tears springing from her beautiful black eyes and streaming down her face.

'I am as much your father's son now as you are his daughter. We are both created from his body and mind. It was the only way for him to revive me. I am literally now the son of his flesh. For us to marry would be a crime against dharma. Your father realized this and he and I exchanged awareness of it without needing to discuss further. He could not bear to tell you, for he knew it would break your heart and plunge you into despair for the remainder of my stay here. He trusted me enough to know I would never violate my dharma by laying a hand in passion upon my own sister. Now that the time has come for me to leave, I am telling you the truth. Yet it is a truth of which you are already aware, even if you have not let yourself acknowledge it. Oh, Devayani. Before this happened, I would still have married you. It would have been hard to do so, with our fathers being preceptors to warring enemies, but I would have found a way. Somehow. Anyhow. But once I emerged from your father's body, I was no less than your biological brother. I am not the same Kacha I was before, not exactly. You have suspected and known this for a long time but perhaps your heart did not permit your mind to accept the truth. Now you must accept it and accept also the fact of our parting.

For we can never be what you wish us to be—man and wife. Therefore it is best that I leave here now and never return. I wish you well, my love. I wish you the best in life. I ask your blessings now before I go. Wish me well too, as someone who never transgressed dharma even when it cost me my own happiness.'

Devayani staggered back, struck by Kacha's words as by a lightning bolt. Her face was twisted with conflicting emotions: love, hate, anger, disbelief, frustration, all warred there and marred her beauty. 'Bless you? I curse you, Kacha! Because you set your dharma and your promise to your father's followers above your love for me, I curse you! The very knowledge you came to seek, the precious, secret sanjivani that everyone prizes so dearly and seeks out so desperately, you shall never be able to put that same method to use, not once, not ever! This I declare as my father's daughter!'

At this, all those watching quailed, for a curse was a terrible thing, and the curse of a woman spurned, a brahmin's daughter no less, was a thing to fear and dread. Even Maharishi Kavya Ushanas, listening to every word of the exchange, bowed his head sadly for he knew that while Kacha had earned only the fruit of his own actions, he did not wholly deserve the suffering meted out to him today.

Still, Kacha did not return fire with fire. Instead, he smiled and bowed his head in acceptance. 'So be it. As I love you and as you are my guru's daughter, I cannot refuse you. If you choose to curse me, then your curse will be fulfilled. I shall never be able to employ the sanjivani for which I came and spent a thousand years, died twice physically, and died once more in every other sense this very day when I broke your heart as well as my own. Let this be my danda.' He joined his palms together and continued, 'But I still possess knowledge of the secret method. And I shall still teach it to my father's followers. And others shall learn its use and put it to work. Therefore my dharma shall be fulfilled.'

And with those final words, Kacha, son of Angirasa, started forward and set out on his way, leaving the ashram of Shukracharya forever. Her heart breaking, Devayani watched him go and, with his departure, love as well as the ability to love itself fled her heart forever.

3

Years passed.

Devayani never truly got over the heartache of losing her first lover. While others who lost love came to terms with the loss and moved on, she remained indignant about being deprived of her beloved. She blamed everyone for the loss and resented everything. It made her a bitter and spiteful person, given to outbursts and tantrums, and on occasion, even vengeful behaviour.

One such instance occurred when a group of asuri were bathing in the river near the ashram of Guru Shukracharya. Among them was Devayani and also her best friend since childhood, Sharmishtha. While they were bathing, a mischievous breeze sent by Lord Indra, king of the devas, sent their garments flying helter-skelter on the bank of the river.

After the women finished bathing and emerged laughing from the river, Devayani picked up the garment nearest to her. The other women did the same, none realizing at first that their clothes were interchanged. As they dressed and saw each other dressing, realization dawned. Most of the other women simply laughed and assumed it was a prank played by some gandharva. Some even called out to whomever might be hiding behind the trees, teasing them about being too shy to come out and play with the girls. None minded the others wearing their garments for they were all asuris and regarded one another as equals. But when Devayani saw Sharmishtha wearing her garments, she lost her temper.

'Asuri! How dare you wear my clothes? Don't you realize you are inferior to me? I shall now have to burn those clothes. I cannot possibly be seen wearing them again! You asuris have no sense of how to behave or conduct yourselves, ignorant women!'

At this uncalled-for rebuke, Sharmishtha lost her temper as well. For though she was indeed an asuri, and as such supposed to treat Devayani with greater respect, she being the daughter of the guru of the asuras, yet her father was none other than Vrishaparva, lord among asuras. She took offence at Devayani's tone and words and lashed out sharply. 'Who do you think you are? Just because you are Shukra's daughter you think you can speak to anyone thus? I would have you know that my father is more respected than your own!'

Devayani stopped in the midst of stripping off the garments she had mistakenly pulled on and glared at Sharmishtha. 'What nonsense are you spouting, asuri? Do you even know what you're saying? My father is the preceptor of your entire race! Everyone bows before him. He is above every single asura, and more respected than anyone else in this realm.'

Sharmishtha made an offensive sound that drew nervous laughter from the other girls and a shocked reaction from Devayani. 'Go speak your wild claims to the fish in the river. They might even believe you! My father is higher than your father among the asura race. Even when seated or lying down, he is still higher! In fact, you should see the way your father, the great Kavya Ushanas, bows and cringes before my father! My father says his compliments are so sweet, they sicken his stomach. Because that is what your father does: he is a man who begs and praises and pleads for alms, and always has his hand out for more droppings. He survives on the generosity of asuras like my father. Without us he would be nothing. And you? You are nothing. You are not even your father! You are just a beggar who is too deluded to realize it. We pity you and let you pretend and keep your airs but nobody here respects you at all! Even your great beloved, Kacha spurned you and left rather than ask for your hand in marriage. And we all know how you begged and pleaded with him. Because that's what beggars do!'

Devayani was furious. She had no words to offer. Twin points of rage burned on her high cheekbones like smouldering coals. Her dark eyes were as venomous as a queen cobra's fangs. Tearing off Sharmishtha's garment, she flung it at the asuri who had been her friend until now. Then she stalked over to where Sharmishtha stood and tried to wrest her own garment from her.

But Sharmishtha was an asuri after all, and no stranger to aggression and violence. She slapped Devayani roughly, and at once a fight broke out between the two girls. Devayani's garment was ripped in half during the struggle. Sobbing and humiliated, Devayani clutched the half garment and began to stumble back homewards. But Sharmishtha followed her and chased her down. They fought again in the forest and while fighting, Sharmishtha saw the open mouth of a well behind the other girl. Manoeuvring Devayani in that direction, she pushed her into the well. Devayani's arms cartwheeled and she struggled to keep her balance, but her feet slipped on the mossy rim of the well's lip and she plunged down into the dark, cold hole, landing with a scream and a splash far below.

Sharmishtha threw the remains of her garment after her. 'Wear this now and see who admires your beauty, you beggar's daughter!' Sharmishtha yelled down the mouth of the well. Her own voice came up, echoing off the stone walls. She remained flat on her belly, listening for several moments, but could hear nothing else, except the gentle slap-slap-slap of the water against the walls. Not a whisper from Devayani, not even a whimper or cry for help. Sharmishtha realized that Shukracharya's daughter must be dead. She had probably struck her head or neck on the way down and either lay with a smashed skull or broken neck. In any case, if she was unconscious down there, she was as good as dead, for she would drown in the water. She already knew that Devayani could not even tread water to stay afloat, for when they played in the river the maharishi's daughter would never dare to venture beyond the reach of her feet.

Looking around, Sharmishtha heard the sounds of the other girls approaching. Acting quickly, she pulled the

wooden cover of the well into place and ran to meet
them. They saw her dishevelled, bleeding face and arms
and exclaimed aloud. She told them that Devayani and she
had fought and that she had beaten the guru's daughter
so badly that she had run home wailing to her father. She
told them she had thrown the rest of the precious garment
after Devayani, telling her to wear it to her marriage if
she liked it so much! They all laughed at that, for every
one of them had felt the sharp edge of Devayani's tongue
at some time or other, and all felt that the brahmin girl
thought much too highly of herself.

Sharmishtha and the other girls went home and
quickly forgot about the incident by the river. Sharmishtha
assumed that Devayani was dead and never went back
to the well again.

4

Around this time, Yayati, one of six sons of the supremely powerful king, Nahusha, happened to visit that same region of the forest, seeking deer to hunt. He rode one excellent horse and was followed by a spare, for he was fond of wandering far and wide in search of good game. This time he had ridden so far, both his horses were exhausted and so was he. Seeking water, he spied the wooden cover of the well into which Sharmishtha had pushed Devayani and moved the cover aside, expecting to find water to slake his thirst and refresh his horses.

Instead of water, he was surprised to see a woman at the bottom of the well. Unknown to Sharmishtha, the well was almost dry, with only a little water and muddy sludge at the bottom. This had broken Devayani's fall and saved her life but the impact had knocked her unconscious. In addition, the sun had been slanted to the west, casting deep shadows into the well, which made it impossible for Sharmishtha to see inside clearly. Assuming the silence to mean death, Sharmishtha had covered up her crime and gone about her way.

It so happened that when Yayati looked in, the sun was exactly overhead, and its light shone directly into the tube of the well, enabling him to see clearly. It was some days after Devayani had fallen in, and while she was thinner from want of food, she was very much alive. If anything, her forced fasting only brought out her inner beauty and the unusual perspective of the well gave her a certain magical appearance, captivating Yayati on sight. What he saw was a beautiful young woman, with lips and fingernails as red as copper, eyes that glittered, high cheekbones and a dusky coal-grey complexion that was set off by a pair of scintillating earrings and a bejewelled nose ring, clad in barely any garments.

When Yayati was met by the unexpected sight of a beautiful young woman looking up mournfully, asking for help, he was taken aback. So unexpected was this discovery, he thought it must be a hallucination brought on by exhaustion or thirst. Then Devayani spoke, her voice echoing softly and mournfully in the muffled confines of the well, and he realized she was no hallucination but a real flesh-and-blood woman. Regaining his composure, he peered down again at the vision of beauty, and asked with all the princely charm he possessed: 'Beautiful woman with the nails of copper, earrings of gold, skin like polished ebony, and eyes like glittering gems, who are you? Why are you crying? What are you doing at the bottom of this well? Are you a gandharva, an apsara or some other beautiful spirit of this forest trapped here for some reason? Tell me honestly for I am new to these parts and am not familiar with the customs and denizens of the region.'

Devayani looked up at the handsome face of the

young man gazing down at her, the sun behind his head flaring like a corona of energy around the head of some supernatural being, and wondered if she was viewing a vision. She decided to answer as honestly as possible without revealing the exact story of what had befallen her until she knew who he was in turn and whether her tormentor was nearby. After days spent in the darkness and damp of the well, she had nursed a great anger towards her former companion. She had vowed to herself that if she survived this experience and was able to emerge from this prison alive, she would seek vengeance against Sharmishtha. She did not know how or when she would do it, but she would be avenged for her humiliation as well as her attempted murder. But as the hours turned into night and night into day and then another night and day, she grew miserable with self-pity and deprivation, her anger turning to a cold fury. By the time Yayati found her, all she desired was to be freed from this hole and to return home. When the cover of the well was moved aside and the handsome young male face peered down she saw it as a benediction of the Almighty Creator upon her. After all that she had suffered, the loss of her beloved Kacha, the humiliation by Sharmishtha—a woman barely fit to be her maid and companion—and the days and nights spent hungry and cold in this miserable well, she saw Yayati as a saviour. Surely he had not come here by accident and merely happened to open the cover of the well to find her. Surely he had been put upon this path by some greater force at work. She saw it as a sign that her fortunes were about to change.

'Great king,' she replied, 'for I can see from your aspect that you are most certainly one of high birth and lineage, I am the daughter of Shukracharya, also known as Kavya Ushanas, preceptor to the asuras, possessor of the fabled sanjivani knowledge that can revive even the dead. I fell into this well by accident and have been trapped here for some time. Neither my father nor anyone else could have realized that I have fallen down here, hence nobody came to my rescue. It is my great fortune to have been found by you. I beg you, save me from this place.'

Yayati needed no further urging. Fashioning a lifeline from hemp ropes, he tied one end to both his horses and the other around his waist before lowering himself into the dark, narrow well. The instant he reached the bottom, Devayani embraced him warmly, relieved and genuinely happy to be saved. Yayati resisted the surge of feelings her proximity provoked in him and focused his energy on securing the rope around her waist, before tugging and clicking his tongue and calling out to urge his horses to draw them out of the well. Soon, they were out of the well and he untied the rope from around Devayani's waist reluctantly. She was even more beautiful in the daylight and though he avoided gazing directly at her lack of modesty and offered her a part of his own anga-vastra to cover herself, he had seen and felt enough of her youth and beauty to be completely infatuated with desire. He had no wish to say goodbye to her.

But while Devayani was equally attracted to her regal saviour, her heart was still fixed on vengeance. She requested Yayati to drop her off near the hut where her companion stayed, not willing to go to the main ashram in her present state. Yayati gladly did as she requested and was frankly disappointed when she bade him a quick if heartfelt goodbye and went into the hut of her friend. But he had been on the hunt for too many days already with little success—unless one counted finding a beautiful doe at the bottom of a well to be good hunting—and it was time for him to return to his capital city. He turned the heads of his horses and rode away, though not before marking in his mind the location of Devayani's friend's hut and the ashram nearby, with every intention of seeing her again soon.

Devayani's friend Ghurnika was shocked to see her appear thus, in her dishevelled and starved condition, oddly clad. 'Where have you been? Your father has been worried sick about you! Everyone has been out looking for you. Where were you these past days?'

Devayani was curt and impatient. 'Where is my father now? I must see him at once.'

'He is in the palace,' Ghurnika said, 'attending to his duties as usual. Worried though he was about you, he could not neglect his tasks.'

Devayani nodded. 'Yes, of course. I must ask you to go and fetch him at once. Tell him what has happened to me. I will coach you on what to say. You must leave immediately.'

'Surely. We can go together. He will be so relieved to see you safe and sound.'

'No!' Devayani's voice was sharp and brooked no

disagreement. 'I cannot go to Vrishaparva's palace, I will not even enter the city! I must ask you to go and fetch him. Will you do this for me?'

'Of course,' Ghurnika said. 'But...'

'I will explain everything later. Right now, do as I say. Tell this to my father...'

Ghurnika followed her friend's instructions to the letter. Reaching the palace of the asuras, she went straight to Maharishi Kavya Ushanas and greeted him deferentially. 'Gurudev, I have brought news of Devayani.'

Shukracharya was immediately concerned. 'What news? Tell me. Is she well?'

Ghurnika glanced around at the asura nobles and ministers present. 'My Lord, what I have to say is for your ears only.'

The preceptor did not question her reasons for desiring privacy. He waited until they were in a place where none other could hear them, then urged her. 'Now tell me, is my daughter well?'

'Yes, great one. She is quite hale and hearty. It was she who bade me come to you in the palace and bring you this message.'

The guru was a wise man. As preceptor of the asuras he had seen and known more in his single lifetime than most people experience in several. He understood that something had transpired which had to be dealt with delicately. 'What is it? Tell me everything. Leave nothing out.'

'Gurudev, Devayani was attacked in the forest by Sharmishtha and left for dead at the bottom of a well.

She escaped from the well only today. That was why she was nowhere to be found.'

Guru Shukra took in this news with equanimity. 'You are certain of this fact?'

'Yes, my lord. She herself told me to pass on this message to you. She asked me to do so discreetly so no one else would hear.'

Kavya Ushanas considered this silently. His daughter had been sensible to have issued that instruction. After all, this palace was Vrishaparva's domain, as was the city itself. And Sharmishtha was Vrishaparva's daughter! Had Ghurnika related this news before anyone else, a scandal would have exploded in the city.

He thanked Ghurnika for her discretion and help, then asked her to take him at once to the place where his daughter was staying. He told no one else what had happened.

When he was with Devayani, he enfolded her in his arms with a father's joy at seeing his offspring safe and sound. Once they had exchanged the emotional relief of being reunited, he asked her gently, 'What happened? Tell me the truth.'

'The truth is that Sharmishtha tried to kill me. It is sheer luck that I survived her assault and the fall into the well. And it is through my own perseverance that I was able to climb out of the well at last today and return to you. She left me for dead, father! She thought she had murdered me and she left me for dead!' Devayani sobbed in her father's arms, but even through her anguish, her voice and face betrayed her rage.

Shukracharya looked at her closely. 'How did this happen?'

'She just attacked me for no reason,' Devayani said. 'She's a murderess!'

The preceptor was too wise not to see something amiss with this overly simplistic explanation. 'People don't just attack one another for no reason. There must have been some cause or provocation. Maybe you said or did something to set her off? Whether knowingly or unknowingly?'

'I did nothing to her, father!' Devayani insisted tearfully.

The guru shook his head slowly, his lined face uncertain, the long greying beard still and stiff. 'I find that hard to believe, beloved daughter. What reason would she have? Perhaps it was some old enmity that she was seeking to avenge? Did you do something to cause her unhappiness a long time ago?'

'Do you not believe me?' she asked plaintively. 'I tell you, I did nothing to cause her to strike me or want me dead! Why will you not believe me?'

Guru Kavya Ushanas sighed and looked away. 'Vrishaparva's daughter would not raise a hand on their preceptor's daughter without some provocation or justification.'

'That is the reason then!' Devayani cried. 'It was because I am your daughter that she attacked me. She said so herself! I did not realize it at the time, but now that you are asking me, I recall it clearly. She said terrible, awful things about you immediately before she began attacking me. Tired from my imprisonment at the bottom of the well and hurt from the beating and the fall, I forgot to tell you this earlier. But now I recall every ugly word she spat at me before she attempted to murder me.'

Shukracharya stared at her. 'Because you are my daughter? Why would that be a reason for Vrishaparva's daughter to attack you? He is a lord of the asuras, king of the danavas, one of my followers. As their preceptor, they look up to me with undying respect. The thought of striking any brahmin would never cross their minds. The idea that they would harm their own guru's daughter is unthinkable!'

'Yet they murdered Kacha, not once but twice,' she pointed out shrewdly, 'and the second time they didn't just strike him and kill him, they cremated him and fed you the ashes mingled in soma!'

Kavya turned his face away in embarrassment. He had never forgiven himself for getting drunk on soma that day. It had been the last time he had ever consumed alcohol but the memory was still fresh in his mind. If not for his vile habit, he would never have had to pass on the secret of sanjivani to the devas. The memory rankled. Devayani's words succeeded in their intention: they made him recall that the danavas had indeed transgressed their bounds and acted with great irreverence towards him. He was silent.

Seeing that she had struck a nerve, Devayani pressed her advantage. 'Father, listen to me. She flew into a rage. It was as if a fit came over her and she began to spout the most horrible untruths and insults! Her eyes were red like a rakshasa's and her voice was shrill like that of an Uraga in heat. She ranted on and on, spewing insults and saying awful things about you. I couldn't bear to hear it!'

Ushanas frowned. 'About me? What did she say about me?' Until now he had assumed that this was the consequence of some disagreement between the two girls. Sharmishtha and Devayani had been friends for years, after all, and friends did sometimes fight, often bitterly. But with the reminder of how the danavas had acted towards his erstwhile disciple and then towards himself, their own guru, the first seed of malice had been sown in his heart. Now, he was genuinely shocked to hear that the daughter of his greatest patron had said untruths about him!

Devayani said in a quivering voice that revealed her own disgust at the words she was repeating: 'She said I was the daughter of one who was nothing more than a beggar for alms, hand always stretched out, asking, always asking, saying whatever he had to in order to curry favour or gain a few coins or grains.'

Shukra stared at his daughter, dumbfounded. 'She said that?'

Devayani went on, emboldened by the fact that she was repeating the truth. Sharmishtha had indeed said all those things. 'She said you only praised the asuras in order to gain their scraps and leavings. She made you out to be a person without pride or dignity, someone no more than a stray dog on the streets of her father's city who would wag his tail and beg dolefully for a morsel of food. Oh, father, it was terrible! I could not bear to hear her say such things. And the tone in which she shouted and ranted. All our friends were there and they heard her as well. It was the most humiliating experience of my life!'

Shukracharya caught his daughter by the shoulders, staring at her intently. His piercing black eyes were wide and alert. 'You say others heard her say these things as well? Your other girl companions?'

She nodded. 'By the river. We had just finished bathing. They were witness to the whole incident. Then she tried to steal my garments and wear them herself. When I tried to take them back, she pushed me away. I was scared. I ran from there. She followed me into the forest where no one else could see and she attacked me. She kept screaming insults at you, saying worse things, that I can never repeat, and she tried to kill me. I stumbled and fell into a dark place, into water and mud which broke my fall. And I lost consciousness. When I awoke, I realized I was at the bottom of a well and she had pulled the cover shut above me, trapping me inside. I screamed until my voice was hoarse but nobody could hear me. It's a miracle that a chivalrous young king happened to be passing by. He heard my cries, helped me out, and thanks to his grace, I was able to come back here alive. He was King Yayati, son of Nahusha.'

Shukra knew now that she was telling the absolute truth. Whatever reason Vrishaparva's daughter might have had to lose her temper at his daughter, she had certainly done and said all these things to Devayani. He could hear and see the truth in her eyes, face and voice. It hardly mattered what Devayani had said to provoke the asuri. This was beyond humiliation or a childish quarrel. It was intolerable! This was attempted murder, no less.

'Father?' Devayani asked, unable to read his mind as easily as he had read hers. 'You do believe me, do you not? I am telling the truth!'

'Yes, my daughter. I believe you,' he said grimly. 'You must know that those terrible things she said were all lies. It is a brahmin's dharma to live off alms as best as he can, not because he is a dog who seeks to curry favour, but because his dharma is to dedicate every waking moment to learning and knowledge. These are reasons to praise brahmins, not insult them! It is I who is always admired, respected, honoured and praised by kshatriyas like Vrishaparva, and in return, I rarely need to praise them for any reason. Whether it is Vrishaparva or any other asura, or a mortal king such as the one who saved you, or even devas such as Indra himself, lord of the gods, it is they who must bow and show their allegiance to me and beg me to accept dakshina, for my acceptance honours them!'

'Father, I know that she was speaking untruth. Even though I am but a girl yet, I know the difference between you and Vrishaparva and the other asuras. That is why I could not stand there and listen to her speak such vile words about you. Even if I were to overlook the fact that she attempted to kill me, I could never forgive her for saying those things about my father!'

Shukra nodded, his high forehead and lined face stern with disapproval. 'You speak rightly. Her speech was unforgivable. Yet know this, Devayani, the one who is able to ignore the criticism of others conquers all obstacles. The wise man is like a charioteer who knows when to rein in his horses and does so at exactly the right moment, never letting them go out of control or pulling on the reins too tightly. As a snake casts off its old skin, thus must we learn to cast off anger through the act of forgiving. Everyone feels hurt when criticized by evil words, but he who is able to restrain himself from retaliating against his critics attains his goals. Compare two men: One performs yagnas continuously every month for a hundred years while another performs no yagnas but is able to restrain his anger perfectly for the same length of time. The one without anger is the superior man. You are young and youth is prone to quarrels and emotional upsets. But that is why you must learn to rise above your anger and emotion and grow into womanhood. That way lies wisdom.'

'Father, you speak great words of wisdom. I shall endeavour always to do as you advise. But was it not you who taught me that a wise man never condones the insults of those who are evil in their intent? If the evil ones persist in their persecution, the wise man knows well enough to move away from them and live elsewhere. Vrishaparva and the asuras are your followers and disciples, therefore it is their dharma to show you respect and honour. Yet his own daughter speaks such vile words against you. As your daughter, how can I tolerate that? You have taught me that the one thing a guru can never condone is disrespect from his pupils. Those who speak ill of people with higher learning cannot be tolerated. In all my life I have never heard anyone speak such terrible things about you. And yet it was the daughter of your own disciple Vrishaparva who said them. How can I forget or forgive her?'

5

Kavya acknowledged the anger of his daughter and her righteousness. He returned at once to Vrishaparva's palace and went before his patron. 'O king, there is a limit to tolerance and forgiveness. I have overlooked your offences and transgressions before, but I can no longer overlook them any more. When you had the brahmin Kacha murdered, not once but twice, you transgressed not only against me but against dharma itself. For he was innocent of any wrongdoing, devoted to dharma, and a loyal pupil, as well as a brahmin. By murdering him you committed a grave offence. Yet I overlooked that sin at the time. But sooner or later the fruits of evil will manifest themselves. Now by causing great hurt and injury to my daughter and nearly murdering her as well, you have exceeded all bounds. This I can never forgive or forget. How could you let such things happen? If this is how you permit your daughter and followers to act then I have no further desire to be your guru. I shall resign as of this very moment and take my leave from this palace, never again to set foot here.'

Vrishaparva was mortified by these accusations. He came down from his throne dais and joined his palms before his guru. 'My lord, my teacher, great illuminator of knowledge. I am not aware of these crimes you accuse me of, yet I know you to be a man of impeccable truth and honesty. If you say these things happened then they must have been done by the persons accused, and I take full responsibility for their actions as well. You are the epitome of dharma and your judgement is indisputable. But I beg you, do not take any action against us for we depend on you as those at sea need the shelter of a boat to stay afloat. We shall drown without your guidance and wisdom.'

When Shukracharya saw Vrishaparva's humility and contrite attitude, he was somewhat appeased. But he knew that he could not simply forgive and let the lapse pass unnoticed, if only for Devayani's sake. 'King of asuras, why should I care any more whether you sink or swim? Your daughter has attempted to kill my daughter. She has said unforgivable things about me to Devayani. Such things are beyond tolerance. I cannot let these transgressions pass.'

Vrishaparva knew how dearly the guru loved his daughter. He had heard from his danavas how the guru had permitted himself to die in order to save Devayani's beloved Kacha, teaching Brihaspati's son the sanjivani secret. He saw that Kavya Ushanas would not be appeased merely by words and appeals. 'My lord, great Bhrigu, tell me how I may make amends for the wrong that has been done to you? All that I possess is yours. My palace, my possessions, my wealth, elephants, cattle, horses, armies… whatever you desire shall be yours. Just as I own all these things, so do you own me.'

But the guru knew his daughter's heart and mind well. Once Devayani had set herself against someone or for someone, she could never be moved to change her stance. 'Vrishaparva, you are a great asura and your offerings are great too. But it is not I who needs pacifying, it is my daughter, Devayani. If you can appease her anger and convince her to forgive your daughter for her sins, then a compromise may be reached. Otherwise, you shall never see me again.'

With those words, Shukracharya left the palace, leaving behind a storm of controversy. Vrishaparva sent at once for his daughter who arrived looking pale and contrite. From her, he learned that Devayani's accusations were true—not that he had ever doubted them—and he realized that if he did not make amends at once, he would lose his preceptor, and the asuras would be without their greatest guide and advisor. Not just a guru, they would lose the means by which they could be resurrected after death, and that alone would surely spell the end of the asuras forever. There was no question or hesitation in his mind. He had to make this right at once. 'I shall go to Devayani and ask her to forgive you,' he told his daughter coldly. 'Whatever she asks, I shall grant. Prepare yourself.' So saying, he left at once with his entourage.

Sharmishtha was certain that Devayani would demand nothing less than her head as punishment. She prepared herself to face her death, knowing there was no recourse. But secretly, she burned with anger for her former friend and in her heart she still carried the bitter seed of resentment.

Vrishaparva arrived at the ashram of his guru with his entourage, coming before Devayani with full pomp and ceremony. He greeted her with no less respect than that shown her father. Queens and princesses had been treated with less formal courtesy than Devayani was that day. At that moment, she knew that she had won. Her moment of triumph was at hand and she was determined to squeeze every last drop of vengeful satisfaction from Sharmishtha for the way she had treated her that day by the river in full view of all their friends and companions.

'Great Devayani,' Vrishaparva said. 'I have already offered your father all that I possess. For as I possess wealth and belongings, so does he possess me. He has asked me to appeal to you. I do so now. Name the price for your forgiveness. Whatever you desire, it shall be yours without question. You have but to say the word.'

Devayani answered primly, 'I desire that Sharmishtha, with a thousand other girls, who are the daughters of all your friends and allies, should serve as my maidservants from this day forth. Even when I am married, they must go with me to my husband's house and serve me for as long as I live. This is my only demand.'

Vrishaparva answered without hesitation. 'It shall be as you say.' He sent his aide to fetch Sharmishtha from the palace. The aide rode back at furious speed, then informed the daii-maa who was matron of the princess to fetch her mistress to the ashram at once. Accompanied by her father's guard, Sharmishtha travelled by palanquin to the forest hermitage where she presented herself before Vrishaparva and Devayani. She was surprised to see other girls her age arriving at the same time, and recognized all her friends, companions and the daughters of other asura nobles and royalty.

'My daughter,' Vrishaparva said, 'You must do as Devayani says. From this day forth, you and these other girls shall all serve as Devayani's maids. Her every wish is your command. Do you follow?'

Sharmishtha answered at once, 'Yes, father. I shall do as you command.'

Devayani added shrewdly, 'No. You shall do as I command. Is that understood?'

Sharmishtha looked up at her father, then at the faces of the other asura nobles and royals gathered around, all sombre and stern-faced. She bowed before Devayani. 'Yes, mistress.'

Once all the thousand girls had assembled, Vrishaparva and the other asuras departed the ashram. Sharmishtha and Devayani were alone again, for the first time since their fight in the forest.

Devayani turned to stare triumphantly at her rival. 'So, here we are again. Do you remember what you said to me the last time we saw each other?'

Sharmishtha knew the only right answer was silence. She hung her head.

Devayani went on. 'You said that day that I was the daughter of a man who begs like a dog for your father's scraps, and lives off alms, saying anything to gain favour. Yet now as you see, you are my slave. How is this possible?'

Sharmishtha tried to stay silent but Devayani strode towards her and commanded, 'Speak! I order you to answer me! You are my servant and will do my bidding!'

Sharmishtha looked up hesitantly, choosing her words carefully. 'You are as my own sister and when one's sister is in need, one cannot refuse to help. I will do everything you say.'

Devayani's eyes narrowed. The answer was a little too circumspect for her liking. 'You do know that your help will be for the rest of your life? This is not a temporary assignment. You will be my servant for as long as we both live. Even after I am married.'

Sharmishtha bowed her head. 'I shall follow you wherever your father bestows you.'

Devayani was still not satisfied. She suspected that Sharmishtha still possessed great pride and resentment. But she had won a major victory. She had no wish to enter into another war of words and wits with the other girl. In any case, Sharmishtha was her slave now. Whatever she said or did not say hardly mattered. What mattered was that Devayani owned her, body and soul, and nothing Sharmishtha said or did could ever change that reality!

She contented herself by gloating over her new-found power and ordering her maids to collect her belongings and prepare for a trip. 'Where to, milady?' they asked. But she did not bother to answer.

She went to her father and said to him, 'Father, I am appeased by Vrishaparva's donation of his daughter and a thousand maids. Now that I possess such a large entourage, we cannot house them here. The king has always offered you apartments in his own palace. Sharmishtha's own palatial residence is lying unoccupied now. Let us go and reside in the palace. I shall live in the princess' palace where my maids can have access to all that is needed to serve my every desire.'

Maharishi Kavya Ushanas was only too happy to agree. They went to the palace and took up residence there. Devayani and her father were welcomed and greeted by all the danavas with great honour and homage, for they were relieved at being forgiven and to still have their guru. Devayani lived in Sharmishtha's own palatial palace within the palace complex, and slept in the same bed as her rival, wearing her rich clothes and jewelled ornaments, while Sharmishtha had to endure the humiliation of living as a servant in her own father's house, sleeping with the other maids in their quarters and watching her most hated rival take her place. But deep in her heart, the bitter seed of resentment still held root.

6

Years passed. To all intents and purposes, Devayani
lived like a princess in the palace of Vrishaparva while
her father conducted his brahminical vocation for the
asuras as before. In this period, Yayati son of Nahusha,
besotted by the vision he had rescued from the well in
the deep forest, returned more than once to the site
of his infatuation, hoping to find her and this time to
progress beyond merely holding her hand and shoulder.
Inevitably, he found no trace of her and could not find
out what had become of her. Even though he knew her
name and her father's name, he hesitated to ask about
her. As she was the daughter of a brahmin, it would not
be proper for him to go around asking after her. In this
way, a young girl's reputation could be ruined. So he
kept his silence and bided his time, returning whenever
he could, or when the hunt permitted, to that same neck
of the deep woods, in the hope of someday encountering
the vision once again.

One day, Devayani awoke and thought how nice
it would be to return to the forest for a few days. She
had grown up in a forest ashram and while she loved
the luxury of life in the palace, she missed the simple

natural pleasures and beauty of that environment. She commanded Sharmishtha to arrange for a trip to the forest. With her thousand maids in tow, she arrived in regal style at the same spot where she had played with many of them in earlier days. They ate fruits and roots, sipped the nectar from madhavi creepers, swam in lotus ponds and enjoyed a delightful holiday. Devayani made it a point to go to the same spot on the riverbank where they had swum that fateful day, and make Sharmishtha stay ashore, holding her richly-brocaded garments and waiting for her to finish swimming and playing in the water. As Devayani silently slipped into the fine garments held out by her former friend, she felt a momentary pang of regret for the friendship they had once shared. But then she recalled the vile words Sharmishtha had shouted at her and the last trace of regret faded away. 'I wish to walk,' she said, and of course Sharmishtha had to follow, along with the rest of the entourage. Devayani took them to the very spot where the fight had occurred, right up to the mouth of the well into which Sharmishtha had pushed her, and she deliberately stood beside it and looked pointedly at her maid. Sharmishtha's face was a mask of wax, betraying no expression or emotion, but the stiffness of her stance and the way she held her shoulders and arms revealed her inner feelings. Devayani shot Sharmishtha a provocative look as if to say, How far we have come since that day, have we not? Now it is you who is trapped, and I who am above you! And it shall stay this way forever. Not once would Sharmishtha raise her eyes and meet her gaze. Their companions chattered and laughed and played around them, unaware of the tension between the two women or the significance of this spot in their lives.

Devayani decided to seat herself in that spot and had her maids make the arrangements. Then she ordered Sharmishtha to massage her feet. The other maids continued to frolic and play, free to do as they pleased, enjoying their holiday. Only Sharmishtha was compelled to wait on Devayani, hand and foot.

The sound of hoofbeats silenced the chatter of the maids. All heads turned as a solitary figure rode into sight, trailing a second horse on a tether. At the sight of the rider, Devayani's heart leaped. She recognized Yayati's handsome features and powerfully-built physique at once. It had been that face and those rock-like shoulders and arms that had been the first things she had seen after the days and nights trapped in the darkness of the well, and to her eyes Yayati was no less than a celestial being descended from heaven to rescue her. She thought, 'It's my saviour! The handsome young king who saved me from the well!'

Yayati froze at the sight of so many women. He had not expected to see this desolate neck of the woods bustling with hundreds of young, attractive women. His first thought was that he had blundered into some queen's entourage and he turned the head of his horse, intending to leave. His destination had been the river and he could find another route to reach it. He glimpsed a richly-dressed young woman seated on luxuriant blankets, getting her feet massaged by a maid and assumed her to be the queen or princess. Rather than risk causing offence by his intrusion, he started to ride away.

To his surprise, a voice called out. 'Yuvaraja! Yuvaraja Yayati! I beg you, please wait!'

He turned around again, surprised at hearing his name called out. He saw the princess or queen who had been having her feet massaged rise and come towards him, her maid accompanying her. It took him a moment or two to recognize the mud-encrusted half-wasted vision he had found at the bottom of the well in this plump, painted and preening princess.

'Yuvaraja Yayati,' she said, laughing as she caught hold of the reins of his horse. 'Do you not recognize me? It is I, Devayani, daughter of Maharishi Kavya Ushanas whom you rescued from this very well! Pray, dismount and speak with me awhile.' She snapped off instructions to her maids to make suitable seating arrangements for the king, letting the sharp edge of her temper show without restraint.

Yayati was conscious of the enormous crowd of curious ogling young girls surrounding them on all sides. From the manner in which they all deferred to Devayani and obeyed her commands, they all appeared to be maids to Devayani. There appeared to be hundreds of them. He knew queens who had fewer maids! Had she not said she was the daughter of a maharishi? And she lived in a simple forest hermitage. How had she come by so many maids? And who was that particular maid, the one who had been massaging Devayani's feet when he rode up, the young girl with the coy, arch look and svelte body? The way she had been bent over as she massaged her mistress' feet, a woman among women and therefore unconcerned with her appearance, had revealed more than a little of her exquisite physique, and even after she saw that a man was approaching, she had been in no haste to conceal her finer points. He found her powerfully attractive. In contrast, the vision he had rescued from the well had turned into an overfed, spoiled and over-decorated princess somehow. He was intrigued by the maid's appearance and by the story of the mistress. It was the only reason he decided to linger awhile.

After pleasantries had been exchanged and suitable decorum shown to the visiting royal, Yayati asked the question that was pressing him. 'How many maids do you have, Devayani? And how did you come by them and by all this luxury? It is not usual for a rishi's daughter, is it?'

She smiled proudly. Her every word and mannerism reeked of the self-indulgent officiousness of the recently enriched or ennobled, and was off-putting in the extreme. He had seen many individuals change and put on such airs overnight when struck by a sudden windfall, inheritance or change of circumstances. He had always found it unsavoury. In Devayani's case, he found it even more unpalatable because he had been so besotted with the vision in the well, and that vulnerable, intense young wraith he had rescued had suddenly changed into this self-indulgent, pompous ass! Almost every word out of Devayani's mouth seemed to be about herself or expressed her views on various things.

She told him briefly that she had suffered a grave
insult by the danavas and as a result her father had
threatened to leave his post as preceptor to the asuras.
King Vrishaparva had offered him anything he pleased
in order to make him stay. 'My father told the danava
to ask me what I wished,' she said proudly. 'I asked for
a thousand maids and to live in a manner befitting one
of my superior status.'

Yayati knew better than to enquire what she meant by
phrases like 'superior status'. He had gained an indication
of Devayani's self-pandering opinions already. He was
more interested in the maid seated immediately behind
her, the one who somehow managed to appear to be
observing his every move and gesture without looking at
him directly. It was a method he knew well as a hunter:
beasts of prey grew conscious of a predator's eyes fixed on
them for too long. Therefore it was important to observe
without staring constantly at them, using one's peripheral
vision. He did the same with her, and because of this,
as Devayani rattled along with her obnoxious prattle, he
began to feel a powerful erotic attraction to the maid.
'How fascinating,' he said politely, interrupting Devayani
in mid-flow as she described at some length the various
luxuries she now enjoyed in the palace of the asuras. 'By
the way, what is that maid's name? Who is she? The one
seated immediately behind you, I mean.'

There was a moment of silence from Devayani,
while the giggly chatter of the maids continued in the
background. Devayani looked frostily at Yayati. 'Why do
you show interest in her, Yuvaraja? She is merely a maid,

one of a thousand who serve me. She is of no importance.'

Yayati licked his lips. 'Yes, of course. I suppose you are right. I just thought perhaps she might be a companion or friend. She is reasonably attractive of face and body. Quite beautiful in fact. And she has lovely...' he stopped himself from saying too much and settled for simply, '... eyebrows.'

He caught a flash of those dark pupils as the one he was speaking of finally acknowledged him with a direct look. And what a look! It was unguarded, smouldering, and openly provocative. There was no doubting that woman's invitation, nor the amusement playing upon those thick sensual lips at his praise of her...eyebrows!

Devayani's eyes narrowed and she snapped her head around as quickly as a cobra lunging. But Sharmishtha was folding a blanket, seemingly intent on the task, her eyes now lowered to the embroidered quilt.

Devayani turned back to Yayati with a disapproving look, made an obvious effort to clear her mind of the irritation she had felt over the interest he had shown in her maid and said, 'Enough about me, Yuvaraja. Tell me about yourself. You are clearly a sovereign of a great kingdom and high birth and upbringing. Your speech and literate manner suggest you are a man of learning. Do tell me about yourself. Whose son are you? Which kingdom do you govern? Tell me everything.'

Yayati was not pleased with her brusque manner and imperious queries. It was obvious that she was jealous of her maid and resented the interest he showed in the girl. That in itself suggested a petty, spiteful nature. But to summarily make demands of him about his father and family was unbecoming. It was the kind of question her parents would have been entitled to ask, and even they would have used a more polite and respectful tone. Devayani acted as if she were an empress and he a visiting suitor. He began to wonder what he had ever seen in this girl. It was quite evident that the vision he had rescued that day was more a creature of his imagining than reality. He wished only to leave and continue with his hunt. Besides, he was genuinely thirsty, as were his horses, and the river was the only source of water for yojanas around. He noticed that Devayani had been dipping her feet in a container of water to wash off the unguents and oils her maid had used to massage them with, so she had water to hand. Yet even with a thousand maids present, not once did she offer him a drink of water or enquire after his needs. Only his breeding kept him from stalking away without a response.

'My name is Yayati. I am a king and the son of a king, and like all kings of my line, I spent the first twenty-five years of my life in brahmacharya-ashrama, by the side of my illustrious guru, steeping myself in knowledge of the Vedas.' He did not elaborate further, deliberately leaving her pertinent questions unanswered. He would rather have taken the maid aside and walked with her through the forest to the river, talking with her. She looked to be much better company than this high and mighty queen of a thousand maids!

She noted his displeasure, and also the direction in which his eyes kept glancing. It irritated her even more.

Instead of changing her attitude, she grew even more arrogant. 'So what brings a great king such as yourself to this aranya? Have you come hunting deer? I know that kings love to hunt down and kill a defenceless doe. Or perhaps,' she added coyly, 'you hoped to collect lotus flowers instead?' Her meaning was underlined by the look she gave him, sidling her eyes sideways to indicate the maid beside her and the many others clustered nearby, some quite pleasing to the eye. 'We are quite famous for the beauty of our lotuses.'

That was as much as Yayati was able to tolerate. There were limits even for a well-mannered king. He stood up slowly, making a show of being weary. 'I was hunting earlier and came by to seek water for myself and my mounts.' He paused, noting that even now she did not bother to offer him a drink of water, or to send some of her many servants to fetch it. 'You are given to speaking a great deal. I will take your leave now.' He turned to go, moving in the direction of the river. At once, the chatter of the maids died down, resulting in a hushed, shocked silence. Everyone knew what had happened and reacted: Devayani had been rude to the handsome young king! And now he was leaving. She felt their eyes judging and assessing her and couldn't stand it.

Devayani sprang to her feet. It was a little more awkward than it used to be as she had put on more than a little weight, thanks to her constant pampering and self-indulgence. She called out to Yayati, stretching her hand out in his direction: 'Raje!'

Yayati paused, glancing back over his shoulder. His

face did not look like the face of a man interested in staying a moment longer. It was only out of sheer politeness that he had even stopped. As far as he was concerned, he had no desire to see Devayani ever again. The maid on the other hand... 'Yes?' he answered curtly, not bothering with her name or even an honorific.

'I was remiss in my hospitality,' she said. 'I was only seeking to exchange a few pleasantries first. I should have realized you must be tired and thirsty from a long ride and from hunting wild game. Pray, do me the honour of seating yourself once more and I shall place all my maids at your service to fetch whatever you wish to eat or drink.'

Yayati looked at her warily, but remained where he was. 'I had best be on my way. A short visit to the river to water my horses and myself, and then I shall return to my kingdom.'

Devayani realized she would have to do more than just be polite now. She saw the direction in which his eyes glanced even now and pounced upon the opportunity.

'Sharmishtha!' she cried.

Sharmishtha frowned and rose to her feet. 'Yes, mistress.'

Devayani gestured towards Sharmishtha. 'This is Sharmishtha,' she said to Yayati directly. 'She is my personal maid. She is enslaved to me for life. She and my thousand other maid servants can fetch you anything you desire. Please, stay a while. It will be pleasant to talk a while longer.'

Yayati turned and came towards the spot where he had sat earlier. His eyes were fixed on Sharmishtha even as he spoke to Devayani. 'Perhaps I shall stay a brief while longer,' he said. 'But only a brief while.'

'What is your pleasure, sire?' Sharmishtha asked, in a voice and manner that were servile yet still provocative, a combination that instantly raised Devayani's hackles and aroused Yayati's emotions. 'Name your desire and I shall fulfil it.'

Devayani raised a hand as if intending to strike out with it, then with visible effort, lowered it again. Her teeth bit into her lips while her eyes glared daggers at Sharmishtha. The maid seemed unaware or unconcerned by her mistress' agitation. She took three steps forward towards Yayati, her delicate silver payals tinkling suggestively, hips swaying, then bent to her knees before the king. He looked down at her, his lips parted slightly.

'May I have some water to drink, please?' he said.

'Certainly,' Devayani said loudly, taking charge of the situation again. 'Sharmishtha...' she began sharply, then reconsidered and corrected herself. 'No, never mind. You girls,' she pointed randomly at a group of girls nearby. 'Fetch water, wine and refreshments for Maharaja Yayati. Move quickly!' She turned back to Sharmishtha. 'Place one of my cushions here that the king may seat himself more comfortably.'

Sharmishtha obeyed without response. Yayati watched her as she moved with swaying hips and tinkling anklets, leaning over, bending down, crouching, stretching out and rearranging the cushions. Devayani watched Yayati as he watched Sharmishtha and two high points of colour began to blaze on her cheekbones. She looked as if she would dearly love to whip the maid. But she settled for changing tack.

'Raje, please refresh yourself,' she said, gesturing at the maids who had returned bearing jugs and bowls and vessels containing every kind of food and drink that was available. Yayati gladly did so, for he had been on the hunt for three days, riding far and wide without food and with scarce water. Devayani was more careful about how she spoke and what she said, and as nourishment entered his body and he felt the warm satisfaction of a full belly and a slaked thirst, he began to look upon her less judgmentally. Devayani could be a fine performer once she set her mind to it. And she had decided that she would outmatch Sharmishtha now. It was her goal to ensure that the king had eyes for none other than Devayani herself. She laughed mellifluously, throwing her head back to reveal her long flowing neck, stretched out languorously, bent over to pick up fruits, kicked out her legs, and did everything she could to demonstrate that she was no less desirable a woman than her enticing maid. She threw herself into the part body and soul and as he ate and drank and was amused by her witticisms and comments, Yayati began to feel that she was not as bad as he had thought after all. He still thought of her as pampered and self-indulgent but she was not without her charms. In some ways, she could even be considered beautiful and desirable.

Devayani persuaded Yayati to linger with her in the forest for a day or two, on the pretext of showing him a rare grove where unusual deer roved, a pond where the most beautiful lotus flowers blossomed and similar ploys. Yayati, for his part, had come this way precisely to see Devayani, if not this Devayani then the vision he had first seen in the well, and as the hours turned into days, and Devayani's masterful performance only deepened in excellence, he could not help but fall under her spell. There was also the added attraction of having Sharmishtha around. From time to time, when Devayani's guard was down or she was momentarily absent, he found his eyes seeking out the alluring maid. More than once, she figured in his thoughts when lying down to sleep at night on Devayani's overly effeminate cushions and blankets. He even mused on the possibility of calling her to his sleeping pallet at night, when Devayani was asleep. But Devayani was too shrewd to let such a thing occur right under her very nose; she took the precaution of having Sharmishtha's wrist tethered to her own, under the pretext that if she, Devayani, happened to wander away in her sleep at night, Sharmishtha would keep her safe.

Sharmishtha knew what Devayani was doing, but could neither object nor do anything about it. She contented herself with shooting knowing glances at Yayati at every opportunity and permitting him glimpses of her when possible. One night, she made sure to change her garments directly in front of a lit lamp, so that her naked shadow was projected onto a flimsy sheet that was hung on a branch to afford her privacy, knowing that Yayati was watching on the other side of the sheet. Another time, after bathing, she did not dress by the river but ran back circuitously so that he would catch a glimpse of her through the trees, just enough to tantalize and arouse his desires, yet never enough to satisfy. It became a game between them to seduce the king. Yayati was aware of it and enjoyed it to the hilt. After all, he could not lose at this particular game! Or so he thought.

It was Devayani who made the killing move. One day, during the visit to the lotus pond, she deliberately permitted a moment of intimacy to blossom into hesitant passion between them.

Even as their bodies brushed against each other fully clothed, hands intertwining, she sighed deeply, then pulled away. The maids had been told to wait a distance away, and even Sharmishtha was not with them, for Devayani had planned her move meticulously.

When she had stayed silent for several moments, Yayati said, 'Devayani? What is it? Why are you so quiet of a sudden?' Being quiet was not one of Devayani's foremost characteristics.

'I was thinking that it is time you met my father,' she said softly.

'Certainly,' Yayati said cheerfully, 'I have heard so much about him, from others and now from you. It would be a great honour. I always respect brahmins of high learning such as he and few can claim a tenth of his knowledge and wisdom.'

'Then it is settled,' Devayani said. 'You shall meet him today itself. We shall go to the city. I shall send a maid at once to announce us.'

In fact, knowing how engrossed her father became with his work as a preceptor and wanting Yayati's reception to be a grand one, Devayani had sent this message to Guru Shukracharya days earlier.

'Why not?' Yayati said. 'Although afterwards, I shall have to return home. I have been away longer than usual and my ministers and people will start to worry.'

Devayani smiled at him. 'Yes, of course, you have a kingdom to govern. Once we have seen my father and he has given his blessings, we shall proceed to your palace at once. It shall be exactly as you wish.'

Yayati frowned at her. Had he missed hearing some part of the conversation? Or was he misunderstanding her meaning now? 'You mean to say, I shall proceed home, do you not? You shall stay in Vrishaparva's palace with your father. And your maids.'

She laughed, a natural full-throated laugh, warm and apparently guileless. 'Why do you tease me so, my love? You know that after I am wed, I cannot possibly stay in my father's house while my new husband goes home without me. Imagine what everyone would say!'

Yayati was taken aback. 'After you are wed? Your new husband? What are you saying, Devayani? Who are you marrying and when is this event to take place?'

Devayani looked at him disconcertedly, a shining brimming in her bright eyes. 'There is a limit to teasing, beloved. Do not torture me now!'

Yayati shook his head. 'I do not understand. What are you saying? You surely don't mean that you and I... that we are to be wed? Us?'

Devayani laughed and clasped her arms around his neck. She had to rise up on her toes to do so, pressing her body against Yayati. He felt a stir of arousal when she did so, and had to force himself to keep his mind on the line of discussion. 'I knew you were teasing! Yes, of course I mean us. You were the one who said you wished to ask my father for my hand in marriage, silly man.'

'I did not,' he began, then thought back through their talk. 'I only meant that I would be honoured to meet such a learned man!'

'And to marry his equally learned daughter?' Devayani asked innocently. 'That is what you implied, did you not? I accepted your proposal of marriage at once, but of course you must meet my father to seal the scroll.'

Yayati began feeling as if he had been manipulated and outmanoeuvred by an opponent shrewder than any enemy general. He turned away, gazing out at the late morning sunlight drifting in through the eaves. 'Devayani, I cannot marry you. It is quite impossible. Surely you know that!'

Devayani cried out as if someone had pricked her heart with a dagger. 'How can you say such a thing? After holding my hand and pulling me from the well, your body so close to my own? No man has ever caught hold of my hand in such a way before, nor given me such a strong indication of his feelings towards me.' She was not telling the whole truth of course, although it was true that even her erstwhile paramour Kacha had never had actual physical contact with her. She would not let herself mark that brotherly caress of her cheek as a lover's touch, even in memory. Kacha had been rigid in his vows to the end. But even Yayati could not deny that he had caught hold of her hand. How else could he have helped her out of that damp dungeon of a well?

'I know that in our culture, when a man takes hold of a woman's hand, it indicates his desire to marry her. But in my case, I had no such desire,' he said firmly. 'I was merely saving your life. In any case, we can never marry. You are a brahmin's daughter and I a raj-kshatriya. It is forbidden for us to cross castes in marriage or childbirth!'

'Not forbidden,' she said evasively, 'merely frowned upon. Besides, you are no ordinary kshatriya, you are a raj-kshatriya of great Vedic learning. Which makes you no less than a brahmin yourself!'

Yayati shook his head, chuckling. 'You would argue that the sun was the moon if it suited your purpose, Devayani. But no amount of learning alone makes a kshatriya a brahmin. There are other conditions and modalities of behaviour. I cannot take the rigid vows of a brahmin. I am a king. I must hunt and kill and do what is necessary to protect my people and kingdom, expand my territories and spread my power. These are things forbidden to any brahmin. If you marry someone like me, your children would become outcastes! They would be shunned by both our people—brahmins would never accept them as brahmins, and kshatriyas would doubt their valour and willingness to take up arms. It would be impossible for me to sire a suitable heir to the throne, and as king, it is my dharma to make an heir suitable to ascend in my stead. No, Devayani, you must give up this foolish notion. We can never marry. It would be against your dharma as well as my own.'

But Devayani was not easily dissuaded once she had made up her mind. When sweet words and persuasion had no effect, she began to lose her temper and revealed her sour, bitter side. In no time at all, she was lashing out at him with the blade of her tongue. 'I have deemed it to be appropriate. Therefore there is no point arguing further. You shall ask my father for my hand in marriage and we shall be wed. I am a proud and honourable daughter. Once a man has caught my hand and then later wooed me as you have these past days, I can never touch another man, on pain of death. You have made it impossible for me to marry any other man now. Dharma clearly says that once a man touches a maiden's hand, he is obliged to marry her. Therefore, by the dharma of the touching hand, you are now obliged to marry me to save me from falling into ignominy!'

At this Yayati realized that he had been entrapped by this young woman as effectively as she herself had been trapped in that cold, dank well. It was up to him to rescue himself. He rose to his feet, preparing to go, knowing that if he did not leave her at once, she would have him. Nonsensical though her arguments seemed, they were nevertheless rooted in sanskriti, the immutable tradition of their culture. If indeed a man grasped a young maiden's hand, he was in fact presumed to be proposing marriage—this was the origin of the phrase 'taking her hand in marriage'. Yet the better he came to know Devayani, the less inclined he was to marry her.

He intended to get on his horse, ride back home and never see her face again.

'Where are you going?' she asked, following him as he walked over to the spot where his horses were tethered.

'I am leaving now,' he said curtly.

'But you cannot! You have proposed marriage to me! I have a thousand witnesses!'

Yayati looked around. The maids were watching them with the avid interest of women treated to a dramatic performance. Which in fact this was. Except that the conclusion of this drama would be very real and it involved two human lives.

He moved closer to Devayani, keeping his voice low. 'This is over, Devayani. I have no intention of marrying you. You tried to trick me but you've failed. I am leaving now and I will not return again.'

At that moment, Devayani's heart filled with utter hatred and rage. Once again, she was being abandoned by a man she loved and desired. Was it not enough that she had been abandoned by her beloved Kacha? Was she to endure this pain and humiliation yet again? Already she was growing past the prime marriageable age. Once some more years passed, even men who were attracted to her would think twice before proposing. Yet instead of making her shrill and agitated, her rage made her cold and perfectly lucid. 'You cannot leave,' she said. 'Dharma is on my side. A king such as you can never transgress against dharma. It will be your ruin!' Yayati cursed silently and turned back from his horses. 'Woman! You test my patience now. I have said I cannot marry you!

Why will you not leave it at that? You are reasonably
attractive, well-attended, influential, the daughter of a
famous brahmin. You will have any number of young
rishis willing to marry you! I am a kshatriya, I cannot
marry you under any circumstances!'

Devayani shrugged. 'I declare you to be a rishi. I can
have my father declare it if you prefer. A brahmin has the
authority to declare another person of any caste a fellow
brahmin. By that brahmin authority, you are made a rishi
with immediate effect. That hurdle is removed. Now you
cannot argue a difference of varna.'

Yayati resisted the urge to punch his fist into the trunk
of the tree to which his horses were tethered. 'Brahmin
authority! I do not care about brahminical authority! You
cannot alter the facts to suit your purpose whenever it
pleases you!'

Devayani replied in a honeyed tone: 'Do you not hunt
with whatever weapons and advantage you possess? A
hunter must fell his prey in any way possible.'

'I am not prey to be downed by you.'

'Certainly not. You are a man of great worth and
stature. You are a prize husband. And I am the daughter
of a great brahmin. It is a match made in heaven.'

'Then go to heaven and find someone suitable! I am
not available to marry you.'

'Why not? Give me one reason at least.'

'I gave you—' He stopped, realizing that she had
effectively negated the varna argument. Brahmins indeed
had the authority to declare a kshatriya also a brahmin,
especially a raj-kshatriya. He sought about desperately for

some way out of his insane trap. Then it occurred to him: If there was one thing a brahmin would not tolerate, it was an insult against their varna. Brahmins were impossibly egotistical. Thus far, Devayani was perfectly in control and had the upper hand. But if he reduced her to anger and tears, compelling her to say something stupid, he could safely ride away with a clear conscience.

'It is said by the learned,' he announced in a voice loud enough to be heard by her maids, all of whom were discreetly or openly listening, 'that a brahmin is always to be avoided.'

Devayani frowned. 'Which learned man says such a thing? All learned men are brahmins, and no brahmin would ever speak against his own varna!'

Yayati smiled to himself. That change of attitude showed him he was on the right path. 'Nevertheless, it has been said by the learned that one must always avoid a brahmin. As you are a brahmin's daughter, I cannot marry you.'

Devayani laughed and waved away the objection deprecatingly. 'Utter nonsense. As a brahmin's daughter, I am all the more desirable. Especially since I am the daughter of not just any brahmin, but of Shukracharya himself, preceptor to the entire asura race, one of the most highly respected and venerated brahmins in the world.'

Yayati shook his head. 'In fact, that makes you least desirable of all.'

Devayani lost her smile and stared at him. 'What do you mean by that? Do you seek to insult my father?' Her voice rose a shrill notch on the last word, and he knew he had found her weak spot.

She cannot bear to hear her father insulted. Behind
Devayani, he glimpsed the other maid, the very attractive
and desirable one that she called Sharmishtha, nodding
vigorously to him, then making hand gestures to encourage
him to go on. So I am right, this is the way to drive her
to anger and tell me to go drown myself. If I insult her
father sufficiently, she will never want to marry me. He
grinned, nodding once to show the beautiful maid that
he understood and appreciated her help.

At the same time, he knew, he could not simply
spout insults and abuse any brahmin, let alone one of
Shukra's stature. It would be unacceptable for a king
of his reputation to do so. He had to tread a fine line
between offending Devayani—and forcing her to lose her
self-control—and not inflicting calumny upon the great
maharishi.

'I only repeat what the learned have already proclaimed
loudly to one and all,' he said smoothly, lapsing into the
familiar diplomatic mode he had been trained to use in
matters of inter-state negotiations, a fine line between
upholding one's own dignity and making sly potshots at
the transgressions of others while never openly provoking
or accusing. 'Brahmins are always to be avoided, the more
famous a brahmin, the more widely one is expected to
avoid him. It is true of all famous brahmins. But if it
applies to you, then by all means take the lesson to heart.'

'That is utter nonsense,' Devayani said sharply. 'You
will stop this at once. No more insults against brahmins
and no further mention of my father! We have reached
an agreement and you must honour it. Marry me.'

Yayati marvelled at how easily she gave orders even though there was no actual contract between them yet and wondered how much more forcefully she would order him about if they were actually married. 'We have no agreement, maiden. As I am saying to you, since you are the daughter of a brahmin, I cannot possibly marry you under any circumstances. This is not my opinion or personal decision, it is merely the lesson of the wise. As a king, I must obey their superior knowledge.' Devayani looked as if she wished to slap him to bring him to his senses. He had no doubt that she was quite capable of doing so. But she restrained herself with a visible effort. 'Stop saying such things. My being a brahmin's daughter can only be an asset. Every young man of marriageable age would give anything to marry the daughter of Shukracharya!'

Yayati glanced around, gesturing casually. 'Oddly, I see no young men of marriageable age here.' He winked at the maids. 'Although there seems to be no shortage of young marriageable women around.' He grinned at Devayani. 'Perhaps the competition is too great? Too many nubile young lovelies to choose from?' He looked pointedly over her shoulder at Sharmishtha, who returned his look with a coy invitation of her own. Devayani saw the direction of his gaze and turned sharply. At the sight of Sharmishtha, her eyes narrowed to slits that threatened to expel thunderbolts of fire.

She turned back to Yayati. 'Enough! There is no reason to avoid the daughter of a brahmin! You are merely speaking ill-thought-out statements.'

Yayati shook his head. 'On the contrary, I can explain the whole argument. The wise have clearly explained why a brahmin is to be avoided at all costs.'

Devayani folded her hands on her chest tightly, glaring at him.

Yayati went on. 'A brahmin is to be avoided even more than a raging fire that spreads in all directions, or a venomous snake that strikes anyone who approaches near. This is the full warning issued by the learned and I merely repeat it as I was taught.'

Devayani started to speak, then held her tongue, choosing to fume instead. Then she changed her mind and sputtered: 'If the learned say so, they must have good reason. Explain!' Yayati smiled and continued, speaking as much for the benefit of Sharmishtha and the other maids, knowing that by doing so he infuriated Devayani all the more. 'The reason for this is a good one. A snake, even if it lunges, can only spend its venom on a single victim. A fire can rage and burn down a forest but cannot cross water or spread to the cities unchecked. Whereas a brahmin, when angered, can issue a curse that kills any number, that can destroy entire cities, even entire worlds. The more famous and powerful a brahmin, the greater his anger, the greater his ability to curse and cause ruin. Therefore the learned have advised that one should always steer clear of a brahmin, and stay even farther away from a famous or powerful brahmin. Such as your father.'

He smiled. 'Now do you see why I cannot possibly marry you, lovely maiden Devayani? I dare not risk incurring the wrath of a brahmin, a very powerful brahmin at that, perhaps the most powerful of all, as you yourself admitted. For if he were to grow wrathful at me, his brahman power could end my dynasty, ruin my kingdom, and wipe out my entire race! I dare not risk such an event. I dare not risk angering your father. Therefore I cannot marry you.'

The peals of laughter from around were suggestive of cheers of approval. Yayati was amused to see that even her own maids did not feel great loyalty towards their mistress. He thought that being enslaved against their will might have something to do with it. Sharmishtha was smiling triumphantly, looking most pleased of all. At the sight of her, his breath caught in his throat, and he thought to himself: I must have that woman. I must!

Devayani was staring at him with an inscrutable expression on her face. He could not read the expression, or even tell whether it suggested rage, frustration or humiliation. In any case, he did not expect her to have any rejoinder this time. He was quite pleased with himself. He had set the woman in her place once and for all. He finished untethering his horses and mounted the first one.

He heard the second horse whinny softly and turned. He was surprised to see Devayani sitting astride his spare horse, sitting as comfortably as any young princess who had ridden horses all her childhood. He assumed she had learned to ride while playing princess in the city of the asuras.

'Very well,' she said.

'Could you dismount from my horse, please,' he asked politely. 'I wish to be on my way.'

'Very well,' she said, louder this time. The giggling and excited chatter died down around them as all the maids noticed their mistress astride the horse. 'I accept your proposal of marriage. We shall proceed at once to my father so that you may ask him.'

'Ask him what?' Yayati said, his brow furrowing with irritation. 'This matter has been settled, Devayani. I have already told you, it is quite impossible for me to marry you.'

'Because I am the daughter of a powerful brahmin, isn't that right?' she asked.

'Yes,' he said doubtfully, wondering what new mischief she was up to.

'And because you fear that he might curse you to ruin and you cannot risk that, being a king and therefore responsible to your people, am I correct?' 'Yes,' he said.

'Then it is settled. We shall go to my father, you shall ask him for my hand in marriage, and you shall lay down the condition that you marry me only on condition that no harm or ill ever befalls you or your future offspring or your city and kingdom and possessions and people... Ask him to ensure spiritual protection for your sewer-cleaners and butchers as well, if you wish. He is a powerful brahmin. His word is immutable. You shall have protection for all that you hold dear. Since that is your only objection, it is best to eliminate it at once. There will be no further obstacle in the path of our marriage. Come now,' she said, urging the spare horse forward, 'let us ride to Vrishaparva and settle this matter. I wish to be married at the earliest.'

7

Yayati was cornered. He had done it to countless prey before and he knew exactly when a beast was left with no way to run, no place to hide, nothing but its own end staring it in the face. He had seen that look on countless animals before he dispatched them with his arrow, sword, javelin or pike. Devayani had taken his own objection and turned it against him. Without actually saying so at any time, she had made him realize that what he said was in fact true: Guru Kavya Ushanas was a powerful brahmin. If Yayati now offended him by refusing his daughter's hand in marriage without a suitable reason, the preceptor of the asuras could indeed curse him to ruin. At the very least, he could invoke the wrath of the asuras against Yayati and his allies. A war with the asuras would be as ruinous as a curse. By taking her hand—albeit to haul her out of the well where she had been trapped—he had indeed offered her protection, and as such, had initiated an offer of marriage. If unaccompanied by any romantic feeling or emotional attachment, perhaps that innocent act of grasping her hand could have been overlooked, but the fact was that he had been infatuated with her, had returned time and again to the site of their first encounter, and had eventually met her, stayed with her, romanced her and been romanced. They had progressed far down the path of courtship and it would be impossible now to deny it to any third person. With a thousand witnesses, it would be equally impossible to disprove her claims. And by raising the spectre of brahminical curses he had given her the very weapon which she was now using to seal the contract. For he had suggested, however indirectly, that by offending her or her father—and what greater offence could a man of good breeding cause a young maiden than to propose marriage and later reject her?—her father would be justified in issuing a curse against him and his people. He had said the very opposite, of course, but it served the same purpose: it had put the idea into her shrewd head. And now that the idea was planted, he would be risking the wrath of the preceptor of the asuras if he rode away from here.

Unable to think of any honourable way out of this situation, Yayati rode in silence to Vrishaparva city with Devayani. She rode surprisingly well for a brahmin, and it only served to remind him that she was not in fact simply a brahmin's daughter. Also, he had observed that over the days he had spent with her, she had reduced her eating considerably, shedding some of those kilos of excess weight, and had begun to look like the same vision he had first seen in the well. The intensity of her arguments, while obnoxiously worded and imperiously delivered, were passionate enough to suggest a woman possessed of great will and life-force. However much he might not want her to be his wife, the fact remained that she could become a formidable queen. As king, one of his responsibilities was to choose a suitable queen, one who was as competent at governance as in spousecraft. There was no doubt that Devayani qualified eminently. And she looks like she would be a tigress in the arts of love, he mused. Perhaps marrying her was not such a bad thing after all. In any case, as king, he was free to spread his seed as he pleased. To take more than one queen if he desired. To maintain a palace full of concubines if he wished. So marrying Devayani was not necessarily the end of his freedom. In fact, this might turn out to be of advantage in time. By marrying the daughter of the preceptor of asuras, he would always be able to count on the support of the asuras, which would strike fear into the hearts of his mortal rivals and challengers. And if the devas objected or crossed paths with him, he need not fear being labelled disloyal since his marriage did not necessarily constitute a military alliance with their enemies. He could play it different ways in different circumstances, using the political and military advantages as he pleased.

By the time they reached Vrishaparva and were shown to Guru Shukracharya's chambers, he had convinced himself that marriage to Devayani was a desirable thing after all.

So when Devayani introduced him to her father as the man who had taken hold of her hand and saved her life, then announced that she wished to marry him, Yayati offered no objection. For one thing, Devayani told the truth, even when it reflected her in an unflattering light.

He saw that her father was accustomed to her imperious way of demanding things.

'Son of Nahusha,' the maharishi said to him thoughtfully. 'So you saved my daughter's life and have now been chosen by her as a husband. Do you agree to this union?' There was a look in his eyes that suggested he wanted to be certain that Yayati was not under coercion.

Yayati nodded. 'Yes, great descendent of Bhrigu, I do.'

Shukracharya nodded thoughtfully. 'You are a brave man.'

Yayati remembered the last part of his argument with Devayani. 'Gurudev, as part of my marriage contract, I wish you to kindly ensure that no harm will ever befall me or my offspring as a result of my marrying a brahmin's daughter.'

Kavya Ushanas considered this thoughtfully. 'A wise request. One that suggests great foresight and planning. You are a good king and will be a good father as well. Your wish is granted. No harm shall ever befall you or your offspring because of our relationship in marriage.'

Yayati bowed low, smiling happily. He had secured a major military, diplomatic and strategic advantage! This alone was worth marrying any woman. 'I thank you, great one.'

'But in return, I have a request of my own,' the guru said quietly. Devayani was not with them at this time, having gone with her maids to make arrangements for the marriage. 'Nay, consider it more a command from your father-in-law.'

Yayati looked up at the preceptor, head still bowed, palms still joined. 'I am listening, Gurudev.'

'The maid named Sharmishtha,' Shukra said. 'She is an attractive girl, is she not?'

Yayati was completely taken aback. What did this mean? Why was his father-in-law-to-be speaking of some other girl, a mere maid at that? Unsure how to answer such an unusual question, he nodded.

'You must vow never to bed her,' said the guru. 'Do you understand?'

Yayati gazed back at the guru. The brahmin had just promised that he would never let harm befall Yayati or his offspring. Even so, like all kshatriyas who knew of the power that could be gained through sustained meditation and austerities, he still feared the maharishi. He dared not even ask why the guru was making this request or what would happen if he refused—besides, how could he possibly refuse the request without seeming boorish and immoral? He could hardly say to his prospective father-in-law that he found the maid named Sharmishtha far more seductive and alluring physically than his own wife-to-be Devayani.

'I understand,' he said simply.

8

Yayati's people welcomed their new queen with great pomp and ceremony. The entire city was coloured with festivities. The celebration was lavish. Yayati instated Devayani in the traditional queen's quarters but immediately commissioned a separate palace for her. Devayani was delighted at the thought of having her own independent residence. Situating the new queen's palace in a beautiful grove of ashoka trees within easy travelling distance of the main palace annexe, Yayati had the structure raised in record time. He made sure that the new palace contained rooms for Devayani's thousand maidservants as well. In addition, he honoured her chief maid and official companion, Sharmishtha, with an additional one thousand maids of her own. This was certainly not pleasing to Devayani but since Sharmishtha was under her command, it effectively put the additional thousand maids under Devayani's command as well, so in a sense, it was she who was being gifted the additional thousand maids. Aloud she did not complain but her eyes shot daggers at Sharmishtha and she increased her demands on the latter, making her work from morning to night without respite.

For his part, Yayati contented himself with that lavish gesture, even if it was but a formality since Sharmishtha still remained a maid, and buried his lust for the beautiful servant deep in his heart. The guru's warning had shaken him to the core and he took it very seriously. He made no attempt to reveal his true feelings for Sharmishtha and at no time let himself lapse.

In time, Devayani conceived and delivered a beautiful baby boy as her firstborn, providing Yayati with an heir.

A thousand years passed. For this was Satya Yuga and the ages of men were far, far greater than they are now.

Sharmishtha, being younger than Devayani, had yet to attain her prime. But in due course, she too attained that flush of womanhood and came into season. Until now, she had accepted her fate reluctantly. But with the blossoming of her womanhood, new emotions stirred within her and she was overcome by a great resentment against her tormentor, matched by an equally powerful lust for Yayati. 'For too long have I lived in Devayani's shadow,' she thought, 'enduring her endless stream of insults and humiliations. How long will I have to suffer for my one lapse? Now I am in season and my body greatly desires the love of a man as well as to bear a child of my own. I cannot stand by and let my youth blossom and fade, unplucked. I am the daughter of a king, a true princess in my own right, not a make-believe one like Devayani. I deserve a king to sire an heir upon me as well. I know that Yayati still has feelings of desire for me. Why should I not pursue him and make him my mate?'

Her mind made up, Sharmishtha began seeking an opportunity to seduce Yayati. One day, she found her chance. The king was passing through the ashoka grove, on his way to see Devayani and their newborn son. Sharmishtha had placed herself in the grove, waiting his chariot. When she felt the ground trembling underfoot she knew he was approaching and stepped in front of his vehicle. Yayati called to his horses as he reined them in. Curious as to why Sharmishtha was barring his way, he dismounted from the chariot and went to her.

He was struck by how much lovelier she now appeared. It had been a long, long time since he had looked upon her with lustful eyes but in the interim she had only grown more beautiful. He saw that while before she had been but an immature girl gifted with certain qualities of womanly allure, now she was a full-blown woman in her prime, lustrous with appeal, ripe with comeliness. Every movement seemed seductive, every gesture, expression, word and sound filled him with desire. Having been absent from Devayani's bed for the past several months of her confinement, his manly desires were unsated and he was most vulnerable to feminine pulchritude. Looking at Sharmishtha at that moment, he was struck by how perfectly she matched his ideal of the most beautiful woman. She was kama itself personified in flesh. It required all his self-control to keep himself from crushing her in his arms and having his way with her there and then.

She greeted him with a formality that was even more appealing than her newly-blossomed ripeness. 'Raje. Great son of Nahusha. You are no less than Soma, Indra, Vishnu,

Yama or Varuna in your aspect and your masculine power. Yet you have always looked upon me and taken me to be but a low-born slave and servant. This is not the case. I was not always a maidservant.'

He caught her joined palms in his hands, enfolding them with careless strength. 'This is known to me.'

She was surprised. 'It is?'

'Indeed. I know that you are Vrishaparva's daughter, a princess of high birth and noble lineage, no less than my own. You are fit to be queen of the daityas. An immaculate asuri without a flaw or blemish on your name or reputation, save the alleged crime of having crossed paths with Devayani, your former friend. For one thousand years I have seen you dutifully serve my wife, doing her every bidding, however undesirable or loathsome. I have admired your fortitude and dedication as well as your sense of dharma. Only a woman of great moral strength could endure such suffering with such dignity. I applaud you for your endurance and must confess a truth I have kept buried in my heart for far too long, with your permission.'

Sharmishtha's heart was already gladdened by the things Yayati had said. She urged him, 'Raje, you are a king of the world. Speak your mind freely to me. I only wish to hear the truth and shall only speak the truth to you.'

'Then hear this, Sharmishtha. I love you. I have loved you since the first moment I set eyes on you. I came back to that forest thinking that I was seeking Devayani, but when I found her, she was not the woman I had assumed her to be. The only reason I agreed to marry her was out of convenience and to avoid her father's wrath. It was you I was attracted to during that time I spent with Devayani in the forest. I desired you more than I have ever desired any woman in my life.'

Sharmishtha lowered her gaze shyly, genuinely moved by the power of Yayati's desire and the evident longing in his eyes. 'And I desired you as well, Raje. But because of my cruel mistress, I could neither openly reveal my feelings for you nor reciprocate the love I saw in your eyes.'

She raised her gaze again to him and the instant when their gazes met was like a physical blow to both, each felt the impact in his or her loins, and was overcome by a great surge of desire.

'Yayati,' she said, and he thrilled to hear his name spoken by her. 'I wish to give myself to you now. I have been patient so long, but I cannot bear it any more. Please, take me and make me your woman this very instant. I desire it.'

Yayati was filled with a great conflict. 'Oh Sharmishtha, you do not know how much your words please me. I desire nothing less than that we be joined this instant. But before I married Devayani, her father cautioned me of one thing. He warned me against ever taking you to my bed. That was the reason why I have avoided you through these many years. I was respecting the wishes of my father-in-law, who is a great sage and powerful maharishi.'

Sharmishtha replied: 'Yet it was not a promise or a vow, merely a caution that you were given, am I right? There would be no sin in ignoring that caution.'

'True, but if he asks me someday, I would have to admit the truth. And who knows what the consequences might be? Remember, he is a great and powerful brahmin and any sane man must fear his wrath. It would not be wise to cross him.'

'Then don't tell him! If he asks you, lie to him. After all, there are circumstances under which lying is not a sin. Specifically, there are five instances when lying is acceptable: in jest, to women, at the time of marriage, when faced with certain death, and in order to avoid losing one's wealth.'

'It is so,' Yayati replied. 'But bearing false witness is also wrong and against dharma. Even if one speaks the falsehood for an ulterior purpose, it is still wrong. I am a king, Sharmishtha, I must be a role model to my people. *Yatha raja tatha praja*, goes the saying. As does a king, so do the people. I cannot set a wrong example. It is forbidden for me to lie, even if doing so can save me from certain destruction.'

Sharmishtha considered the matter then replied: 'Then do not consider it a lie at all. Our rites of marriage declare that a close friend's marriage is equal to one's own nuptials. By law, a friend's husband is equivalent to one's own husband. It is acceptable for me to regard you as my own husband and call you to my bed. In addition, I am your wife's slave, therefore I am your slave as well, for when you married her you took possession of me as well. I regard it as my dharma to mate with you and produce a child from our union. Therefore I do not ask you to commit any sin or crime, merely to enable me to uphold my dharma. As my owner's husband, and friend's husband, it is your duty to help me uphold my dharma. Legally, this logic is unassailable. None can question the right of a man to have sexual congress with his own slave. In fact, by doing so, and by fostering a child upon me, you perform your right as a king as well, enabling me to fulfil my dharma. There can be no wrong in this act. Make love to me now, king. All doubts are dispelled. Take me in this scented arbour. My season is ripe, my body is ready, and it is the righteous thing to do for both of us.'

Yayati was persuaded. Inflamed by his long-suppressed desire for Sharmishtha, he laid her down upon a bed of soft springy grass and made passionate love to her in the ashoka grove. Both enjoyed the pleasures of each other's bodies and satisfied their desires completely. Their union was not merely one of lust but of genuine love, far greater than the forced bond which united Yayati and Devayani. After an afternoon of rich passion, he lovingly bid her farewell and continued on his way. She returned home as well, and was certain that she had conceived that very day.

She was right. From that union, Sharmishtha conceived and gave birth to a son with eyes like blue lotuses, matching her own darkly beautiful eyes.

9

Devayani had watched her maid like a hawk all these years. Temporarily distracted by the birth of her first child, she had ceased the constant visitation of torment on Sharmishtha. Her life and routine had changed and she failed to notice Sharmishtha's state of motherhood until it was almost time for her to give birth. Only after Sharmishtha had delivered herself of the child did Devayani come to realize that Sharmishtha was also a mother now.

She came to see Sharmishtha, hoping to catch her off guard and was quite unhappy to see her nursing a beautiful baby boy no less resplendent than her own son. 'What sin have you committed now, Sharmishtha?' she asked without preamble or greeting. 'With whom have you been rutting in dark corners to produce this proof of your misbegotten lust?'

Sharmishtha had expected this confrontation and had prepared her answers carefully. 'I was visited by a rishi, mistress. A great man, learned in the Vedas and devoted to dharma. He offered me a boon and I asked for a son. He granted my wish and this is the result. Surely there can be no sin in what I did?'

Devayani was taken aback. Of all the answers she had thought to hear, this was least expected. She could hardly find fault with such an explanation. 'Yes, yes, of course,' she admitted grumpily. 'This is all very well. But I wish to know the name, lineage and birth details of this brahmin.' She thought to check the details with her father and verify Sharmishtha's story. She did not put it past her to lie blatantly to her!

But Sharmishtha was prepared for this as well. 'You look more radiant than ever after delivering, Devayani. Motherhood suits you well. It has brought out your natural beauty.' Before Devayani could repeat her request, she added, 'I wish I could provide the details you ask for, but this rishi was so radiant and awe-inspiring. I never thought to ask him such questions. It hardly seemed to matter. After all, he was clearly some great being, possessed of magnificent spiritual energy and luminescence. I was overcome by his spiritual splendour.'

Devayani was frustrated. But she could not accuse Sharmishtha further without some basis in fact. Such births were quite common, and it was no crime for any unmarried woman to ask a visiting brahmin to seed her with child. Her own father had probably seeded hundreds of such women in his time. It was regarded as a blessing and a benediction. The child remained the mother's legitimate child, the father's name being of no relevance at all. In fact, as she thought about it further, Devayani realized, this was the perfect end to her long-lasting fears of Sharmishtha becoming a rival. Now that Sharmishtha was an unwed mother with a child to raise, and still a maidservant, her desirability had been further reduced. No man would want her, let alone King Yayati. In the end, Devayani decided, this was a wonderful stroke of good luck. She could finally stop worrying about Sharmishtha stealing her man away.

In the wake of this confrontation, rather than dividing the two women, the birth of Sharmishtha's fatherless child brought them closer together. Rid of the constant anxiety that Sharmishtha might steal her husband away, and flush with her own motherhood, Devayani was pleased to share her present situation with her former friend, and inasmuch as such a thing was possible under the circumstances, their old friendship revived and flourished again. They spent hours together, sharing information on baby care, caring for one another's infants, and otherwise enjoying each other's company at every waking moment. The change in the relationship was striking: no more was Sharmishtha Devayani's slave and servant. She was almost treated as an equal and friend once more! Devayani in turn altered her outlook and became sweet-smiling and good-tempered again, as she had once been. The other maids marvelled at the change in their mistresses. Soon after the birth of her first son, Sharmishtha was permitted to build a house of her own and reside near the ashoka grove. Over time, she was careful not to invite Devayani to her house or to let her mistress meet her son as he grew older.

In time, Yayati had another son through Devayani. Their two sons were named Yadu and Turvasu. Through

Sharmishtha he fathered three sons—Druhyu, Anu and Puru. All five boys were magnificent, healthy and possessed of strikingly beautiful features and strong bodies. If placed in a row together, there would have been no mistaking the fact that they were all sons of Yayati, but because of Sharmishtha's care, that never happened. She took great pains to ensure that Devayani never saw her sons closely once they had grown old enough for the resemblance to be obvious.

One day, by pure chance, Devayani was travelling with Yayati and they happened to visit the same ashoka grove near Sharmishtha's house. Devayani insisted on stopping there to rest awhile. As they were sitting there, she saw three handsome young boys playing nearby. Struck by their appearance and by the similarity in their features to her own two sons, Devayani grew suspicious. She asked Yayati: 'Who are these boys? Why do they resemble our sons so much?' Understandably, Yayati did not answer.

Devayani went over to the boys and asked them, 'Who is your father? Where does he live?'

Innocently, the boys answered, 'Our father is right here. There he is.' And they pointed at Yayati. He was trying to dissuade them with gestures and refused to accept that they were his sons, only because he was afraid of Devayani finding out the truth. He denied their claim before Devayani. 'They are just children, my love. Why do you ask them such questions?'

Devayani went pale. Her legs lost their strength and she sat down suddenly on the grass. It took her a moment to find her voice and wits again. When she had recovered a little, she asked the question to which she already knew the answer: 'And your mother? What is her name?'

They answered cheerfully with the innocence of children. 'Sharmishtha!'

Devayani was stunned. All her fears and doubts and anxieties came rushing back and she realized that she had been made a fool of all this while. Yayati had been sporting with Sharmishtha under her very nose for years, without her realizing. And she in turn had befriended Sharmishtha once more and spent her days in her company, never once suspecting that the boys she was raising were sired by her own husband! Most unbearable of all was the realization that the man she loved and whom she believed loved her exclusively had been sharing his body and his passion with her best friend—who was also her maid! The fact that Sharmishtha's sons were three to her own two sons, and were handsomer and taller in appearance, thanks to their mother being more attractive than Devayani, was the final insult.

Devayani flew into one of her old rages. She saw Sharmishtha emerge from the house to call back her sons. At the sight of her betrayer, she began shrieking like a wild thing. 'How dare you? You are my slave! My servant! How dare you do this to me?'

Sharmishtha had no intention of backing down before her old nemesis. 'I am far more than just your slave and servant. I am the true princess and if not for your manipulations, it would have been I whom Yayati married. He would never have looked at you twice if not for me. Even your first meeting was due to me! But since you regard me only as your slave and property, you should know that my being your slave means that I am also your husband's slave. And that in turn means he is free to enjoy me if he pleases. And it pleases him very greatly, does it not, Yayati, my love?'

Yayati did not have the courage to reply and take either side in this battle of women, but Sharmishtha continued, speaking up for both of them. 'You once had Yayati declared a rishi by your own father, so that he would be equal to you in status and you could be married. You chose him as your husband and insisted that he wed you. I did the same thing. If what you did was right in dharma, then how can I be wrong? But while you did everything out of selfish greed, thinking of none other than yourself, I did what I did with mutual love and respect. Yayati may be your husband in name and law, but he is mine in love and affection. He goes to your bed only because he must, because it is his dharma as a husband to please you and his dharma as a king to sire heirs upon you. But to my bed he comes willingly and eagerly each afternoon, filled with desire, passion and love. These three children are the fruits of that love and that is why they blossom more brightly than even your own two sons!'

Devayani could not bear to hear any more. Sharmishtha's words had the ring of truth, and for Devayani, this was the culmination of years of self-doubt. She rose from there and went back to her palace. When Yayati followed her there, he found her preparing to leave.

'Where are you going?' he asked. 'You have caused me the ultimate insult,' Devayani said. 'I cannot live here another day. I am going home to my father.'

She left that very day, returning to Vrishaparva and prostrating herself before her shocked father, weeping miserably as she poured out her tragic plight. 'Adharma has won over dharma,' she wailed. 'The inferior have won, the superior have lost. My husband Yayati has betrayed me by fathering three sons on Sharmishtha, my maid and slave! In addition, he has deliberately fathered only two sons on me, seeking to elevate his illicit mistress over his own lawful wife.'

Yayati was alarmed at the thought of how Shukracharya would react to this terrible news. He followed close on Devayani's heels, arriving immediately after her. He arrived just in time to hear the tail end of Devayani's impassioned plea to her father.

Shukra turned to Yayati with a face like stone. 'What do you have to say to this?'

Yayati hung his head in shame, unable to summon up any words. Anything he might say would only compound his guilt further and he could not deny the truth to the great preceptor of the asuras.

Shukracharya took his silence and shamefaced aspect as proof of his guilt. 'I see. You will recall that I once forbade you this very thing, knowing the distress it would cause my daughter. Had you copulated with any other woman, it might have been forgivable. But to have violated my sole request to you, made in trust and in good faith of your sense of dharma, this is an insult to me as well. You have succumbed to lust and indulged yourself without care for the consequences. By slaking your lust on two women you have lived two lives at once. Therefore, let your own lifespan be shortened to half. Even though you are yet young, let old age come upon you at once and may your youth be ended at this moment.'

No sooner had the guru pronounced the curse than a shadow passed across the sun shining through the palace windows, even though no cloud or bird was visible in the clear blue sky. When the shadow passed, Yayati's handsome young face was lined and wrinkled, his body bent over with age and infirmity, his joints stiff, his back curved, his hair whitened, his eyes rheumy.

Staring down at himself, he cried out pitifully. 'Do not punish me so harshly, great one. I did nothing on my own. Sharmishtha commanded me to make love to her and said that she had vowed to bear children, therefore as her mistress' husband she was within her rights to demand that I sire children upon her. Countless men do so in the exact same way, will you punish them as well? You yourself agreed at your daughter's request that I was no less than a brahmin and therefore had to concede to your daughter's request to wed her and sire children upon her. If I did no wrong then how could I have done wrong by fathering children upon Sharmishtha? Is it not said by the learned that he who refuses to sire a child upon a woman who desires one is no less than a murderer of an embryo? What wrong have I committed in the eyes of dharma? How can you punish me thus unfairly?'

Kavya Ushanas rose to his feet, pointing a bony outstretched finger at the king. 'Even if this were the case, you should have consulted me. Having been forbidden by me specifically to avoid bedding Sharmishtha, you had no business doing just that! You have no right to ask me for mercy now. It was my specific instruction that you disobeyed. By doing so, dharma itself has blinded her eyes to you!'

Yayati joined his wizened palms together, weeping pitiful tears, but the guru would not be moved.

Finally, Yayati struck upon an argument that even Shukra could not ignore. 'By punishing me thus, you punish your own daughter as well, Gurudev! For if I am old and decrepit now, then your wife has lost her young virile husband. What will she do with this ancient feeble body as her companion? You have cursed her as well.'

Shukra looked at his daughter's face and realized that Yayati spoke truly. By cutting down Yayati's youth, he had deprived his own daughter of her husband. But now that the curse had been uttered and taken effect, it could not be taken back. He thought quickly, arriving at a compromise.

'You may exchange your condition for any other youth if you desire,' he said gruffly. 'The only condition is that he must accept this state of old age willingly and without protest. You cannot force it on anyone.'

Yayati saw a ray of hope in his desperate state. He decided to press his advantage. 'Then let me offer this willing person in exchange for his youth the kingship of my own land. For I must give him something to compensate for the loss of his prime years!'

Shukracharya nodded. 'So be it. But make this arrangement only with one of your own sons. In exchange for his youth, he shall rule your kingdom in your stead. As I have already promised to protect your heirs and see that no harm ever befalls them, I shall add to that the promise that whichever of your sons agrees to exchange his youth for your old age and infirmity shall enjoy long life, great success and fame, and produce numerous offspring of his own. These are my final words.'

10

Yayati's change of condition made even the journey back home seem like an epic undertaking. Every jolt of the chariot, every hour of sunshine or of damp, cold nightfall, every minor deprivation and physical discomfort felt like torture. In moments he had gone from a robust young man in his prime, filled with strength and virility, proud of his body's abilities and his youth, to a decrepit, sagging, bent-over old man, barely able to walk straight, plagued by a dozen aches and weaknesses, beset by failing eyesight, hearing, impaired bodily functions. The full weight of old age had descended upon him like a boulder fallen from above. He struggled to merely cope, one moment at a time. He knew that if he remained in this condition, a quick death was assured. He would not be able to live for long in the state he was in. All men grow old in their time, over time, with years and decades to gradually adjust to failing senses and impaired organs. Yayati had not even had a moment to register the full impact of Shukracharya's curse before he was struck down by his condition. Even now, he was still struggling to accept the reality.

Somehow, he made it home, shivering with chills and fever, racked by pains and sprains, struggling to breathe,

see, think, speak. It was all the royal vaids could do to
keep him sane and functional. He was prone to ranting
and raving, to berating the world for his condition, to
self-pity and remorse.

But he was inherently a strong, determined man.
Gradually, he overcame the mountainous weight of his
afflictions and summoned his eldest son, Yadu, child of
Devayani and dearest to his heart. He sought to soften
the blow of his condition by having his servants draw
the drapes and dim the lamps in his chamber, covering
his body with a blanket. But the overall effect was worse:
the dim lighting, subdued atmosphere and attendants
with faces that revealed their own sorrow at their king's
condition only served to heighten the impact of the
revelation. Yadu reacted at the sight of his father very
badly. He reared back as if struck by a snake, gaping with
wide open eyes and mouth, nostrils flaring. He stared at
his father as if confronted by an imposter, unable to accept
the radical change. He could barely believe that this was
in fact his own father. It took several moments for him
to accept the fact of the curse and its terrible outcome.

When Yayati spoke, in a wheezing voice wholly unlike
his robust baritone, Yadu was even more dismayed.

'Son, my first-born, my best-born. Do not fear me.
All this you see, the old age, the wrinkles, the grey hair,
are the result of a curse imposed on me by my father-
in-law, Kavya Ushanas.' 'Grandfather did this?' Yadu
said, astonished.

Yayati nodded, breaking into a coughing fit that
alarmed the young Yadu even more. Barely grown to

manhood, he was of that age where all old people appear to be of a different race or species, barely human. To see his own father thus, the same father whose powerful physique and commanding personality had provided a model to which he himself aspired, altered overnight, was the worst shock of his young life. He wondered if Yayati was going to die as a result of the intense coughing.

He looked dead already.

'Yes,' Yayati said at last, clearing his throat with difficulty. Unnoticed by him but observed by Yadu with great disgust, he had spots of blood on his chest and chin from the intense coughing. An attendant wiped it away but Yadu thought he could still see the places where the spots stained his father's garment. 'Grandfather did this to me. It is a long story and I shall explain it all later. But first I have something to ask of you.'

'What is it?' Yadu asked doubtfully. He was still wrestling with the realization that this was now his father, this old, broken-bodied, feeble being who seemed barely able to survive a coughing fit.

Yayati was taken aback by his son's abrupt tone. He had envisioned his son as his saviour, imagining that Yadu would throw himself upon his chest, weeping out of sorrow for his father's plight, and offer to do anything in order to restore his father to his former state. Instead, Yadu was staring at him with horror, keeping a safe distance and acting as if he were possessed of a disease that was contagious. 'There is only one condition under which the curse may be rescinded. If my son agrees to exchange places with me. I wish you to do this for me, my son. Take this condition upon yourself willingly for a thousand years. Let me be young again. When the thousand years are over, I shall again return your youth to you and accept my fate as an old man.'

Yadu stared at his father silently for a long moment. 'Why not accept it now? You are already made old.'

Yayati was irritated by the question. He had expected unconditional support and acquiescence, not this suspicious hostility. 'Because I am in my prime! I still wish to enjoy life, to live fully. You know what I looked like yesterday, son. Now look at me! White hair, white beard, flabby flesh, wrinkled skin, ugly, thin, weak, worthless as a man or a warrior, incapacitated by ailments and infirmities, beset by failing organs and countless aches and pains... I do not deserve to be like this!'

'And I do?' Yadu asked.

Yayati was struck dumb. What could he say to such a question?

Yadu took a step forward. 'Father, I love you, this you know already. But do you mean to say that you deserve your youth and strength, but I do not? Do I deserve to be like this? With white hair, beard, flabby, wrinkled, ugly, thin, weak, worthless...all the rest that you describe?' He shook his head slowly. 'No, father. I cannot do this for you. It is too much! I cannot become old in your place!'

He turned his face away, both disgusted and ashamed. Disgusted by the very thought of becoming like the creature in the bed before him—for Yayati's abrupt change made him seem less like a man and more like some creature that had suddenly taken his father's place overnight—and ashamed at his own weakness.

Yayati felt shock, pain, disappointment. He had thought his son capable of giving up his life for him. He knew he would have given his own life to save Yadu, if the circumstances arose. It was another matter that the only scenarios in which he had expected to have to sacrifice his own life were those entailing battle and combat. Not a sacrifice of this magnitude. This was more than mere death, it was living hell. But despite his understanding of his son's decision, he was overcome by a wave of self-pity and anger.

'If that is so,' he shouted feebly, his voice cracking and turning hoarse, 'if you will not aid your father in his time of need, then you deserve no share in this kingdom, Yadu! You and any offspring you have in future shall have no part in my domain. I disinherit you from this moment onwards!'

Yadu cried out in anguish and ran from his father's chambers. Yayati's heart broke as well and he knew his judgement was harsh, much too harsh. But he was now overcome with righteous conviction. He felt that it was the duty of his son to do as he asked, and that by refusing to do so, Yadu had failed his dharma as a son and as a prince. He deserved to be disinherited.

Turvasu, Devayani's second son, was next to be summoned. He reacted much as Yadu had to his father's appearance and condition—and to his demand as well. 'No, father! I cannot do such a thing. Old people feel no desire or pleasure. They have no strength, beauty or intelligence, they are like the dead, though they live.'

This time, the disappointment was even more crushing. Yayati could scarcely believe that even the younger Turvasu, who doted on his father's every word and deed, could refuse him. In his son's words, he heard his mother's voice and phrasing, and he felt certain that Devayani had warned both her sons against acceding to their father's request. The anger he unleashed now against Turvasu was in fact intended for Devayani.

'Everything you possess—your eyes, heart, strength, your senses—were created by me. I am the father of that body! Yet you refuse me! Foolish boy, I disinherit you as well! Even if you become a king, you will rule over subjects who will be inferior and impure. Women of high birth shall cohabit with men of low birth. People in your reign shall eat meat and drink alcohol, mate with their own guru's wives, or even animals when they cannot find humans to mate with! People will behave like animals or worse, like mlechchhas! Only a barbarian would refuse his father, therefore you shall only rule over barbarians. I banish you to the barbarian provinces.'

After Turvasu had left, weeping copiously, Yayati decided to send for Sharmishtha's eldest son, Druhyu. Surely she would have no reason to caution her sons against him. If anything, she would have made them sympathetic to his plight and one of them would surely agree to do as he asked.

With renewed hope, he sent for Druhyu. But when the boy came, it was a repetition of the same scene that had taken place with the previous two boys. Druhyu was more sympathetic but said, 'Father, I love riding elephants, chariots, horses—I am a warrior and wish to do great things in war and combat. I love women and wish to enjoy their love as well. I am not ready for this sacrifice. Please forgive me.'

Again, Yayati was enraged at this insubordination. 'Oh Druhyu, you should not have refused me. Now, I have no choice but to disinherit you and banish you as well. You are hereby sent to the kingdom of Bhoja, where you shall have no elephants, chariots, horses to ride or women to love. Your only means of transport there shall be rafts, boats and swimming. And you are forbidden from entering into liaisons with women. Go now from my sight.'

The fourth son to be summoned, and Sharmishtha's second, was Anu. With him too, it went much the same way. The difference was that Sharmishtha's sons tried to explain and justify themselves at least, which suggested that the reasons were their own and that they were refusing their father despite their mother's urging, not because of it. 'Father, I love to eat and to look smart and dress well,' Anu said plaintively. 'If I am old I will barely be able to eat with that toothless mouth, and I would drool and dribble on myself. My garments would be stained and unclean, and I will not be able to stay clean long enough to perform a single yagna. No, I cannot accept your condition. Please understand.'

Yayati was tired and weary now, exhausted by the emotional disappointment and sense of despair that had overcome him. 'In that case, I forbid you the wearing of new or clean garments henceforth. You will be given unpalatable foods to eat. And you are forbidden from performing yagnas ever again.'

Now Yayati feared that even his last and youngest son, Puru, would surely refuse him. All that had transpired pointed to that likelihood. Still, he clung to the final straw of hope like a dying man clinging to a reed on a riverbank to save himself from drowning.

When Puru, his youngest, stood before him, Yayati said, 'Son. You are my youngest and most beloved. A terrible curse has been put upon me by your own grandfather, Kavya Ushanas. I am condemned to this state of old age that you see before you. Yet I still desire to live and enjoy life in a young body. I wish to enjoy many pleasures still. Therefore I entreat you to grant me your body and youth for one thousand years. After the thousand years have passed, I shall take back my condition along with the pain and infirmity that accompany it. What do you say to my request?'

To his astonishment, Puru said, 'Father, my life is yours. You sired me and everything I possess is given by you, including this body and its strength. If this is what you desire, then take it. I shall accept your curse and live a thousand years, or as long as you wish, in that frail old body. It is my privilege to serve my father in his time of need.'

Yayati's ancient eyes could barely see, yet tears sprang from them and rolled down his withered cheeks. Through blurry vision, he reached out to his youngest son, clasping him to his sunken chest, and said, 'Puru, my son. This is a great sacrifice you have made. You are truly Arya in the best sense of the word, a noble and pure soul. Your sacrifice will be richly rewarded. You and your offspring alone shall inherit this kingdom, achieve great prosperity and achieve all their ambitions and desires. This is part of the condition of the curse and hence it is no less than a decree of destiny.'

Then Yayati reached out and took his son's hand, and in an instant, both father and son were transformed, Yayati regressing in age until he was once more the virile man he had been before the curse, and the boy Puru aging until he became bent, wrinkled and withered like an old man. Both father and son exchanged places.

11

Enjoying the gift of renewed youth gifted to him by his son Puru, Yayati appreciated life more than ever. He relished every kala and kashtha of time that passed, using it to its fullest. He had vowed that if he was given this opportunity he would do nothing that transgressed against dharma and would accomplish all the tasks that he had planned. For a thousand years he worked hard, building and consolidating his kingdom until it became one of the most powerful in the world. He made sure that his people were cared for, that nobody slept hungry or wanted for anything, that law and order were upheld and crime was curbed, that traditions were maintained, arts, crafts and culture patronized. He took special care of the aged and infirm and incapacitated, since he now knew what it meant to be one of them, making sure that they were given all the aid possible. He performed every duty and responsibility diligently. In his spare time he enjoyed himself as well, but never did he act against dharma. His was a golden reign and not only the four varnas of the earth, but even the gods and ancestors were pleased with his efforts and showered blessings upon him.

Eventually, the time allotted to him drew to a close. He worked harder than ever, seeking to complete as much as possible before he had to go back to his sickbed. When the day finally came, he went to his son's bedchamber and presented himself before the wasted, withered figure that lay outstretched on the bed, racked by pain and ailments. He clasped the withered, bony hand of the ancient Puru and said, 'My son, my great and wonderful son. Thanks to you, I have lived life more fully than ever before. I have fulfilled my heart's every desire. Now, as I promised, I have returned to give you back your youth. In recognition of the great sacrifice you made, I shall honour my commitment to you. You shall now rule the kingdom and I shall retire to my sickbed. Before this day is ended I shall crown you king and before the eyes of all, we shall complete the ceremony of succession.'

Knowing that there would be political resistance, Yayati then sent for his advisors, his ministers, and other members of the court, representing all the four varnas. The brahmins objected most vociferously: 'How can you install Puru as your successor? Yadu, son of Devayani, grandson of Shukra, is your eldest son and legitimate heir!'

Others added loudly, 'Even if you discount him for any reason, there is a clear line of succession: after Yadu comes Turvasu, then Sharmishtha's sons Druhyu, Anu, and only then can Puru's name be counted. This is against tradition and all laws of succession. It is against dharma!'

Yayati was prepared for this opposition. He raised his hand to command silence. Calmly he responded: 'What you say is not incorrect under ordinary circumstances. But these are extraordinary times. I was stricken down by a curse of aging long before my prime was ended. I had important work to do to build, consolidate and strengthen this kingdom. My sons were all too young at the time to shoulder this mountainous responsibility. The kingdom would have fallen apart, chaos and ruin followed and today you have had no king to hear your complaints!'

The court was silent. Yayati's efforts these past thousand years had been admired and appreciated by all. They conceded that he had done far more than any king in his place would have for them. They listened with respect and affection.

'Due to the rigidity of Shukra's curse, the only way for me to extend my youth was for one of my sons to exchange places with me for a duration. Yet when I asked each of them in turn, all refused. This you know already. Our sanskriti clearly states that a son who disobeys his father is no son at all. Therefore I disinherited four of my sons who refused to do as I asked: Yadu is banished to another part of the kingdom, as are Turvasu, Druhyu and Anu. Only Puru was immediately responsive and obedient to me. He was more than willing to undertake this sacrifice for my sake and for the sake of the kingdom.'

Yayati pointed to his four sons standing on the throne dais, all four grown to young manhood now and in their prime, strong, handsome, virile. 'Look upon these four sons of mine. They have enjoyed their childhood and youth these past thousand years, playing, cavorting, hunting, loving, fighting and doing as they pleased. Now look at my youngest son, Puru.'

At Yayati's pre-arranged signal, Puru came out onto the dais, bent and bowed, walking with the aid of a stick, his long white hair and beard covering most of his features, his withered limbs like twigs in autumn, his rheumy eyes peering at the court. People gasped to see him in this state.

'For the past thousand years, while his brothers played and cavorted, hunted and dallied, and did as they pleased, Puru has lain in my sickbed, suffering the curse that was meant for me. By the pronouncement of Guru Shukracharya himself, he consented to take the curse upon himself willingly—for it could not be done by force—and spent the best years of his life suffering thus for my sake, and for your sakes as well. What greater son could any father have? What greater king could any kingdom wish for? Therefore, I entreat you all, accept my choice of successor, Puru as the king of this land, for I believe that none but he can govern you as wisely and justly. This is my final edict as a king.'

And with those words, Yayati, son of Nahusha, touched the hands of his son and exchanged their conditions once more. Yayati became old and withered again, and Puru stood tall and strong and handsome.

Without further arguments, the court and the people gladly accepted Puru as their new king and the rite of succession was completed without delay. Thus was the line of Puru established over the kingdom originally built by Dushyanta and Shakuntala's son Bharata and named after him, Bharat.

When all was done, Puru went to his mother and bent his back before her to ask her blessings. All watched as Sharmishtha, the woman they knew only as Queen Devayani's maid, blessed and then embraced her proud son tearfully.

The old king Yayati turned his eyes to his queen. Devayani looked away, eyes flashing with anger. But the force of his will compelled her to look at him at last whereupon he said to her, not without kindness: 'In the end, love conquers all. It was only natural that the child born of love should make the sacrifice that earned him the right to rule the kingdom. For one may make a child, a marriage, or a kingdom out of ambition, but one can govern them well only through love and compassion. You may be my queen, Devayani, but it was Sharmishtha's love that infused her son's heart from birth and brought him to this shining day. She shall always be queen of my heart to the end of my days.'

Taking the hand of his paramour and ignoring the muffled whispers of consternation among the nobility, Yayati and Sharmishtha left the palace together and went into the forest to live the rest of their mortal days in togetherness. They would never be parted again, except by death.

BRIDE OF THE FOREST
The Untold Story of Yayati's Daughter

Madhavi Mahadevan

The myth of Drishadvati appears in the *Mahabharata* as the 'story of the salvation of kings by a maiden'. While tales of surrogacy abound in the Indian epics, this is the first known example of a womb-on-rent. This strange story—of a girl whose fertility was bartered repeatedly in exchange for priceless horses—has intrigued modern scholars, playwrights and authors for its cultural significance. While earlier adaptations have cast its theme as the exploitation of a helpless woman, *Bride of the Forest* presents it as the story of girl who is surprisingly radical in her ultimate rejection of patriarchy.

Staying true to the original myths and springing entirely from the world of the *Mahabharata*, the novel brings to life several other characters: Garuda, the divine bird who flies Lord Vishnu around the world; the proud kings of Ayodhya, Pratisthan and Kashi; the arrogant queen, Devayani, and her duplicitous maid—whose stories reveal an intricate tapestry of human and divine relationships. Intertwined in the tales of traditional rivalries is the age-old war between the asuras and the devas that gave rise to the perennial male quest for immortality, transmuted into the human desire for sons that lies at the root of commercial surrogacy even today. However, it is the story of Drishadvati, her sacrifice and her nobility that will enchant the reader.

YASODHARA
A Novel About the Buddha's Wife

Vanessa R. Sasson

Who was Yasodhara? The Buddha's forgotten and abandoned wife? The mother of his only son? Or an enlightened being in her own right, denied her rightful place in the stories and histories about the Buddha? A long time ago, in a far-off kingdom, a boy and a girl, born on the same day, were destined to be together and then painfully wrenched apart. The boy was Siddhattha, heir to the Sakya kingdom and the future Buddha; the girl was the beautiful and precocious Yasodhara, his friend who became his loving wife. In this exquisitely crafted narrative, we encounter Yasodhara as a fiercely independent, passionate and resilient individual. We witness her joys and sorrows, her expectations and frustrations, her fairy-tale wedding and her overwhelming devastation at the departure of her beloved.

It is through her eyes that we witness Siddhattha's slow transformation, from a sheltered prince to a deeply sensitive young man. On the way, we see how the gods watch over the future Buddha from the clouds, how the king and his ministers try to keep the suffering of the world from him and how he eventually renounces the throne, his wife and newly-born son to seek enlightenment.

Resurrecting a forgotten woman from the origin stories of the Buddha, Vanessa R. Sasson combines the spirit of fiction and the fabulism of Indian mythology with impeccable scholarship to tell the evocative and deeply moving story of an extraordinary life.